H o u g h t o n   M i f f l i n

# IMAGINE

## LITERACY ACTIVITY BOOK


**Senior Authors**
J. David Cooper
John J. Pikulski

**Authors**
Kathryn H. Au
Margarita Calderón
Jacqueline C. Comas
Marjorie Y. Lipson
J. Sabrina Mims
Susan E. Page
Sheila W. Valencia
MaryEllen Vogt

**Consultants**
Dolores Malcolm
Tina Saldivar
Shane Templeton

INVITATIONS TO LITERACY


**Houghton Mifflin Company • Boston**

Atlanta • Dallas • Geneva, Illinois • Palo Alto • Princeton

*Illustration Credits*
Elizabeth Allen 81, 82, 116, 131; Susan Aiello 3; Gary Antonettti 28, 61; Andrea Barrett 120, 128, 208; Shirley Beckes 121, 135, 131; Karen Bell/Carolyn Potts & Associates 44; Ka Botzis/Melissa Turk 223; Cindy Brodie/Square Moon Productions 53, 65; Ruth Brunke 43, 130, 139, 142, 152, 155, 157, 178, 200, 210, 217, 220, 224, 251, 259, 260; Robert Burger/Deborah Wolfe 7, 10, 16, 54, 71, 77, 79, 119, 145, 153; Jannine Cabossel 8, 29, 114, 129, 225, 232, 237; Tony Caldwell/Cornell & McCarthy iv, 203; Estele Carol/HK Portfolio 20, 23; Olivia Cole/Asciutto Art Reps iii, top left, 4, 240, 250; Mark Corcoran/Asciutto Art Reps 241, 243, 247; Laura D'Argo 143, 219; Ruta Daugavietis 46, 70, 112, 137, 229, 235, 237; Susanne Demarco/Asciutto Art Reps 19, 27, 253, 256; Tom Duckworth 25, 66, 122, 140, 165, 187, 192, 198, 204, 245; George Eisner/Steven Edsey 90, 159; Kate Flannagan/Cornell & McCarthy 156; Bryan Friel/Steven Edsey 166; Dave Garbot iii, top right, 27, 45, 92, 215, 245; Steve Gillig 230, 234; Susan Greenstein 76, 183, 190; Paul Hoffman 117, 118, 147, 161; John Jones/Cornell & McCarthy 80; Gary Krejca/Steven Edsey 193; Bob Lange 2, 17, 88; Jared D. Lee 151; Bert Mayse 51, 55, 63, 123, 145, 148, 195, 202, 221; Lori Mitchell 94, 97; Mas Miyamoto/Square Moon Productions 125, 154, 209; Paul Moch 141; Andy Myer/Deborah Wolfe 176; Steven Nau/Deborah Wolfe 87; Laurie Newton-King 239, 242, 248; Karen Pritchett/Cliff Knecht 91; Stephen Schudlich/Ceci Bartels Associates 15, 18, 93, 101; Neil Shigley/Carol Chislovsky 153, 188; Darren Thompson 83; Lynn Titleman/Cornell & McCarthy 213, 214; Stan Tusan/Square Moon Productions 64, 96, 99, 100; George Ulrich/HK Portfolio 148; Dave Winter 32, 33, 41, 79, 95, 111, 115, 158, 205, 207, 222, 233, 238, 255, 261, 262.

*Photo Credits*
©Bill Bachman/Photo Researchers 102, top left; ©Jen & Des Bartlett/Photo Researchers 47, bottom; Photo by Hillel Burger/ Peabody Museum, Harvard University 160; ©B. Dobos/H. Armstrong Roberts, Inc. 244; ©Stan Elms/Visuals Unlimited 140, top center; David R. Frazier Photolibrary, Inc. 119, 210, right center top; ©David R. Frazier Photolibrary, Inc./Photo Researchers 24; ©Tony Freeman/PhotoEdit 255; ©John Gerlach/Visuals Unlimited 140, top right; Grant Heilman Photography 47, top right; H. Armstrong Roberts, Inc. 39, top, 85, top right, 132; Image Club Graphics Inc. 21, 101, 143, 229; ©Breck Kent/Animals/Animals 210, left bottom; ©Larry Lefever/Grant Heilman Photography 252; ©Zig Leszczynski/Animals/Animals 210, right top; ©Ted Levin/Animals/ Animals 210, right center bottom; ©Robert Maier/Animals/Animals 210, right bottom; ©Felicia Martinez/PhotoEdit 199, top; North Wind Picture Archives 139, top left; ©Richard Passmore/Tony Stone Images 124, bottom left; ©Robert & Eunice Pearcy/ Animals/Animals 210, left center bottom; ©Robert Pearcy/Animals/Animals 210, left center top; ©Pelton & Associates, Inc./ WestLight 201, right; PhotoDisc iii, iv, 14, top left, 23, 103, top, 196, 250; ©F. Prenzel/Animals Animals 158; Stamp courtesy of Japan Ministry of Posts and Telecommunications iii, 124, top; ©Trent Steffler/David R. Frazier Photolibrary, Inc. 195; ©Reneé Stockdale/ Animals/Animals 210, left top; Tony Stone Images 124, bottom right; All other photographs by Ralph J. Brunke Photography.

1997 Impression


Printed in the U.S.A.

ISBN: 0-395-72485-6

14 15 16 17 18 19 20-WC-02 01 00 99

# CONTENTS

# CONTENTS

Name

# My Reading Strategy Guide

| As I read, I **predict/infer** by . . . | |
|---|---|
| Looking for important information. | ☐ |
| Looking at illustrations. | ☐ |
| Thinking about what I know. | ☐ |
| Thinking about what will happen next. | ☐ |
| **As I read, I monitor by asking . . .** | |
| Does this make sense to me? | ☐ |
| Does it help me meet my purpose? | ☐ |
| I try fix-ups: | |
| • Reread | ☐ |
| • Read ahead | ☐ |
| • Look at illustrations | ☐ |
| As I read, I **think about words** by . . . | |
| Figuring out words by using context, sounds, and word parts. | ☐ |
| Reading to the end of the sentence or paragraph. | ☐ |
| As I read, I use **self-question** strategies by . . . | |
| Asking myself questions, then reading ahead to find the answer. | ☐ |
| As I read, I **evaluate** by . . . | |
| Asking myself how I feel about what I read. | ☐ |
| Asking myself if this could really happen. | ☐ |
| I **summarize**, during and after reading, by . . . | |
| Thinking about story elements. | ☐ |
| Thinking about main ideas and important details. | ☐ |

Name

# Ali Baba's Birthday Words

**Did Roger forget his best friend Ali Baba's birthday? Find out by drawing a blue line from Start to the vocabulary word that has the same meaning as the underlined words in each clue. Keep following the clues until you come to the last box that tells where Roger was.**

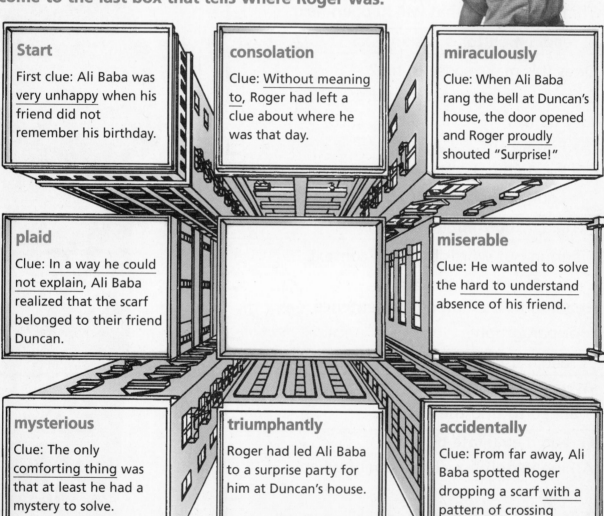

**Start**
First clue: Ali Baba was very unhappy when his friend did not remember his birthday.

**consolation**
Clue: Without meaning to, Roger had left a clue about where he was that day.

**miraculously**
Clue: When Ali Baba rang the bell at Duncan's house, the door opened and Roger proudly shouted "Surprise!"

**plaid**
Clue: In a way he could not explain, Ali Baba realized that the scarf belonged to their friend Duncan.

**miserable**
Clue: He wanted to solve the hard to understand absence of his friend.

**mysterious**
Clue: The only comforting thing was that at least he had a mystery to solve.

**triumphantly**
Roger had led Ali Baba to a surprise party for him at Duncan's house.

**accidentally**
Clue: From far away, Ali Baba spotted Roger dropping a scarf with a pattern of crossing stripes.

**Write a sentence describing how Ali Baba reacted when he discovered the surprise party. Use at least two vocabulary words.**

Name

# It's on the Map

Complete the following story map for *Hurray for Ali Baba Bernstein*. Then write how you feel about the story.

**Title:**

**Characters:**

**Setting:**

**Plot:**

**Conclusion:**

**My Feelings:**

Name

# The Writing Process

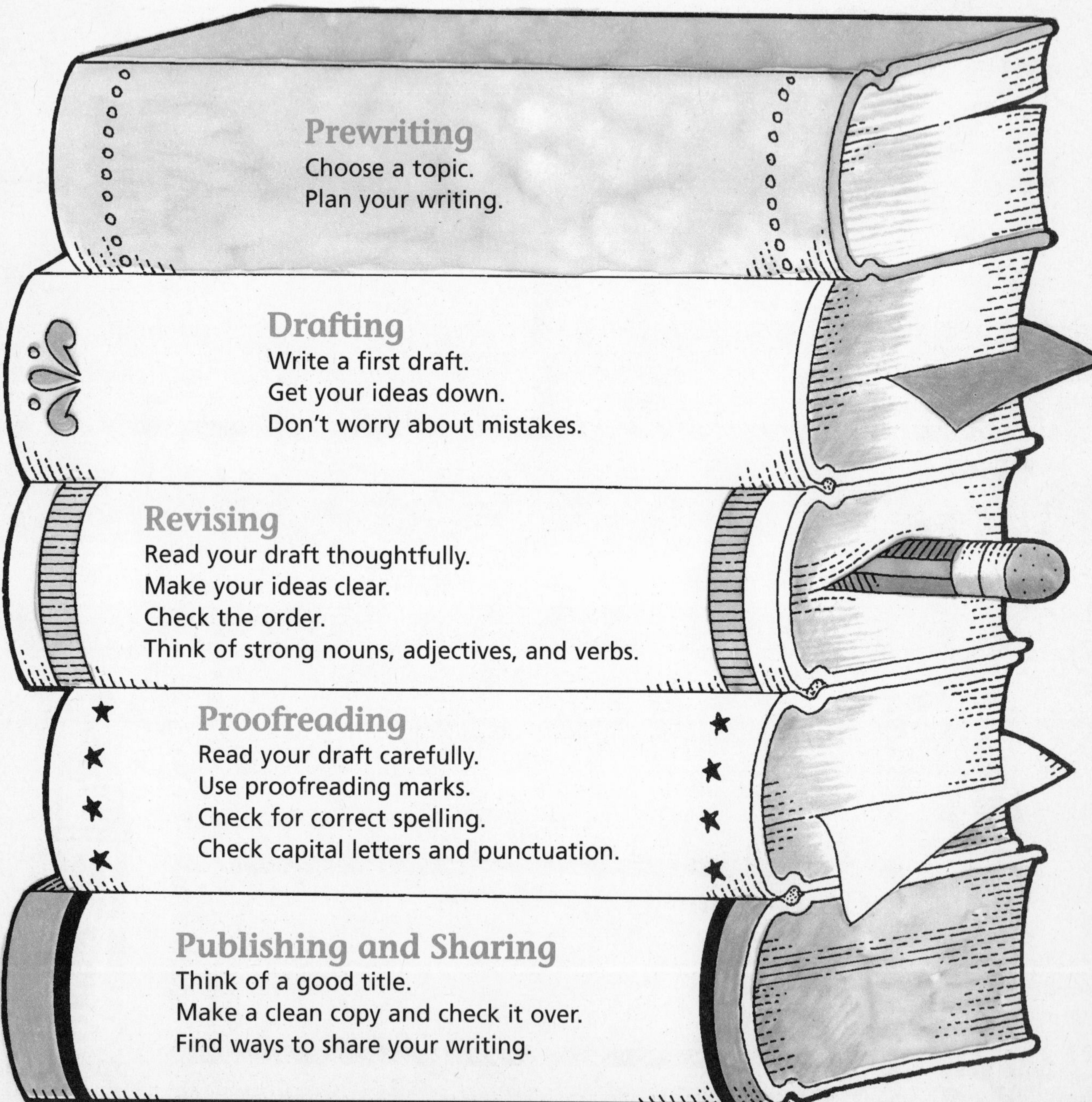

Prewriting
Choose a topic.
Plan your writing.
Drafting
Write a first draft.
Get your ideas down.
Don't worry about mistakes.
Revising
Read your draft thoughtfully.
Make your ideas clear.
Check the order.
Think of strong nouns, adjectives, and verbs.
Proofreading
Read your draft carefully.
Use proofreading marks.
Check for correct spelling.
Check capital letters and punctuation.
Publishing and Sharing
Think of a good title.
Make a clean copy and check it over.
Find ways to share your writing.

Name

# Ready, Set, Plan!

**Choosing a Topic** List three or four topics that you could write about. Put a check mark next to the one you will be writing about.

**Plan Your Writing** Write your topic in the center box. In the outer boxes put big ideas about your topic. Add details below the outer boxes. Keep adding details as you think of them. Use another sheet of paper if you need more space.

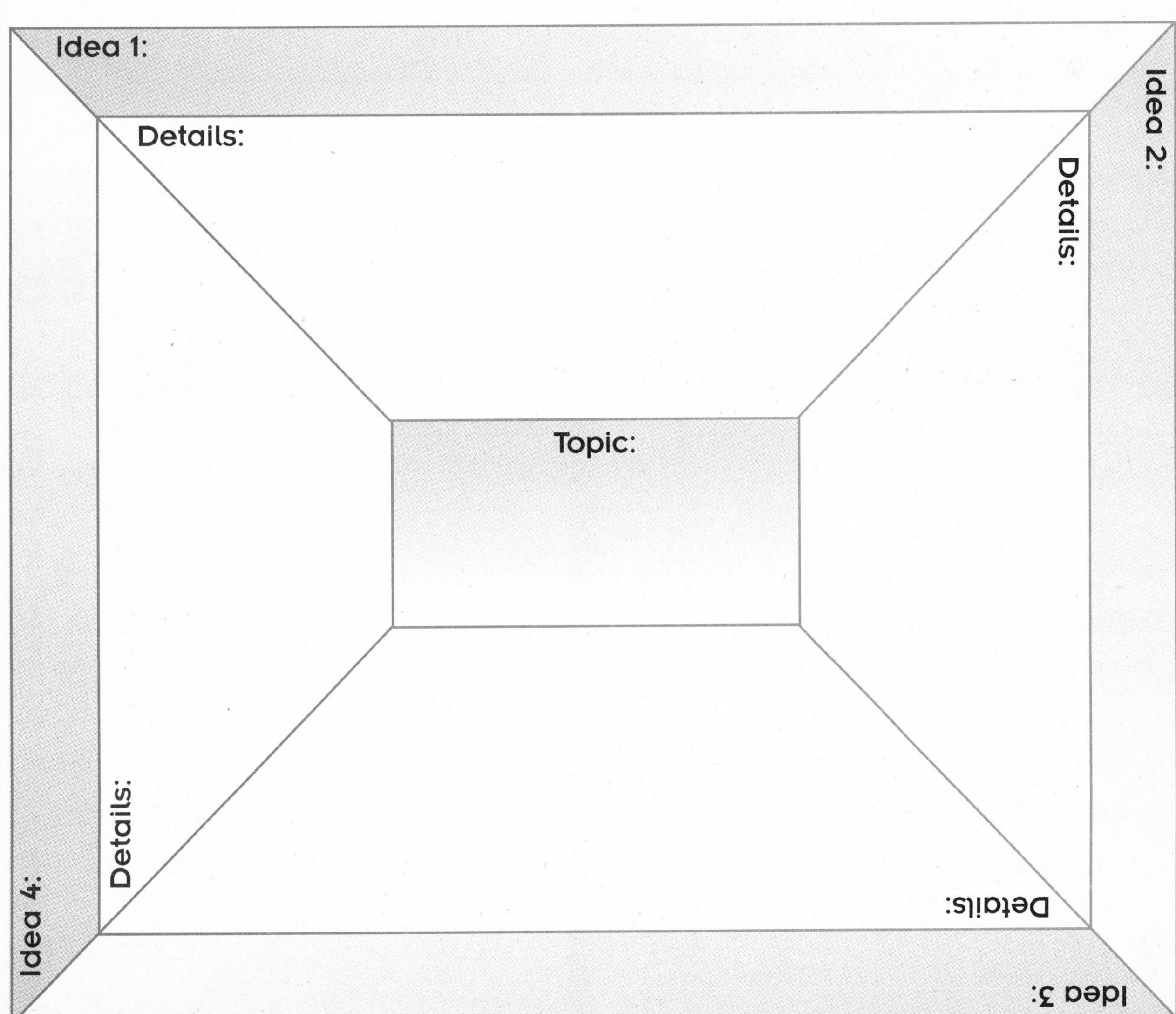

Name

# Revising Your Writing

**Reread and revise your page of the class book. Use the Revising Checklist as a guide. Then have a writing conference with a classmate. Use the Questions for a Writing Conference to help your partner.**

## Revising Checklist

- ❑ Have I stated my main ideas clearly?
- ❑ Are there enough details and support?
- ❑ Is there anything I should leave out?
- ❑ Are my ideas in good order?
- ❑ Have I used interesting words?

### Questions for a Writing Conference

**Use these questions to help you discuss your writing.**

- What is the best thing about this piece?
- Does it stay on the topic?
- Does it seem well organized?
- Does it help me learn about what this person enjoys?
- What additional information would I like to know?
- What information seems unclear?
- Does it end in a strong way?

**Write notes to remember ideas from your writing conference.**

My Notes

Name

# It's Cool. It's School.

What has been the most important school day for you? What made it important? Was it something you learned? Was it a relationship with a friend? Write about that day. Be sure to answer the five "w's."

Write the name of your school here.

Who?

What?

Where?

When?

Why?

Name

# It's Cool. It's School.

As you read the stories in It's Cool. It's School., you'll get to know the characters. After you finish reading each story, fill in this chart and compare the characters' experiences with your own.

| | Tales of a Fourth Grade Nothing<br>realistic fiction | I'm New Here<br>narrative nonfiction | Koya DeLaney and the Good Girl Blues<br>realistic fiction |
|---|---|---|---|
| How the Story Compares with Real Life | | | |
| Main Character | Peter | Jazmin | Koya |
| Main Events | | | |
| Similar Experiences You've Had with Your Friends | | | |

Name

# Take On This Assignment

**Match each word to its definition by writing the letter on the line beside the word. Then choose a vocabulary word to finish each sentence.**

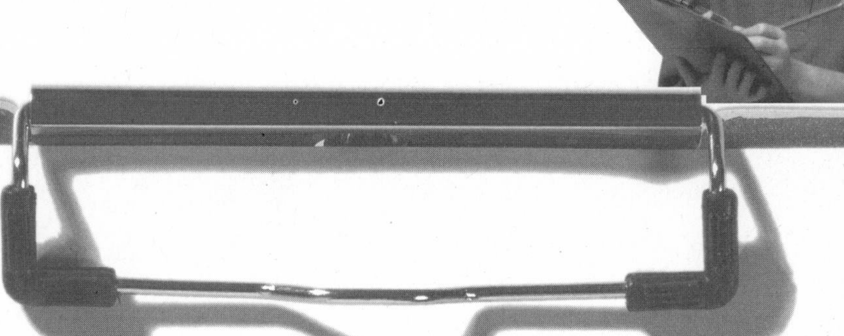

_____ project — **a.** a group of people formed to complete a task

_____ committee — **b.** a plan or process for doing something

_____ arranged — **c.** a task to be done or a problem to be solved

_____ solution — **d.** made ready or put into order

_____ method — **e.** a plan with a time line for completing a project

_____ schedule — **f.** the answer to a problem

1. Zach worked to find the ______________ to his math problem.
2. Marta read the bus ______________ to plan her trip.
3. Theo couldn't decide which ______________ was harder: making a volcano or writing a report on earthquakes.
4. The food ______________ met to plan the snacks for the party.
5. Does anyone know the best ______________ for learning to throw a baseball?
6. Before she left town, Janna ______________ to have Irene take care of her cats.

Name

# Check Your Memory

**Think about the selection. Then complete the sentences.**

1. The committee decided that Sheila would copy all their written work into the booklet because

2. At times the committee had a hard time getting along because

3. Peter became furious with Fudge when

4. Sheila decorated the booklet with flowers because

5. The story could be called "The Flying Train Committee" because

Name

# Recess Racers

**Read the story about some fourth graders. Then answer the questions.**

Steve challenged Julie to a race at recess. Steve loved to race, and he usually won. Julie didn't like to lose races so she agreed to the contest on one condition. "I'll race with an apple on my head, and you have to balance an orange on yours."

"That's fine with me," said Steve. "I'll win no matter what."

"Here are the rules," Julie explained. "If the fruit falls off your head, you're allowed to pick it up and put it back. However, you have to continue racing from where it fell off. Mike can watch to make sure no one cheats."

On the call, "Ready, set, go!" Julie and Steve began walking as fast as they could. It wasn't easy. About every three steps or so, one racer lost his or her piece of fruit. Before they were halfway around the track, both racers were spending more time picking up their fruit than actually racing. It also didn't help when they started laughing.

"Hurry! The bell's going to ring!" Mike jumped up and down.

Just then, Julie and Steve noticed that someone else was watching the race. It was their teacher, Mrs. Wilson. She was laughing as hard as they were.

1 Why does Julie want the racers to balance fruit on their heads? ______________

______________________________________________

______________________________________________

2 What happens when the school bell rings at the end of recess? ______________

______________________________________________

______________________________________________

3 How do you think the race will end? ______________

______________________________________________

______________________________________________

Name ______________________

# Sentences Only!

Fudge cut up Peter's homework! Help Peter separate the five complete sentences from the five fragments by marking each with a **C** or an **F**.

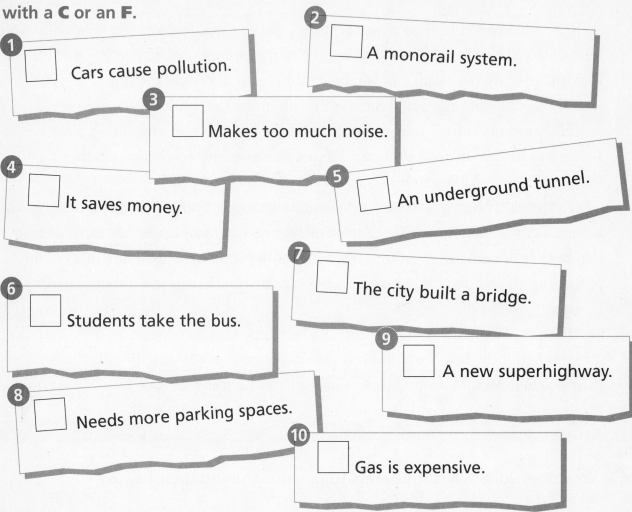

1. ☐ Cars cause pollution.
2. ☐ A monorail system.
3. ☐ Makes too much noise.
4. ☐ It saves money.
5. ☐ An underground tunnel.
6. ☐ Students take the bus.
7. ☐ The city built a bridge.
8. ☐ Needs more parking spaces.
9. ☐ A new superhighway.
10. ☐ Gas is expensive.

Make each fragment into a sentence by adding missing subjects or predicates.

11. ______________________
12. ______________________
13. ______________________
14. ______________________
15. ______________________

Name

# Getting to Base

Peter felt that having Fudge as a younger brother was one of life's little unfairnesses. *Unfairnesses* is a long word, but look how it is formed.

u n f a i r n e s s e s
u n f a i r n e s s
f a i r n e s s
f a i r

Now you try it. The base word should be at the bottom.

1 unpopped

_ _ _ _ _ _ _ _

_ _ _ _ _ _

Base word: _ _ _

2 disagreement

_ _ _ _ _ _ _ _ _ _ _ _

_ _ _ _ _ _ _ _ _

Base word: _ _ _ _ _

3 lovingly

_ _ _ _ _ _ _ _

_ _ _ _ _ _

Base word: _ _ _ _

4 reviewers

_ _ _ _ _ _ _ _ _

_ _ _ _ _ _ _

_ _ _ _ _ _

Base word: _ _ _ _

5 unenjoyable

_ _ _ _ _ _ _ _ _ _ _

_ _ _ _ _ _ _ _ _

_ _ _ _ _

Base word: _ _ _

**Wishing You Success!** Create your own step-by-step puzzle with the word *unsuccessfully*. Use another piece of paper.

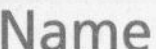

Name

# A Science Assignment

**Use the words to complete the story.**

| project | committee | present | method |
|---|---|---|---|
| arranged | schedule | solution | cooperation |

In science class, Ms. Holloway gave Julia, Darnell, Rodney, and Melinda an assignment on the life cycle of a caterpillar. Ms. Holloway made a plan, or ____________________, that gave students three days to research the topic. They were to make a series of posters and show the posters to the class the following week. Ms. Holloway told the students to form a ____________________ to decide how to divide the work. The four students ____________________ to meet three times after school to work on the ____________________. They decided to use this ____________________ to divide the work: Darnell and Melinda would do the research, Julia and Rodney would make the posters, and they all would ____________________ the posters to the class. However, they had a difficult time figuring out a time and place to work together. After they talked it over, their ____________________ to the problem was to meet in the science classroom for a half hour right after classes. The four of them got along well, and their assignment was very successful. Ms. Holloway said the ____________________ of group members was the key to their success.

Name

# Short Vowel Transport

**Short Vowels** Each Spelling Word has a short vowel sound spelled with the short vowel pattern. This pattern is usually spelled with a single vowel followed by a consonant sound.

| | | |
|---|---|---|
| short a | /ă/ | class |
| short o | /ŏ/ | drop |
| short e | /ĕ/ | desk |
| short u | /ŭ/ | dull |
| short i | /ĭ/ | still |

## Spelling Words

1. class
2. plan
3. desk
4. still
5. check
6. dull
7. drop
8. trust
9. snip
10. knock

**My Study List**
What other words do you need to study for spelling? Add them to My Study List for *Tales of a Fourth Grade Nothing* in the back of this book.

**Help Peter, Jimmy, and Sheila transport short vowels. Write two Spelling Words that have the same short vowel sound as the underlined vowel in each picture name.**

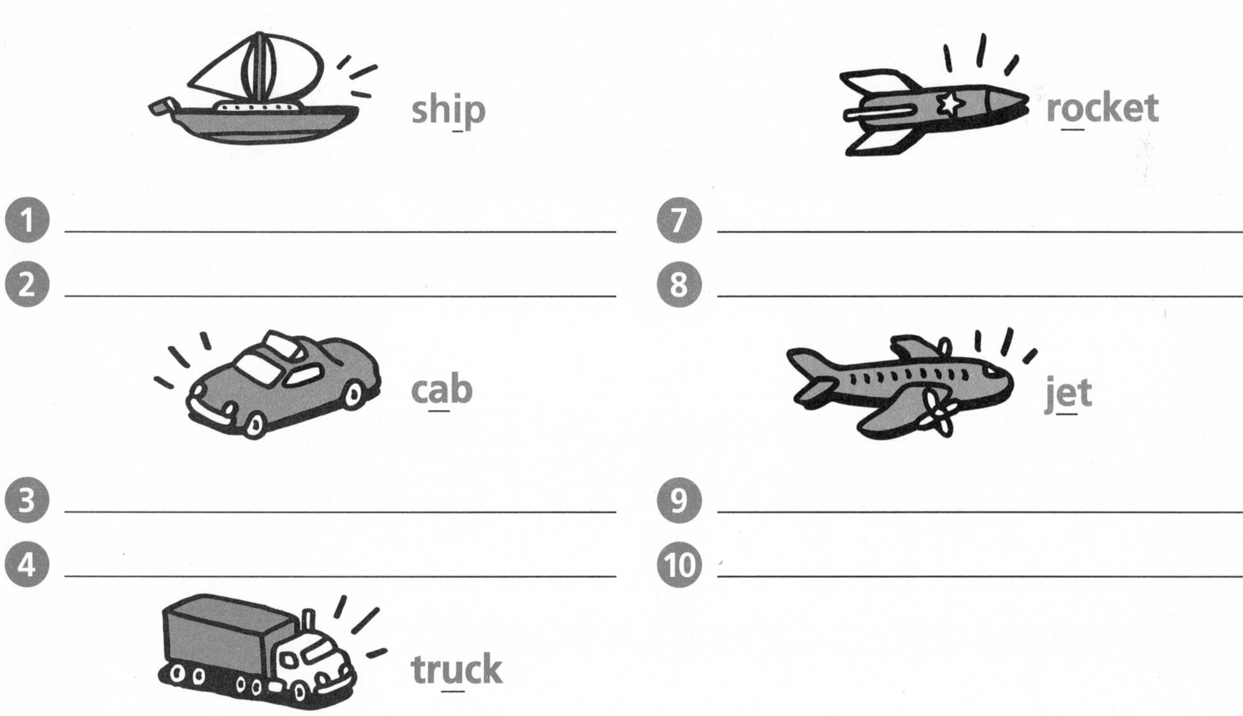


1 ______
2 ______
3 ______
4 ______
5 ______
6 ______
7 ______
8 ______
9 ______
10 ______

Name

# Spelling Spree

**Proofreading** Circle four misspelled Spelling Words in these notes on a school project. Then write each word correctly.

**Spelling Words**

1. class
2. plan
3. desk
4. still
5. check
6. dull
7. drop
8. trust
9. snip
10. knock

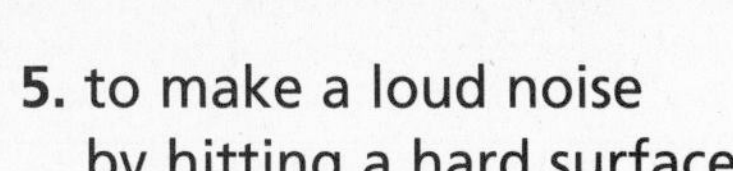

Notes on Project

We are to plan an oral report and a poster.
Must chek ideas with teacher before starting.
Has to be interesting, not dul.
Can snipp out magazine pictures for poster.
Have to give report in clase next Friday.

1 ______
2 ______
3 ______
4 ______

**Monorail Messages** Write the Spelling Word that fits each clue.

5. to make a loud noise by hitting a hard surface
6. a piece of furniture used for reading or writing
7. to have confidence in
8. yet
9. to think out or arrange ahead of time
10. to let fall

**A Private Place** If you had your own bedroom, what rules might you want to post on the door? On a separate piece of paper, write some of the rules. Use Spelling Words from the list.

Name

# Subject-Predicate Puzzle

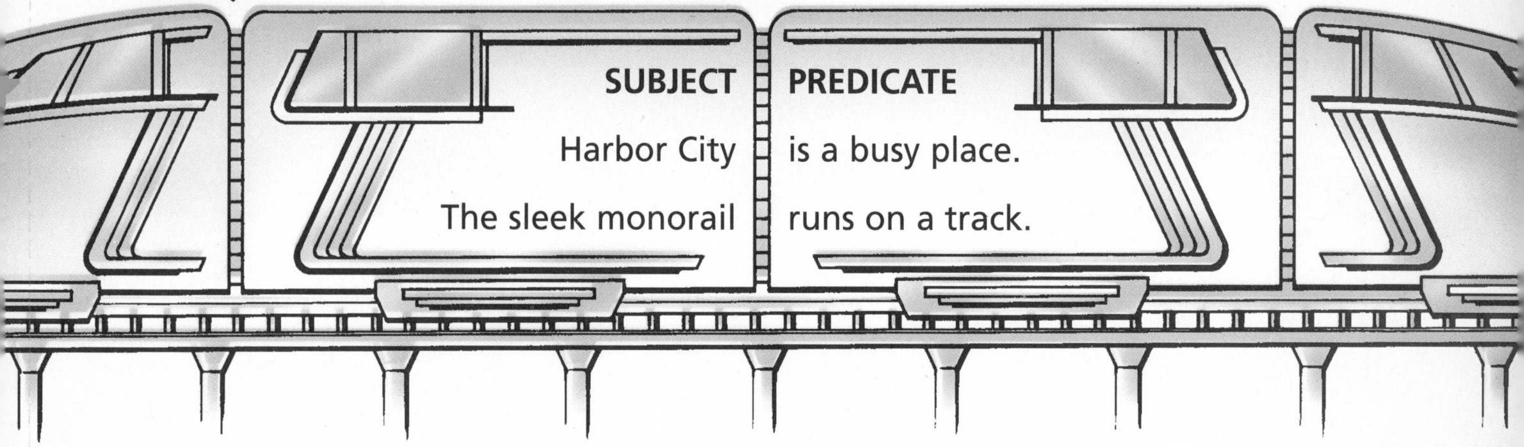

| SUBJECT | PREDICATE |
|---|---|
| Harbor City | is a busy place. |
| The sleek monorail | runs on a track. |

**Subjects and Predicates** In each sentence, draw a line between the complete subject and the complete predicate. Then write the simple subject across and the simple predicate down to complete the puzzle for each sentence.

1. A huge city is an exciting place.
2. Joggers in running gear race through the park.
3. The city's buses bring workers to their jobs.
4. They ride elevators to their offices.
5. Many bikes weave through the traffic.
6. The Super Express speeds along steel tracks.

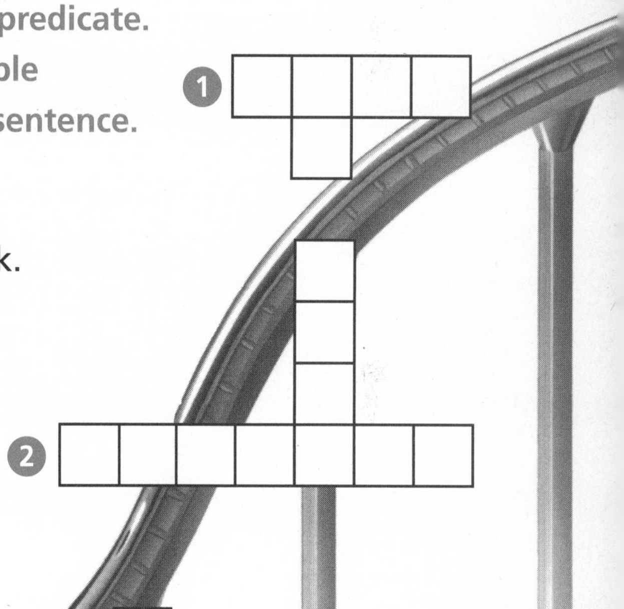

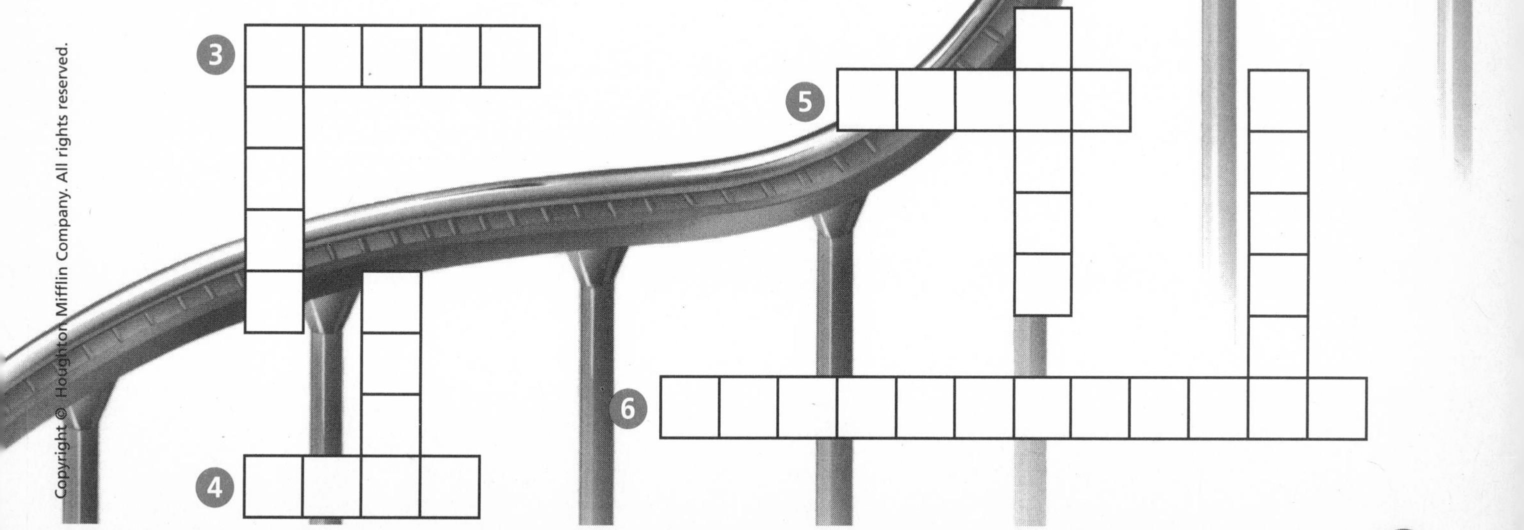

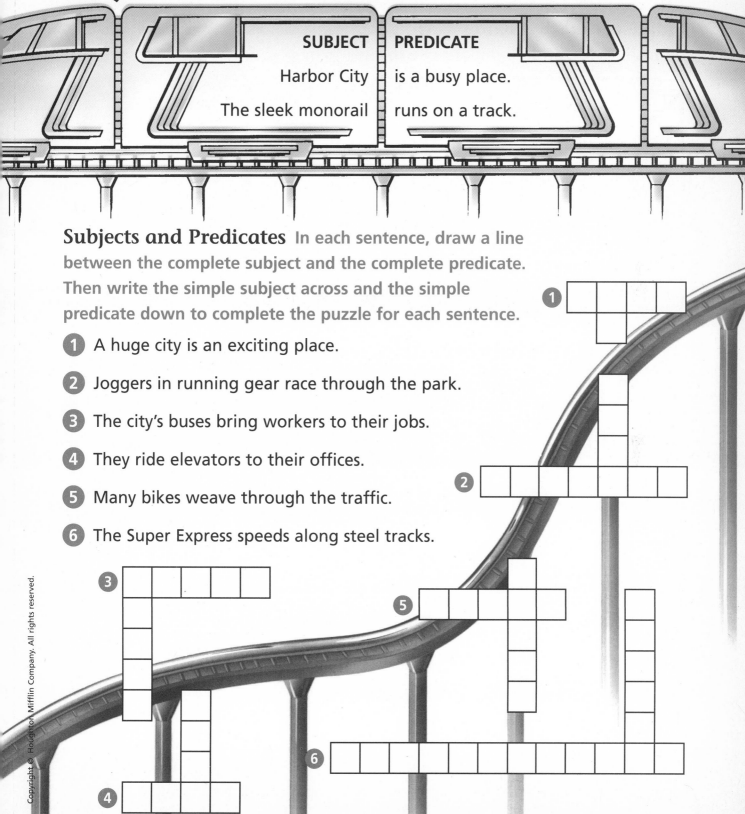

Name

# Symbol Sentences

**Subjects and Predicates** Rewrite each sentence, using words in place of the symbols. Use the key to help you.

**Example:** The [bus station] is W of [24].

**The bus station is west of Route 24.**

1. The [railroad tracks] cross [24].

_______________

2. Two [bridge] span the [Carey River].

_______________

3. The [Carey River] flows N and S.

_______________

4. The [airport] is E of the [bus station].

_______________

5. A large [ship] docks in the [harbor].

_______________

Now, draw a line between the complete subject and the complete predicate. Circle the simple subject and the simple predicate.

Name

# Life in a New Place

**Read the definitions and answer the questions by writing the letters of the correct answers in the blank spaces.**

customs: the inspection of a person's baggage when traveling between countries. Customs inspections are carried out by government officials who collect taxes on certain items that are brought into one country from another.

1. _____ What is customs?
   a. a set of baggage
   b. the inspection of baggage
2. _____ Who carries out the customs process?
   a. government officials
   b. airline flight attendants

papers: documents that verify a person's identity or give other information about the person who carries them. People who move from one country to another often need to have papers with them when they start school or go to work.

3. _____ What information do a person's papers contain?
   a. information about the person's neighbors
   b. information about the person who carries the papers
4. People who move ________ often need to have papers with them.
   a. from one country to another
   b. from one state to another

register: to enroll officially at a school as a student. Every student must register to be allowed to attend classes.

5. A person who registers can ________ .
   a. attend classes at school
   b. enroll in after-school programs

Name

# Be True to Your New School

**Mark a T if the statement is true and an F if it is false. If the statement is false, on a separate sheet of paper, correct it to make a true statement.**

| | True | False |
|---|---|---|
| 1 Jazmin moved to her new home from El Salvador. | | |
| 2 Jazmin could not go to fourth grade in El Salvador because she was sick. | | |
| 3 Jazmin was not nervous about the first day of school because she had visited school the day before. | | |
| 4 Mrs. Edwards failed to make Jazmin feel a part of the class. | | |
| 5 The first day of school turned out to be a good one for Jazmin. | | |
| 6 Even though she was good at math and reading, Jazmin had to remain in fourth grade. | | |
| 7 Jazmin's classmates thought she was a good soccer player. | | |
| 8 Allison made fun of Jazmin and called her names. | | |

**Read and answer the question.**

9 What is the main problem that Jazmin faced at her new school?

______________________________

______________________________

Name ______________________________

# What a Nightmare!

Write different Clue Words to complete the sentences.

**Clue Words**
- At the same time
- After that
- Next
- Finally
- Then
- First

*My Bad Day*

*__________, I burned my toast. __________, I spilled my glass of juice. __________, I missed the school bus. __________, I stepped in a mud puddle. __________, I found that I had lost my homework. __________, I woke up and realized that it was all a bad dream.*

Write about a good or a bad day you once had. Use as many of the Clue Words as you can.

______________________________

______________________________

______________________________

______________________________

______________________________

______________________________

______________________________

______________________________

______________________________

______________________________

______________________________

Name

# Start Now!

**Answer these questions. Then use the answers to start your own journal!**

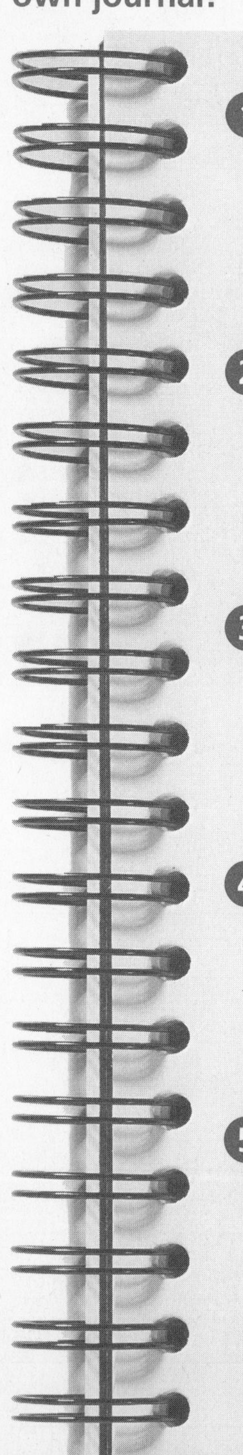

1. Write one new word, fact, or idea that you learned today.

______________________________

______________________________

2. If you could ask anybody in the world a question, who would it be and what would you ask?

______________________________

______________________________

3. Look around you. What object catches your eye? Name the object and write a few words to describe it.

______________________________

______________________________

4. Name a movie or television show that you have seen lately and give your opinion of it.

______________________________

______________________________

5. Name one thing that worries you.

______________________________

______________________________

Name

# A Neat Trick

Help Jazmin learn new words by showing her a little trick. Break down each word into its base word and ending.

| Story Word | Base Word | -ed, -ing, -s, -es, -er, -est |
|---|---|---|
| 1 called | | |
| 2 teaches | | |
| 3 safer | | |
| 4 greatest | | |
| 5 saying | | |
| 6 crayons | | |

ending
end ing

Write the correct word in each sentence.

7 Jazmin's new school would be ________________ than her old one.

8 She couldn't understand what anyone was ________________.

9 Some boys teased Jazmin and ________________ her names.

10 Mrs. Edwards gave Jazmin some bright ________________ to color with.

11 Jazmin is the ________________ soccer player in the class.

12 Jazmin's friend ________________ her new words.

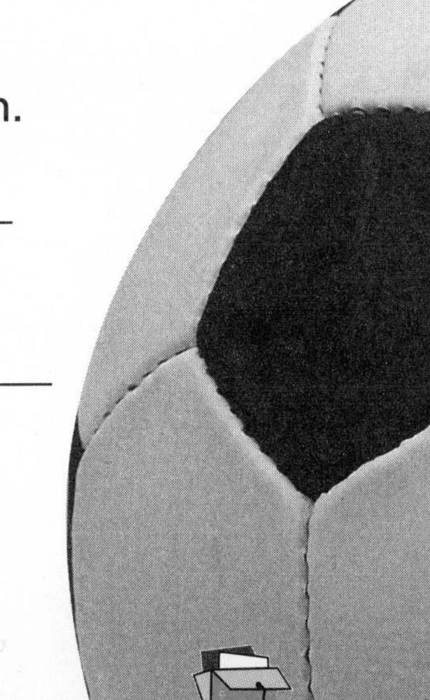

Name 

# New Experiences

**Complete the puzzle.**

customs new papers hello register smile nervous

**Across**

1. Jazmin had to _____ as a student before she could attend school.
2. At _____ , a person's luggage and documents are examined and approved.
3. Jazmin felt this way about starting school in a new place.

**Down**

3. Jazmin didn't feel _____ anymore after meeting Allison.
4. Jazmin's mother had to fill out _____ on Jazmin's first day of school.
5. A word of greeting
6. A friendly look

Name

# Soccer Sort

**Long *a* and Long *e*** Some Spelling Words have the long ***a*** sound, which is written as /ā/. The /ā/ sound can be spelled with the pattern ***a***-consonant-***e***, ***ai***, or ***ay***.

/ā/ grade, wait, away

The other Spelling Words have the long ***e*** sound, which is written as /ē/. It is often spelled with the pattern ***ea*** or ***ee***.

/ē/ neat, meet

**Spelling Words**

1. grade
2. meet
3. seem
4. neat
5. wait
6. away
7. safe
8. afraid
9. least
10. crayon

**My Study List**
What other words do you need to study for spelling? Add them to My Study List for *I'm New Here* in the back of this book.

**Help Jazmin get control of the ball! Write each Spelling Word in the soccer ball with the correct pattern.**

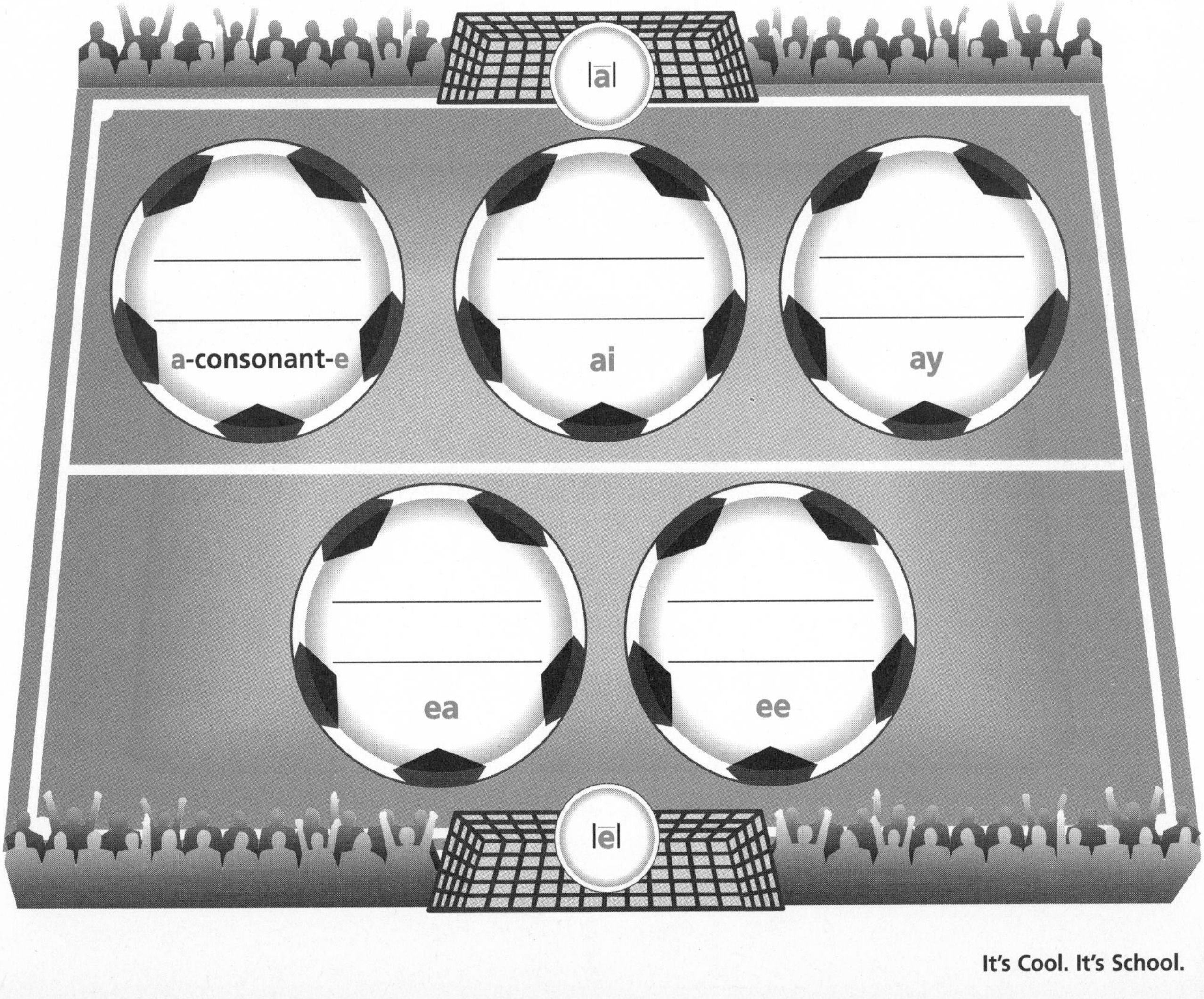

/ā/

a-consonant-e
__________
__________

ai
__________
__________

ay
__________
__________

ea
__________
__________

ee
__________
__________

/ē/

Name

# Spelling Spree

| Spelling Words | |
|---|---|
| 1. grade | 6. away |
| 2. meet | 7. safe |
| 3. seem | 8. afraid |
| 4. neat | 9. least |
| 5. wait | 10. crayon |

**New-School Blues** Complete this story by writing the Spelling Words that fit the blanks.

I don't ___ ___ ___ ___ like the nervous type, but on my first day at my new school, I shook like a leaf. I wanted to ___ ___ ___ ___ new kids, but I didn't know how to go about it.

Just as I was thinking how ___ ___ ___ ___ and clean the room was, I stepped on a ___ ___ ___ ___ ___ ___. My feet flew out from under me, and I landed with a thud in another boy's lap. "Well!" he said, startled. "Welcome to fourth ___ ___ ___ ___ ___!" With that, we both began to laugh. What on earth had I been ___ ___ ___ ___ ___ ___ of?

**Proofreading** Circle four misspelled Spelling Words. Then write each word correctly.

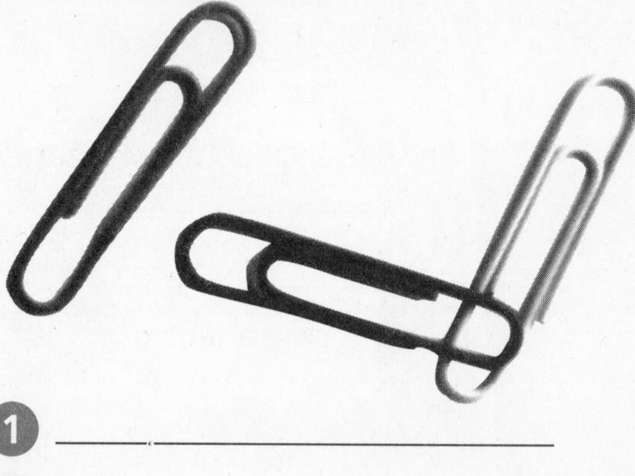

Dear Berta,

I'm glad you have come to our town from so far awey. It is saif here, so you'll never have to be afraid again. I can hardly wate until summer, when we will have a lot of fun. It will be here before we know it. (At leest I hope so!)

1 ______________________

2 ______________________

3 ______________________

4 ______________________

**Welcoming Words** On a separate piece of paper, write a dialogue in which you welcome a new student from another country. Remember to capitalize and punctuate your dialogue correctly. Use Spelling Words from the list.

Name

# Name That Sentence!

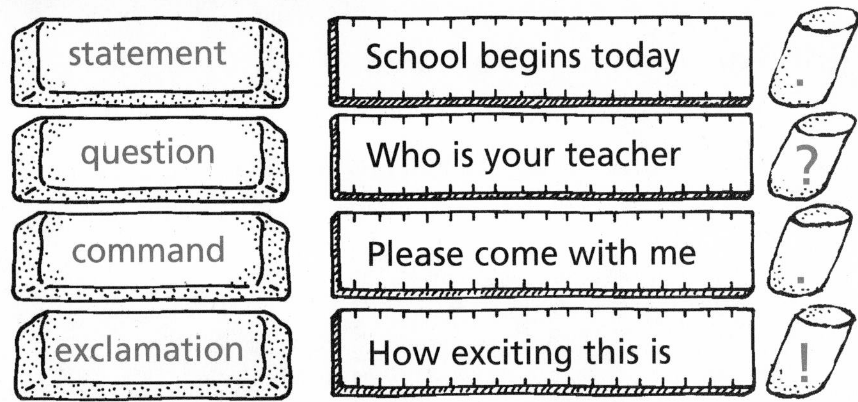
statement
School begins today
.
question
Who is your teacher
?
command
Please come with me
.
exclamation
How exciting this is
!

**Kinds of Sentences** Add the correct end mark to each sentence. Then write what kind of sentence it is.

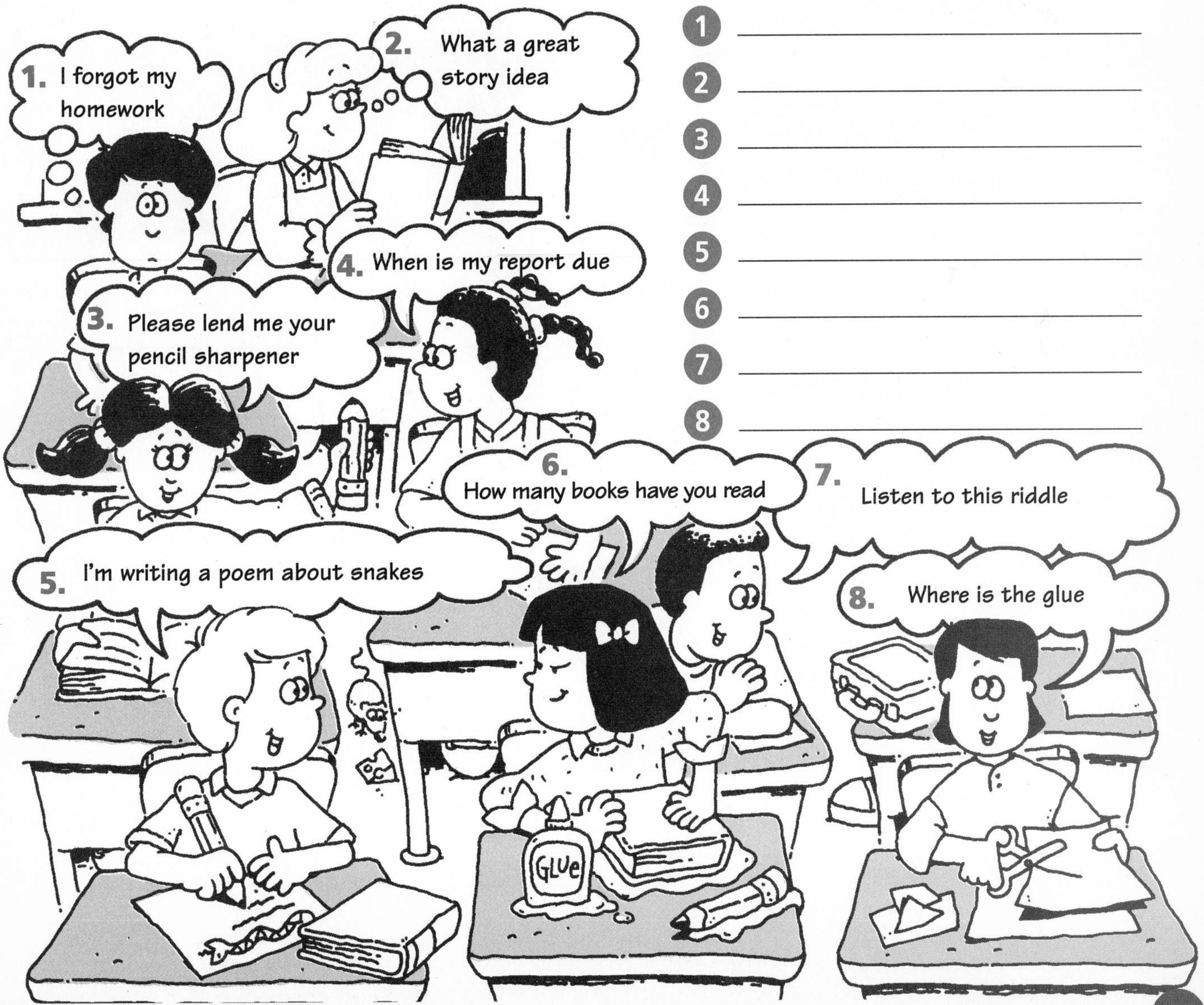

1. I forgot my homework
2. What a great story idea
3. Please lend me your pencil sharpener
4. When is my report due
5. I'm writing a poem about snakes
6. How many books have you read
7. Listen to this riddle
8. Where is the glue

1 ______________________
2 ______________________
3 ______________________
4 ______________________
5 ______________________
6 ______________________
7 ______________________
8 ______________________

Name

# Splendid El Salvador

**Kinds of Sentences** Read the facts about El Salvador. Use the facts to write six sentences. Write at least one command, one question, one statement, and one exclamation.

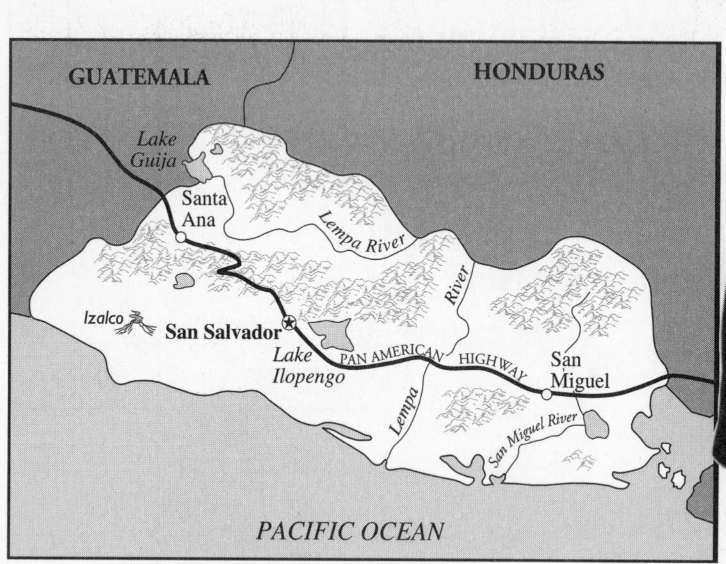

## FACTS

- smallest country of Central America
- wet season from May to October
- two high mountain ranges
- many important ancient ruins
- some volcanoes active
- most roads not paved
- twenty major volcanoes
- over 300 rivers
- capital—San Salvador
- Spanish language

1. ______________________________
2. ______________________________
3. ______________________________
4. ______________________________
5. ______________________________
6. ______________________________

Name ..............................................................

# I Remember the Time I . . .

## Topic Ideas

Make your own BEST and WORST list!

**What was the . . .**

weirdest
happiest
funniest
most serious
stupidest
proudest
most embarrassing
most important
most surprising

**. . . moment of your life?!**

## My Personal Narrative Ideas

List five ideas for a story about yourself.

1 ______________________________
______________________________

2 ______________________________
______________________________

3 ______________________________
______________________________

4 ______________________________
______________________________

5 ______________________________
______________________________

Think about each idea you wrote.
Ask yourself . . .

Would someone else enjoy reading about this?

Can I make this experience come alive for my readers?

Do I remember this clearly?

Circle the topic you would most like to write about.

Name

# Search Your Memory

Use this chart as you list the details of your experience. It will help you when you write your draft.

**Draw pictures and write notes to answer these questions.**

- What happened?
- Who was there?
- What did you see?
- What did you hear and say?
- What did you feel?

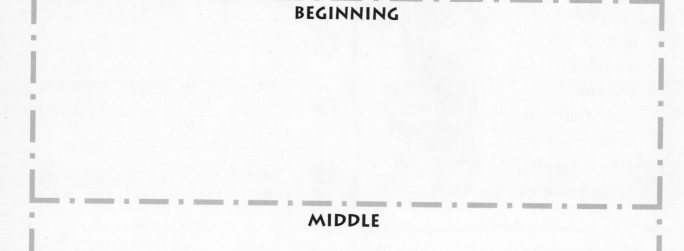

BEGINNING

MIDDLE

END

Name

# Check Your Story

Read your story to yourself. Use the questions on this page to revise it.

## Revising Checklist

Ask yourself these questions. Make changes in your story.

- ☐ Will the beginning catch my readers' interest?
- ☐ Is the order of events clear?
- ☐ Where could I add more details?
- ☐ Where could I add dialogue?
- ☐ What other changes could I make to improve my story?

## Questions for a Writing Conference

Use these questions to help you discuss your story with a partner.

- What is the best thing about this story?
- Does the beginning make the reader wonder what is going to happen?
- Is the story easy to understand?
- Are there places where more details would make the story clearer or more interesting?
- Where could dialogue be added to tell the story?
- How could the story be improved?

Write notes to help you remember the ideas from your writing conference.

**NOTES**

_______________________________________

_______________________________________

_______________________________________

_______________________________________

_______________________________________

_______________________________________

_______________________________________

_______________________________________

Name

# Jump To It!

Do you know what the words on the poster mean? Use the words in the box to finish each word web.

- somersaulted
- routine
- rhythm
- poised
- participants
- competition

DOUBLE-DUTCH COMPETITION
October 17, 8 PM
Walsh School Gym
Teams will perform one routine each.
Participants: Rhythm Runners
Poised Ponies
Somersaulting Susans

( ______ ) — contest; game or event

( ______ ) — players; people who join in

( ______ ) — confident; balanced

( ______ ) — sound with a beat; movement that repeats

( ______ ) — series of movements; pattern

( ______ ) — flipped; went head over heels

Name

# You Be the Judge

**You're a judge at the double-dutch competition. Answer the reporters' questions.**

What is double-dutch?

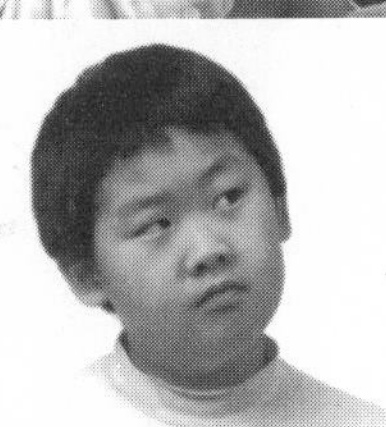

I noticed Loritha DeLaney did not take part. Why not?

Why did Barnett School lose points during the freestyle routine?

Who won?

Name

# Where Are They Going?

**Read the story. Then take a closer look at Ms. Robbins's class by filling in the chart.**

"Okay, I want all of you to line up next to the wall with your partners," said Ms. Robbins. "Remember that you and your partner will stay together all day." Ms. Robbins put on her coat and hat.

"Now, I want you all to check that you have your bus money, your lunch, some paper, and crayons," Ms. Robbins added. "Did everyone remember to read the handout about paintings? We'll be seeing some beautiful paintings today."

"What about the mummies? Aren't there going to be mummies?" asked Koya.

"Yes, there will be mummies, too, and statues, and many other interesting works of art," Ms. Robbins replied calmly.

Koya was looking through her backpack. "I can't find my crayons." She started to search for another box, opening drawers and looking on the cubby shelves.

"You can share mine," said Koya's friend Aletha. They were going to be partners.

"That's a great idea. Thanks, Aletha," said Koya, looking relieved.

| WHERE do you think the class is going? | WHY did Koya look relieved when Aletha offered to share her crayons? | HOW would you describe Aletha? | WHAT kinds of things will the students do today? |
|---|---|---|---|
| | | | |

Name

# Who Called?

The DeLaney family is out celebrating Barnett's second-place double-dutch prize! Read about each telephone call that comes while they are gone and write a message for each one.

1. Ms. Harris calls at 6:00 P.M. on Saturday. She says Loritha has double-dutch practice at 3:00 P.M. next Wednesday. She would like Loritha to bring a jump rope. She wants Loritha to call her back. Her number is 555-2350.

2. Coach Dickinson calls at 7:30 P.M. on Saturday. He says that Koya left her jacket at the gym, on the Barnett bench. He says to call the school as soon as possible. The number is 555-6792.

3. Dawn calls at 8:00 P.M. on Saturday to speak with either Loritha or Koya. She wants to know what they're doing tomorrow afternoon. She says she'll call them back tomorrow morning.

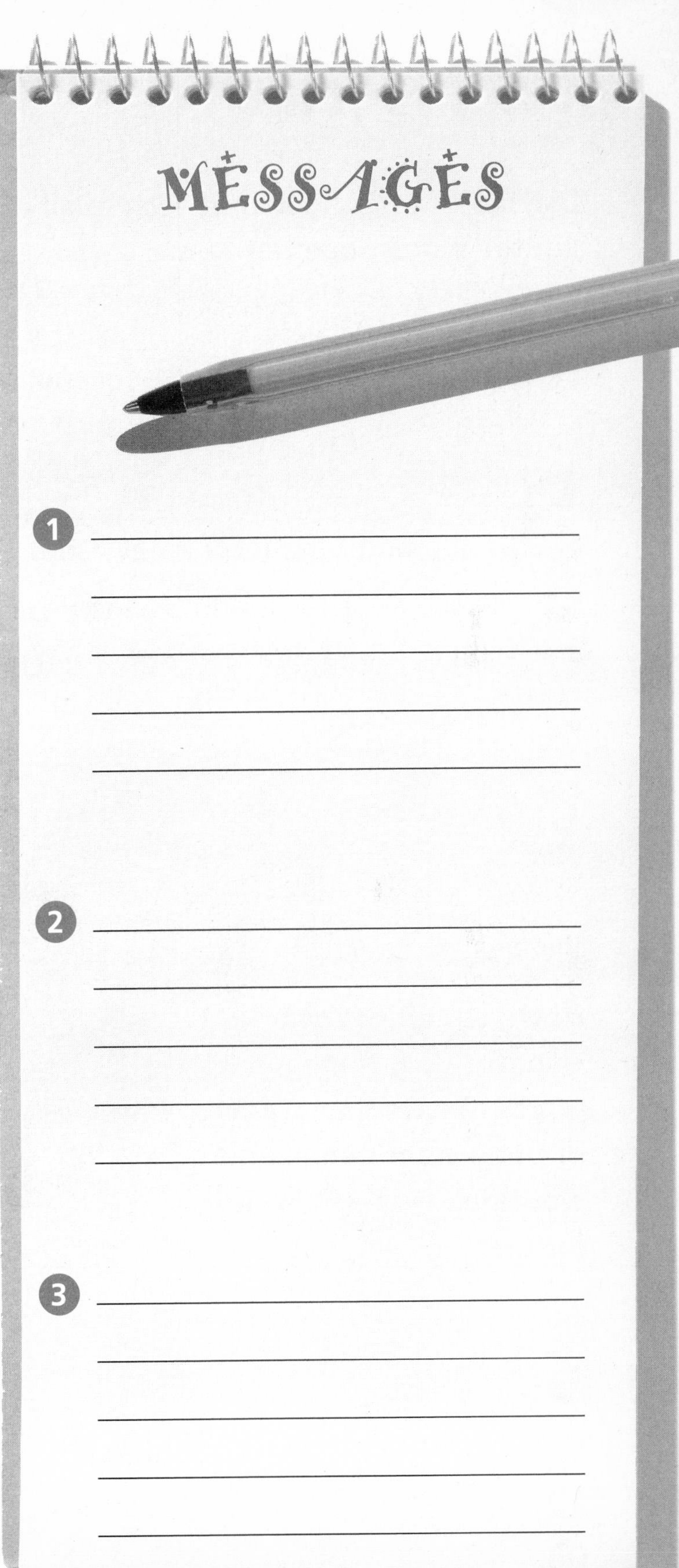

Name ______________________________

# Get It Together!

Use the clues to figure out each small word.
Put the words together to make a compound word.

**Example**: a group of students + a friend = **classmate**

1. a woven container + a bouncing toy = ____________________
2. to hop on both feet + heavy cord = ____________________
3. the season after spring + noon, for example = ____________________
4. sudden brightness + what a bulb gives off = ____________________
5. the letter after *s* + a piece of clothing = ____________________

Now you try it. Write clues for each compound word shown. Then think of three more compound words, and make up clues for them.

6. ________________ + ________________ = toothpick
7. ________________ + ________________ = jungle gym
8. ________________ + ________________ = ________________
9. ________________ + ________________ = ________________
10. ________________ + ________________ = ________________

Name

# Doing Double-Dutch

**Some new kids in town are at a double-dutch meet. Sammi is explaining what's going on. Fill in the blanks with words from the box.**

| rhythm | routine | participants | poised | somersaulted | competition |
|---|---|---|---|---|---|

Double-dutch is great! Teams from all over the city are here for this ______________. My sister and my cousin are two of the ______________. You have to be ______________ and ready to go when you start your ______________.

Here comes our team. Look at them stomp their feet to the ______________. Wow, did you see that? Those girls just ______________ out of the rope! It must be hard to go head over heels like that.

Name

# Jumping Jumble

**Long *i* and Long *o*** Some Spelling Words have the long ***i*** sound, which is written as |ī|. The |ī| sound can be spelled with the pattern ***i***-consonant-***e*** or ***igh***.

|ī| side high

The other Spelling Words have the long ***o*** sound, which is written as |ō|. The |ō| sound can be spelled with the pattern ***o***-consonant-***e***, ***oa***, or ***ow***. The ***oa*** pattern is usually followed by a consonant sound.

|ō| rope coach know

**Spelling Words**

1. rope
2. coach
3. know
4. side
5. spoke
6. high
7. blow
8. bright
9. wipe
10. goal

**My Study List**
What other words do you need to study for spelling? Add them to My Study List for *Koya DeLaney and the Good Girl Blues* in the back of this book.

**Join the double-dutch teams! Write the pattern that spells the |ī| or the |ō| sound in each Spelling Word. Then write each word under the correct sound in the ropes.**

sp__________

g__________l

br__________t

kn__________

h__________

r__________

s__________

c__________ch

w__________

bl__________

|ī|

1. __________
2. __________
3. __________
4. __________

|ō|

5. __________
6. __________
7. __________
8. __________
9. __________
10. __________

Name

# Spelling Spree

**Spelling Words**
1. rope
2. coach
3. know
4. side
5. spoke
6. high
7. blow
8. bright
9. wipe
10. goal

**Trophy Crossword** Complete the puzzle on the trophy by writing the Spelling Word that fits each clue.

Down
**1.** a person who trains a team
**2.** to send out a stream of air
**3.** not the top or the bottom

Across
**4.** not low
**5.** to clean or dry by rubbing

**Proofreading** Circle five misspelled Spelling Words in this paragraph from a news article. Then write each word correctly.

**Double-Dutch Jumpers Thrill Crowd**

Yesterday, a big crowd attended a double-dutch contest at the school gym. Under brigt lights, the teams jumped and twirled the roap with amazing speed. One coach spowk after the event, saying, "These kids really now how to dazzle a crowd! Their gole is to put on a good show."

6 ______________________

7 ______________________

8 ______________________

9 ______________________

10 ______________________

Name

# Double-Dutch Delight

**Run-on Sentence:** Contests do not just happen they take a lot of planning.

**Correct:** Contests do not just happen. They take a lot of planning.

**Run-on Sentences** A student committee is making up the schedule for the double-dutch contest. Use proofreading marks to correct their run-on sentences. Then write the events correctly onto the schedule in the correct order.

**Proofreading Marks**

≡ Make a capital letter.

⊙ Add a period.

**Example:** Everyone is ready⊙ the contest will begin.

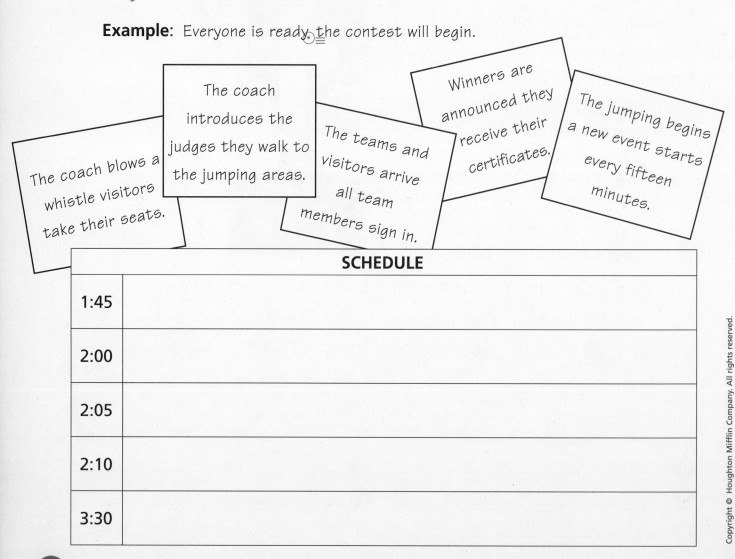

The coach blows a whistle visitors take their seats.

The coach introduces the judges they walk to the jumping areas.

The teams and visitors arrive all team members sign in.

Winners are announced they receive their certificates.

The jumping begins a new event starts every fifteen minutes.

| SCHEDULE | |
|---|---|
| 1:45 | |
| 2:00 | |
| 2:05 | |
| 2:10 | |
| 3:30 | |

Name

# Ladies and Gentlemen . . .

**Run-on Sentences** The announcer is so excited that she ran some sentences together. Use proofreading marks to correct the run-on sentences.

| Proofreading Marks | |
|---|---|
| ≡ | Make a capital letter. |
| ⊙ | Add a period. |
| ? | Add a question mark. |
| ! | Add an exclamation mark. |

**Example:** Attention! please take your seats.

May I have your attention, please! I want to welcome you to this event an important day in the life of our school has arrived. Your talented classmates will show their skills nobody knows how hard they have worked some of them will leave this event with trophies. Can you guess who team members will now take their places. Give them a big hand stand up now for the school song.

The announcer forgot to say what event it was! Write the first letter of each sentence in the boxes below.

Unscramble the letters and write the word to name the event.

Name

# Creating a Skit

Work with a partner to create a skit about Sheila and Jimmy from *Tales of a Fourth Grade Nothing.* Imagine that Sheila and Jimmy are spending an hour after school helping Mrs. Haver prepare for the school Open House. In order to help, they must (1) clear away the desks, (2) arrange the food, and (3) decorate the classroom. Think about *Tales of a Fourth Grade Nothing* and about what Sheila and Jimmy are like. Fill out the chart to help you plan your skit.

| Character | What Each Character Is Like | Job(s) Each Character Will Do | Problems or Disagreements They Will Solve |
|---|---|---|---|
| Sheila | | | |
| Jimmy | | | |

Use what you know about Sheila and Jimmy to create a skit about what might happen as they get ready for the Open House. Use the checklist to make sure you're ready to present your skit.

**Checklist**

- ☐ My skit makes Sheila and Jimmy seem like real people facing a real challenge.
- ☐ In my skit, Sheila and Jimmy behave like the same characters in *Tales of a Fourth Grade Nothing.*
- ☐ The order of events in my skit makes sense.





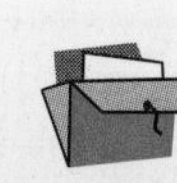

Name

# Earth Patrol: Preserve and Protect

**Starting Off** Three kinds of environment are pictured below. For each picture, draw the beings that live in that environment. Then draw the problems that trouble that environment.

Air

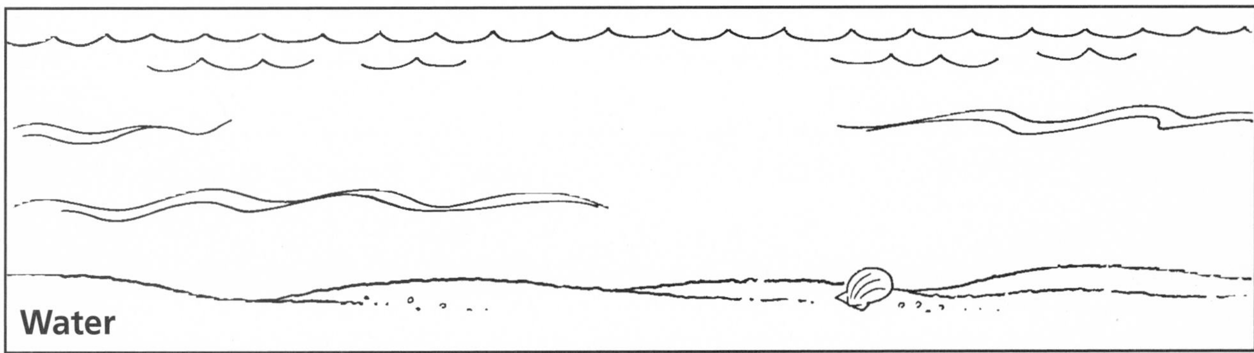

Water

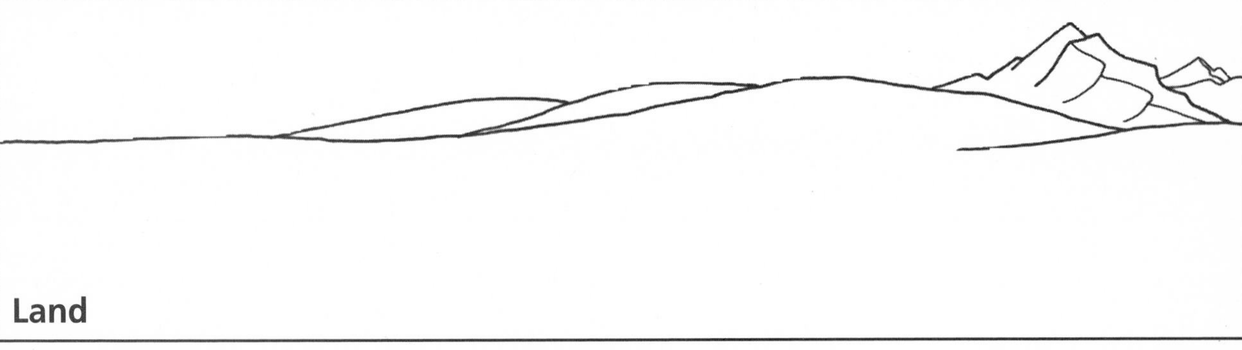

Land

How can human beings restore these environments?

Name

# Earth Patrol: Preserve and Protect

As you read each story in Earth Patrol: Preserve and Protect, fill in the boxes of the chart below that apply to the story.

| | The Great Yellowstone Fire | The Great Kapok Tree | Just a Dream |
|---|---|---|---|
| Where does the story take place? | | | |
| What happens to this place in the story? | | | |
| What do the human beings or characters do in the story? | | | |
| What kind of story is it? | | | |

Choose your favorite story and explain why you liked it best.

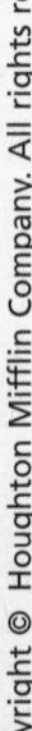

Name

# Fire Words from the Forest

Unscramble the vocabulary words. Then unscramble the circled letters to solve the riddle.

singeing kindled charred smoldering ignited scorching

EGSIIGNN __ (__) __ __ __ __ __ __
Hint: means "slightly burning surface features such as hair or fur"

LEDDINK __ __ __ (__) __ __ __
Hint: means "started a fire"

REDARCH (__) __ __ __ __ __ __
Hint: means "burned but left remaining parts"

REDINGMOLS __ __ (__) __ __ __ __ __ __ __
Hint: means "burning slowly with smoke but no flame"

NITEDIG __ __ __ __ (__) __ __
Hint: means "caught fire quickly"

CHINGROCS __ __ __ __ __ __ __ __ (__) __
Hint: means "burning the surface with great heat"

WHAT DID THE CRANKY LODGEPOLE PINE DO TO PUT THE SASSY LODGEPOLE PINE IN ITS PLACE?

__ U __ __ T __ __ W __

Name

# Extra! Extra!

Write the headlines to show the order in which the events occurred. Then write your answer to the question.

**Headline Bank**

- Lightning Sets Small Fires
- Officials Say Fight Fires
- Plants Grow in Blackened Earth
- Firefighters Save Inn
- Snowfall Dampens Flames
- Park Officials Let Natural Fires Burn

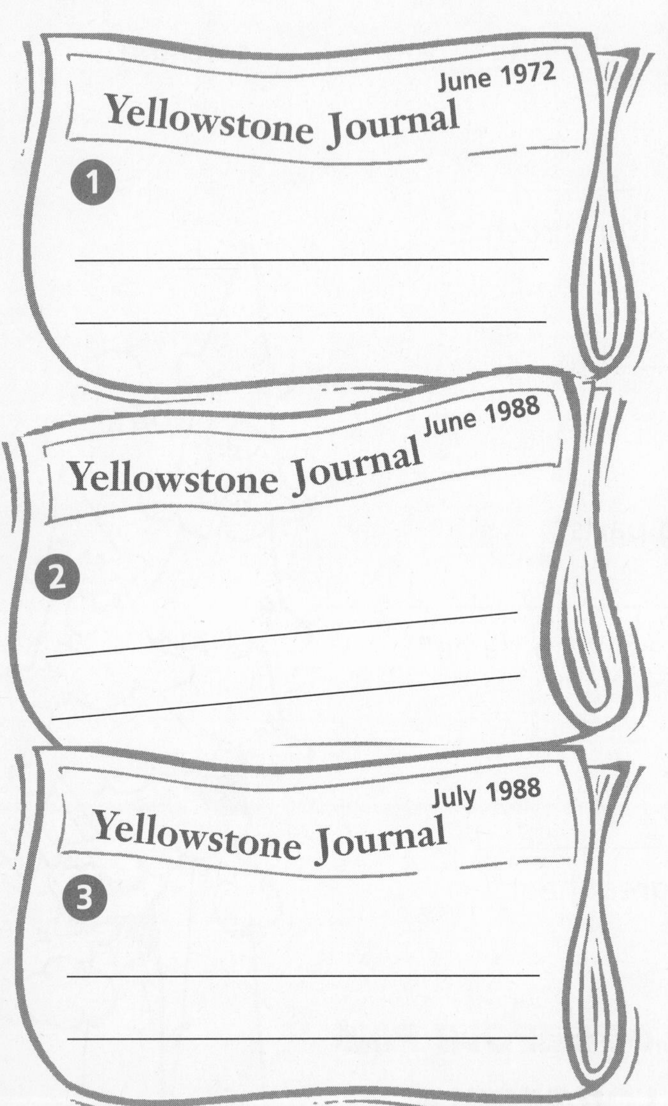


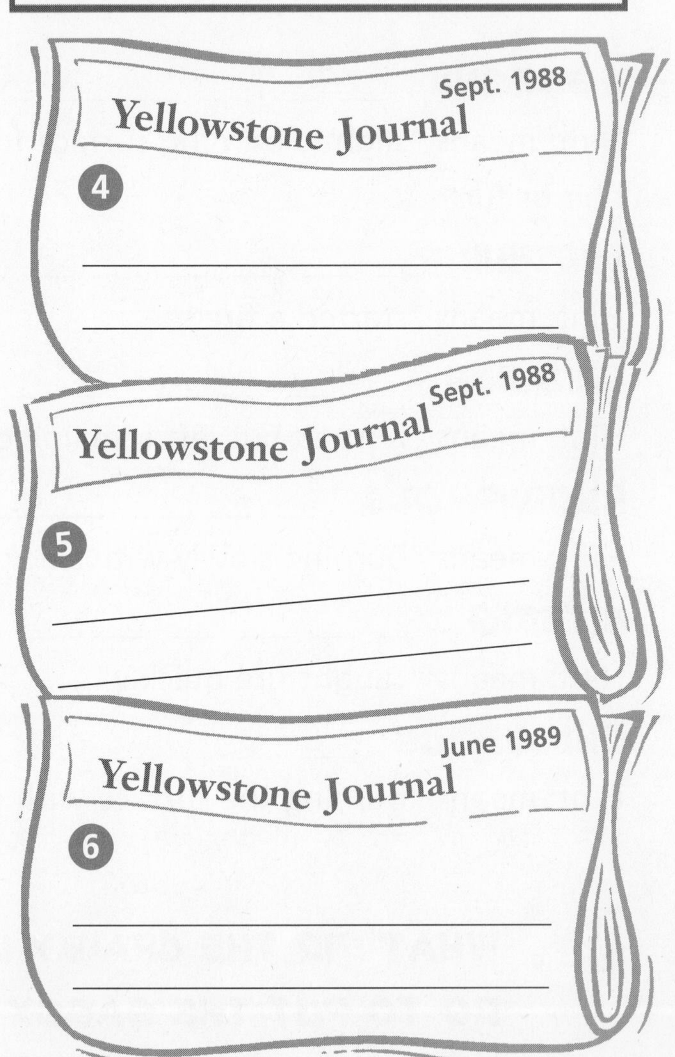


How have officials' opinions of forest fires changed over the years?

Name

# Is That a Fact?

**Read the brochure about Yellowstone National Park. Write F if the sentence is a fact. Write O if the sentence is an opinion.**

## About Yellowstone National Park

- ____ Yellowstone National Park was founded in 1872.
- ____ It covers 2.2 million acres.
- ____ The geysers are the most amazing sights in the park.
- ____ Old Faithful erupts every sixty-six minutes.

- ____ Everyone has lots of fun at Old Faithful Village.
- ____ Many kinds of wildlife live in the park.
- ____ You'll want to spend your whole vacation at Yellowstone.
- ____ The park has more than two million visitors each summer.

**Explain the difference between a fact and an opinion.**

______________________________________________

______________________________________________



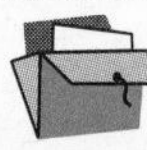

Name

# A Yellowstone Adventure

**Read the draft of a letter the Old Faithful Adventures Company will send to people who plan to visit Yellowstone. Look for sentence pairs that have the same predicate. Combine each pair into one sentence with a compound subject. Use proofreading marks.**

**Proofreading Marks**

| | |
|---|---|
| ⌒ | Delete words |
| ∧ | Insert words |
| / | Make a letter small |

Old Faithful Adventures Company
1234 Canyon Road Yellowstone Park, WY 82190

February 3, 1996

Dear Adventurer:

Thank you for your request for information about Yellowstone National Park. Yellowstone is an adventure for everyone. There is much to see in the park. Lodgepole pines blanket much of Yellowstone. Spruce trees blanket much of Yellowstone. Moose graze in open meadows. Deer graze in open meadows.

Even in summer, it can be cool in the park. Long pants are good to have on hand. Sweatshirts are good to have on hand. You will want to be comfortable while you are here.

There are several places to stay. Inns are located near the park. Cabins are located near the park. We hope this information is helpful. We look forward to seeing you this summer!

Sincerely,

Old Faithful Adventures





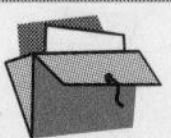

Name

# Know What I Mean?

**Read the newspaper article about the Yellowstone fire. Use context clues to answer the questions.**

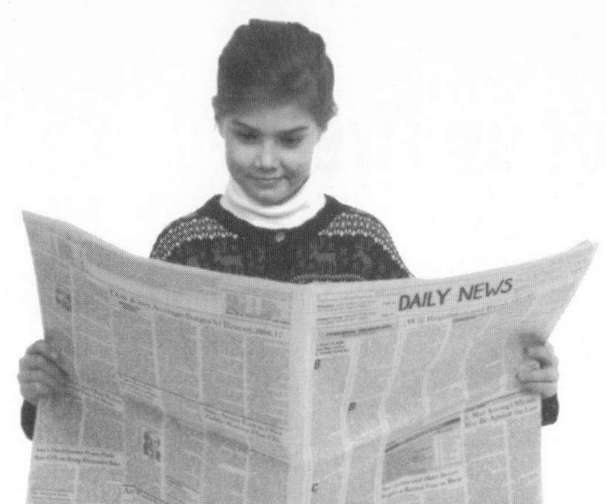


Firefighters did their best to subdue the flames, but the fire spread too quickly. In the end, only smoky and charred stumps remained where once great forests had stood. Even though the landscape looked barren, life soon began to flourish again. New grass, shrubs, and trees provided a bounty of food for the animals.

1. What might you do to **subdue** a fire?

_______________

2. What do **charred** stumps probably look like?

_______________

3. What might you see in a **barren** landscape?

_______________

4. When living things **flourish,** are they growing or are they dying? Why do you think so?

_______________

_______________

5. What word or words could be used in place of **bounty** to mean the same thing?

_______________

**Bonus** Choose two words and use them in sentences. Write the sentences on a separate piece of paper. Clearly show what each word means.

**smoldering** **shriveled** **detonated**



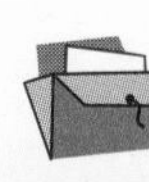

Name

# Words on Fire!

**How well do you understand forest fires? Complete the survey. Use the underlined words in your answers.**

1. Why is it unsafe to leave a campfire that is still <u>smoldering</u>?

___

___

2. What materials <u>kindled</u> the 1988 Yellowstone fire?

___

___

3. Why was the fire <u>scorching</u> some trees but leaving others untouched?

___

___

4. What <u>ignited</u> the fire in Targhee National Forest?

___

___

5. What finally stopped the Yellowstone fire from <u>singeing</u> even more land?

___

___

6. How did the <u>charred</u> trees and plants help the forest grow back?

___

___

Name

# Parachute I.D.

**Long *u*** Each Spelling Word has the long ***u*** sound. This sound can be said two ways, as in ***grew*** and ***few.*** The long ***u*** sound you hear in ***grew*** is shown as |**oo**|. The long ***u*** sound you hear in ***few*** is shown as |**yoo**|. The long ***u*** sound can be spelled with the pattern ***u***-consonant-***e***, ***ew***, ***ue***, ***oo***, or ***ui***.

|oo| or |yoo| rule grew true roots fruit

## Spelling Words

1. grew
2. roots
3. rule
4. few
5. June
6. tool
7. true
8. fruit
9. glue
10. suit

**My Study List**
What other words do you need to study for spelling? Add them to My Study List for *The Great Yellowstone Fire* in the back of this book.

**On each smoke jumper's parachute, write the Spelling Words that match the given long *u* spelling pattern.**

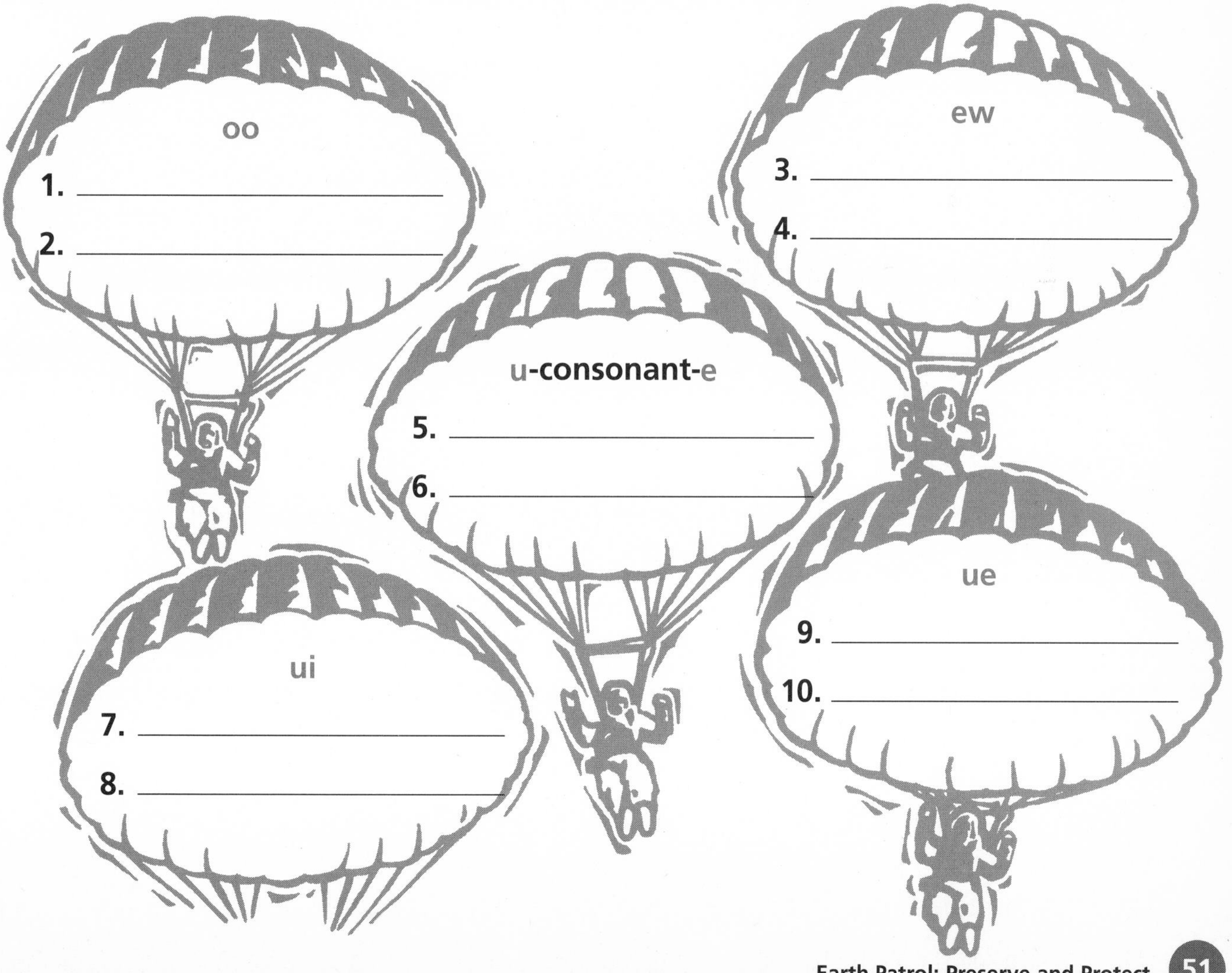

oo

1. ______________________
2. ______________________

ew

3. ______________________
4. ______________________

u-consonant-e

5. ______________________
6. ______________________

ui

7. ______________________
8. ______________________

ue

9. ______________________
10. ______________________

Name

# Spelling Spree

**Spelling Words**

| | |
|---|---|
| 1. grew | 6. tool |
| 2. roots | 7. true |
| 3. rule | 8. fruit |
| 4. few | 9. glue |
| 5. June | 10. suit |

**Fire Crew Quotations** Write a Spelling Word to complete each quotation from a firefighter.

1. "Sometimes, I grab an orange or another piece of ________________ for extra energy."
2. "It's really ________________ that firefighters work hard."
3. "This fire is worse than the one we fought last ________________."
4. "That hot pine tar is as sticky as ________________ ."
5. "A firefighter lives by that old ________________: Be prepared!"
6. "These trees are burning from their tops down to their ________________."

**Proofreading** Circle four misspelled Spelling Words in this bulletin. Then write each word correctly.

**FIREFIGHTER BULLETIN** June 29

**Yesterday, the forest fire grue by many acres. Now, spot fires are springing up from the roots of burned trees. Be careful! Never go near the fire without your suite. Take a fyew moments to dress properly. Your best firefighting tule is common sense.**

7. ________________
8. ________________
9. ________________
10. ________________

**Fiery Words** You are a reporter covering a fire. On a separate piece of paper, write a short article about the fire. Use Spelling Words from the list.

Name

# The Birth of a Park

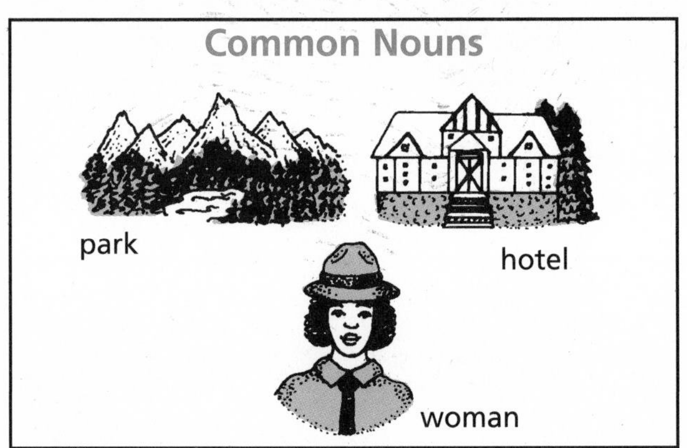


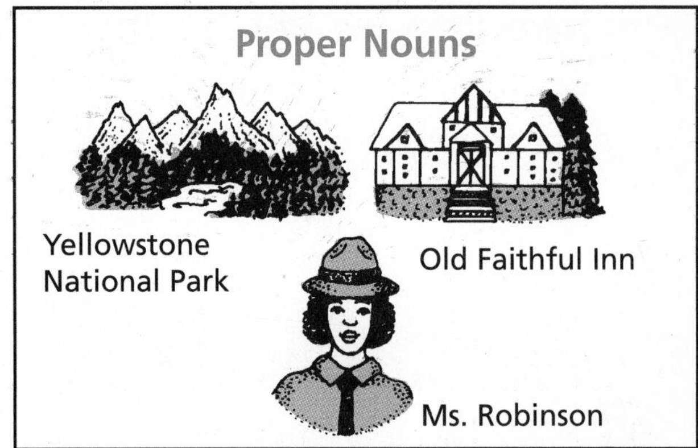


**Common and Proper Nouns** Proofread the paragraph. Find common nouns that have capital letters. Find proper nouns that need capital letters. Use the proofreading marks to show the corrections. Then write each common and proper noun correctly.

**Proofreading Marks**

/ Make a small letter

≡ Make a capital letter

Early Explorers, such as John colter, described the geysers, but People thought their tales were not true. Later groups took photographs. Then many americans felt that the land should belong to the Nation. In march of 1872, a law made yellowstone a Park. Now the national Park service runs this beautiful place.

| Common Nouns | Proper Nouns | |
|---|---|---|
| *explorers* | *Colter* | |
| | | |
| | | |
| | | |

Name

# Notable Nouns

**Common and Proper Nouns** Fill in the blanks on this historical marker with common and proper nouns of your own choice. Remember to use capital letters with proper nouns.

## Of Historical Note

On this spot one of the greatest fires in the state of ____________________ accidentally started. People came from cities as far away as ____________________ and ____________________. They worked during the month of ____________________. Many ____________________ were lost, and many ____________________ and ____________________ were destroyed. The last blaze was finally put out on ____________________. This day is a local holiday known as ____________________. Mayor ____________________ of the city of ____________________ placed this marker to honor the brave ____________________ and ____________________ who risked their lives fighting this terrible ____________________.

Name

# Rain Forest Words

Help the rain forest animals complete their sentences by writing the correct word.

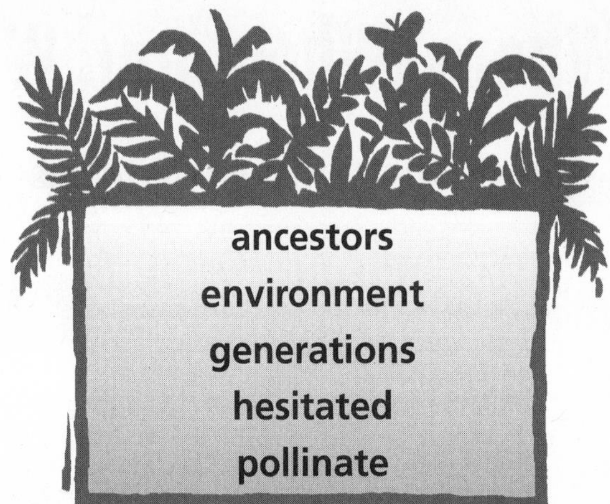

ancestors
environment
generations
hesitated
pollinate

1 I go from blossom to blossom to help ______________________ the flowers.

2 Visitors have ______________________ at the base of my tree to watch me swinging above.

3 Many ______________________ of my family have lived in this tree.

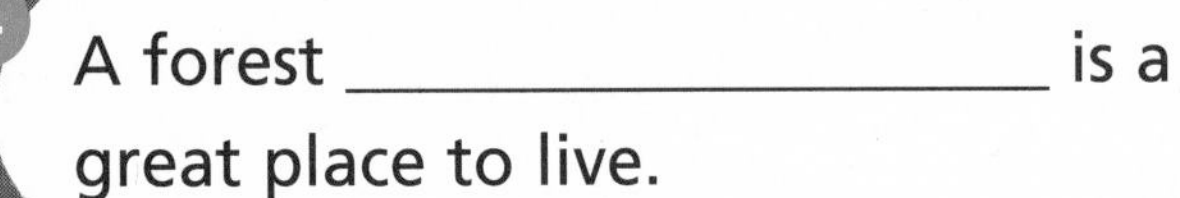

4 A forest ______________________ is a great place to live.

5 My ______________________ from years ago made their home in this forest.

Name ____________________

# Where, When, and What?

Complete the story map to tell about *The Great Kapok Tree.*

## SETTING

Where does the story take place? ____________________

____________________

Most of the animals live in the top layer of the rain forest, called the ____________________.

## EVENTS

The man came into the rain forest because he intended to

____________________.

When the man grew tired, he ____________________

____________________.

The monkeys told the man that if he cut down the Kapok tree, the heavy rains would ____________________ the soil.

The porcupines told the man that trees provide ____________________, which living things need to survive.

## ENDING

What did the man do when he woke up? ____________________

____________________

____________________

____________________

Name

# Woody's Generalizations

**The great explorer Woody Parks spent a week in the Amazon rain forest. Read the following page from his journal.**

Tuesday

This morning I watched monkeys swing on branches and vines while they chattered to each other. Most monkeys I have seen here and in other places are lively and playful. They chatter almost all the time. Where does their energy come from?

I'm glad that I brought shorts. It is always hot here. You can get a steam bath every day.

Later in the day, I heard the distant sound of trees being cut down. This made me very sad. Destroying the trees in the rain forest will destroy many lives here.

How many generalizations does Woody make in his journal entry? ___________

**Complete the chart.**

| Topic | Generalization |
|---|---|
| Monkeys | Most monkeys are lively and playful. |
| Monkeys | |
| Climate | |
| Destroying trees | |

**Write a generalization describing how Woody feels about the rain forest.**

_______________________________________________

_______________________________________________

Name

# Zoo News

**Tina read about the animals in *The Great Kapok Tree* and decided to visit the zoo. Later, she wrote an article about it for the school newspaper. Tina's article is too long. Help her make it shorter. Find sentences that share the same subject. Combine each pair into one sentence with a compound predicate. Rewrite the article.**

I went to the zoo last Sunday with my family. We saw some amazing animals. We learned many new things.

First, we went to the monkey garden. The monkeys were chattering. The monkeys were leaping through the trees. Then we went to see the lions. The lions rested on the grass. The lions bathed in the pond. They were exciting to watch.

Next, we went to the building where snakes and other reptiles live. We looked at each reptile. One of the boa constrictors had the hiccups.

My favorite animals were the elephants. They ate peanuts out of my hand. They let me pet their trunks.

Name

# It's Wonder + *ful*!

**Each item has two sentences. In the first sentence, one word is a clue. Add the suffix *-ful, -less,* or *-ly* to the word, and it will complete the second sentence. Write the letters of the word with the suffix on the blanks.**

**Example:** Do not cut down the trees. If you do, the forest will be t r e e l e s s.

1. Does the monkey have a name? Without one, it is ___ ___ ___ ___ ___ ___ ___ (___).
2. Thank you for sparing the Kapok tree. We feel very ___ ___ ___ ___ (___) ___ ___ ___.
3. The forest was quiet. The animals moved very ___ ___ (___) ___ ___ ___ ___.
4. Owl gave wise advice. Owl spoke ___ ___ ___ ___ (___) ___.
5. The birds made loud calls. They squawked (___) ___ ___ ___ ___ ___.
6. I hope the rain forest can be saved. I feel very ___ ___ ___ ___ (___) ___ ___.
7. A sudden storm came upon the forest. The storm came ___ (___) ___ ___ ___ ___ ___ ___ ___.
8. Animals need a home. Without one, they are ___ ___ ___ ___ (___) ___ ___ ___.

**Write the circled letters in order. Find a message.**

___ ___ ___ ___ ___ ___ ___ ___ work, ______________________ !
your name

Name

# Words on South America

Cut out the puzzle pieces. Match words and definitions. Complete the puzzle and glue the pieces down. Use the key to answer the question.

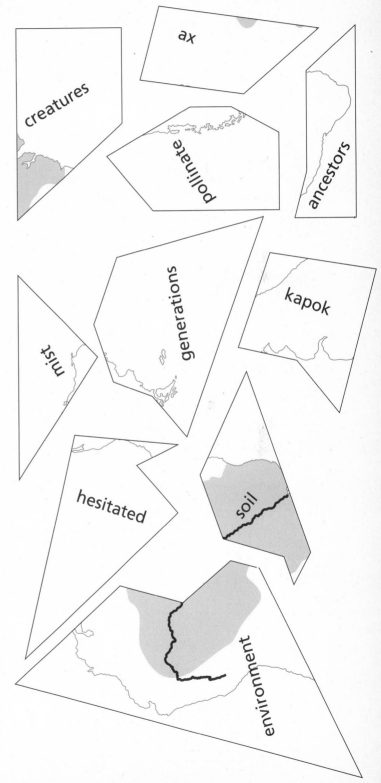

tiny drops of water

living things

dirt

surroundings

relatives of long ago

a chopping tool

a rain forest tree

paused

groups of people of about the same age

fertilize

Key

0 1000 mi.

Amazon Rain Forest

Amazon River

ax

creatures

pollinate

ancestors

generations

kapok

mist

hesitated

soil

environment

About how long is the Amazon River? ______

Name

# Proud Voices

## Vowel Sounds in *ground* and *point*

Some Spelling Words have the vowel sound you hear in ***ground.*** This sound, written as /**ou**/, is often spelled with the pattern ***ou*** or ***ow.***

/ou/ gr**ou**nd fl**ow**er

The other Spelling Words have the vowel sound you hear in ***point.*** This sound, written as /**oi**/, is often spelled with the pattern ***oi*** or ***oy.***

/oi/ p**oi**nt enj**oy**

**Spelling Words**

1. ground
2. flower
3. sound
4. soil
5. howl
6. voice
7. about
8. point
9. enjoy
10. loyal

**My Study List**
What other words do you need to study for spelling? Add them to My Study List for *The Great Kapok Tree* in the back of this book.

**Help the animals save the rain forest! Write each Spelling Word on the sign with the matching sound and spelling pattern.**

/ou/ **ou**

______
______
______

SAVE

/ou/ **ow**

______
______

OUR

/oi/ **oy**

______
______

RAIN

/oi/ **oi**

______
______
______

FOREST!

Name

# Spelling Spree

| Spelling Words | |
|---|---|
| 1. ground | 6. voice |
| 2. flower | 7. about |
| 3. sound | 8. point |
| 4. soil | 9. enjoy |
| 5. howl | 10. loyal |

**Proofreading** Circle the five misspelled Spelling Words in this speech. Then write each word correctly.

I am here to talk to you about the rain forest. Imagine that you are walking across the grond of a steamy, lush forest. You don't hear a single vois. But you can hear the houl of a monkey. You stop and look abowt. Springing from the rich soil, a brightly colored flour catches your eye.

1 ________________
2 ________________
3 ________________
4 ________________
5 ________________

**Snake Search** Write the Spelling Word that fits each clue. Then find and circle the word in the snake.

**Clues**

6. to direct; aim
7. faithful
8. the loose layer of earth in which plants grow
9. to get pleasure from
10. something that is heard

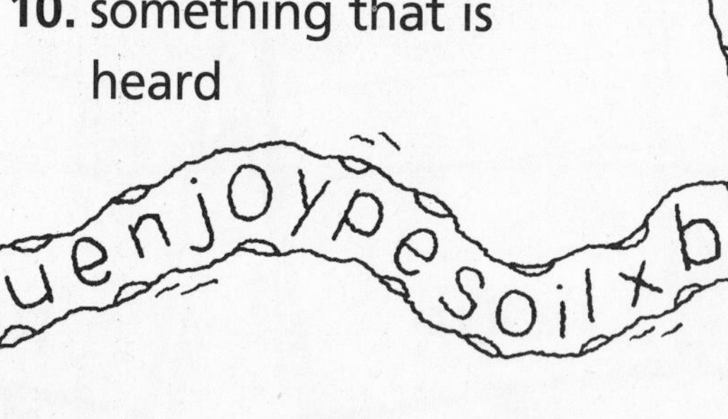

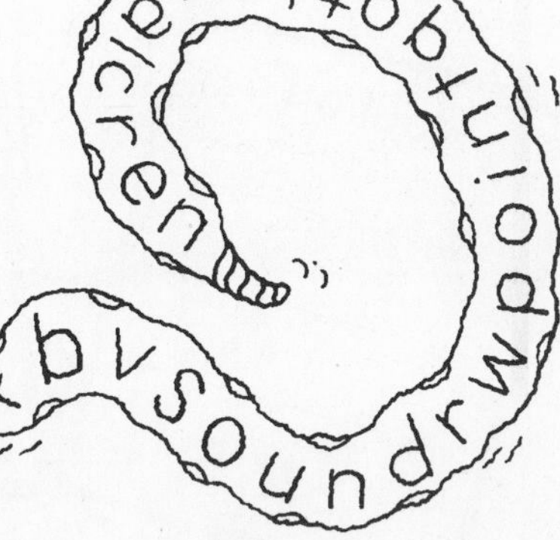


6 ________________
7 ________________
8 ________________

9 ________________
10 ________________

**Rain Forest Rules** Rain forests need protection. Visitors can damage them. Imagine that you give tours of a rain forest. On a separate piece of paper, write a set of rules for tourists to follow while they're there. Use Spelling Words from the list.

Name

# Nouns in the Rain Forest

| | Most Nouns | | Nouns ending with *s, x, ch, sh* | Nouns ending with consonant + *y* | Nouns that change | Nouns that stay the same |
|---|---|---|---|---|---|---|
| **Singular** | rose | moth | class | family | goose | sheep |
| **Plural** | roses | moths | classes | families | geese | sheep |

**Singular and Plural Nouns** Identify the people and things in this rain forest scene. Write the plural form of each noun below to label the nouns in the picture.

| | | | | |
|---|---|---|---|---|
| baby | tree | woman | monkey | deer |
| mouse | branch | butterfly | bush | berry |

Name

# Noun Puzzle

**Singular and Plural Nouns** Complete the puzzle about things you could see in a rain forest by using the clues and writing the plural form of these nouns.

| branch | crocodile | parrot | vine | sloth |
|---|---|---|---|---|
| child | deer | fly | moss | tooth |

**Down**

1. very slow-moving animals
2. young human beings
3. small green plants that form dense growth on the ground or on trees
8. what you chew with

**Across**

4. large animals with sharp teeth
5. insects with wings
6. animals with hoofs
7. plants with long, thin stems that twine around something for support
9. parts of trees
10. colorful birds

1 2 3 4 5 6 7 8 9 10

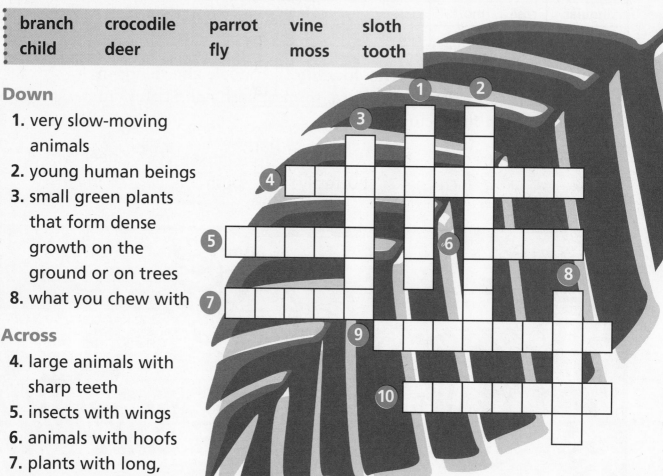

**Solve It!** Use a dictionary to find the plural forms of these nouns that name more things in the rain forest. Then use the plurals to create a crossword puzzle on another sheet of paper. Trade puzzles with a classmate, and complete each other's puzzles.

| toucan | coati | iguana | cashew | mahogany |
|---|---|---|---|---|

Name

# If I Had My Way . . .

## Persuasion Ideas

What change would you make if you were in charge of the following places—or any other place that you can think of?

| | |
|---|---|
| **If I ran the shopping mall . . .** | **If I ran a TV station . . .** |
| **If I ran the school . . .** | **If I ran the cafeteria . . .** |
| **If I ran the playground . . .** | **If I ran the neighborhood . . .** |

## My Persuasion Ideas

Write five ideas you have for persuading someone about something. Beside each idea, write who your audience would be—whom would you have to persuade?

| My goal is to . . . | The person or people I will try to persuade . . . |
|---|---|
| 1. ______________ | ______________ |
| 2. ______________ | ______________ |
| 3. ______________ | ______________ |
| 4. ______________ | ______________ |
| 5. ______________ | ______________ |

Think about each idea you wrote. Ask yourself . . .

Do I care a lot about this?

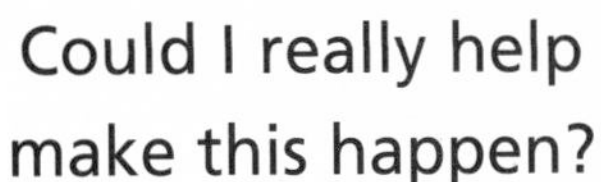

Could I really help make this happen?

What would be the best way to deliver this message? a letter? a speech? an editorial? a poster?

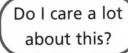

Can I think of good persuasive reasons?

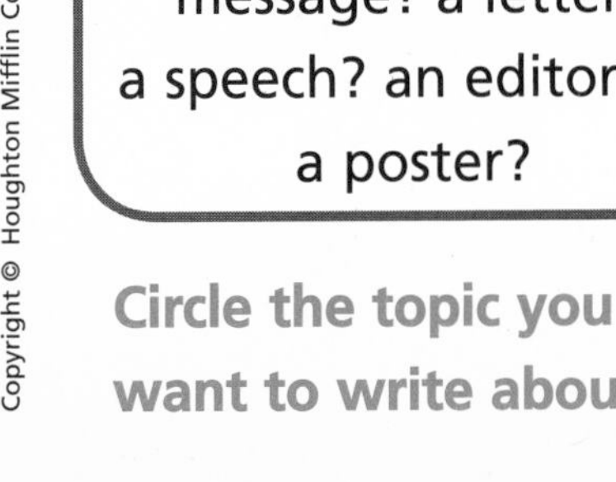

Circle the topic you want to write about.

Name

# How Convincing Can You Be?

Plan your argument. Write your goal, three reasons, and facts or experiences to support each reason.

| GOAL | | |
|---|---|---|
| | | |

| Reason #1 | Reason #2 | Reason #3 |
|---|---|---|
| | | |
| Facts or Experiences | Facts or Experiences | Facts or Experiences |
| | | |

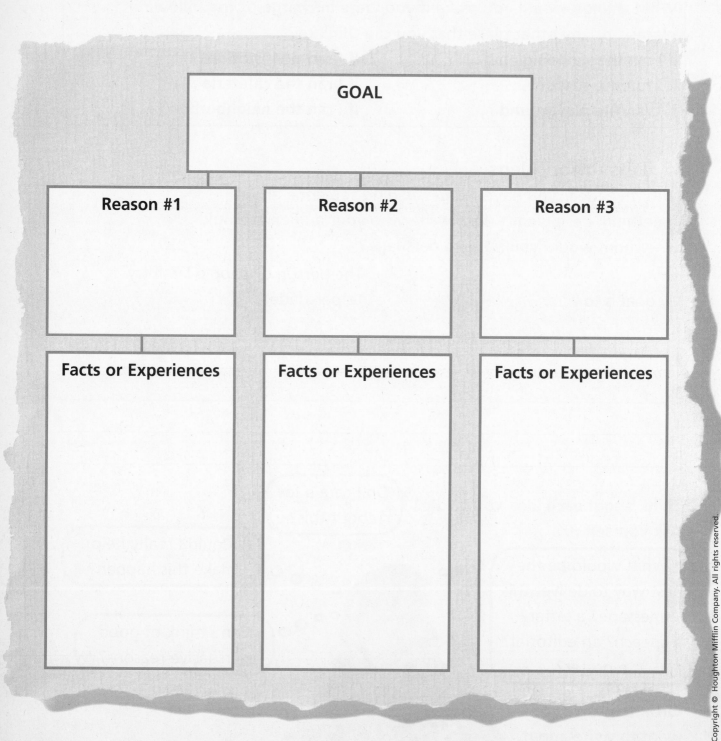

Name

# Take Another Look

## Revising Checklist

Ask yourself these questions about your persuasive writing.

- ❑ Could I state my goal more clearly?
- ❑ Is each reason convincing?
- ❑ What other facts or experiences could I add?
- ❑ How could I strengthen my conclusion to make my reader want to act?
- ❑ What other changes could I make to be more persuasive?

## Questions for a Writing Conference

Use these questions to help you discuss your persuasive writing.

- What is the best part of this piece?
- Is the goal clear?
- Are the reasons clearly stated?
- Where are more facts and experiences needed to support the reasons?
- How could the conclusion be stronger?
- Is the argument convincing? How could it be made more persuasive?

Write notes to remember ideas and comments from your writing conference.

## My Notes

Name 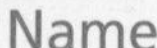

# Unscramble It!

| sort |
|---|
| haze |
| suspected |
| foul |
| enormous |

**Write the word that fits each definition.**

1. to arrange according to characteristics

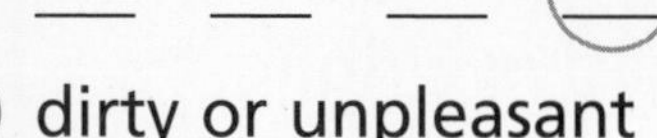

2. dirty or unpleasant

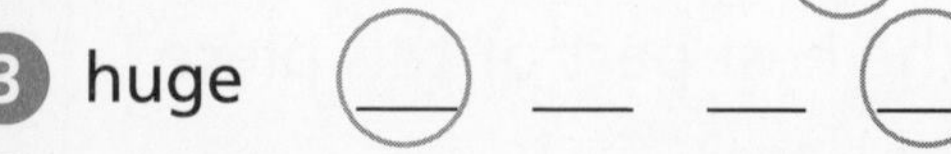

3. huge

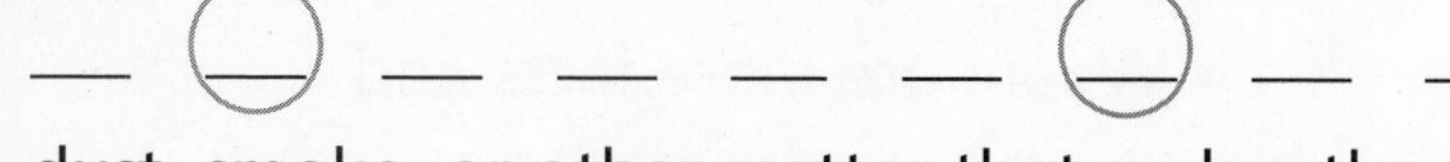

4. imagined that something was true

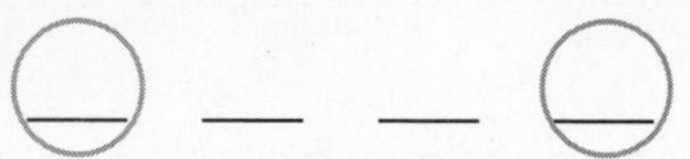

5. dust, smoke, or other matter that makes the air less clear

**Now unscramble the circled letters to make two words to complete the sentence.**

6. Protecting our environment will make

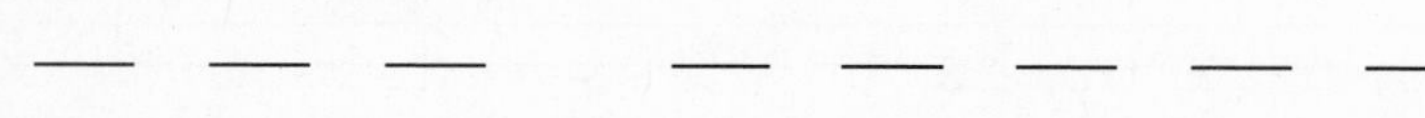 brighter.

**In each group, write the word from the box that belongs.**

7. Words about size (from small to large)

*tiny small medium* ______________ *vast*

8. Words that tell how pleasing something is (from pleasing to unpleasing)

*wonderful nice ordinary* ______________ *repulsive*

Name ______________________________

# Is That True?

**Help write a paragraph for a book jacket for *Just a Dream.* Read each sentence. If the sentence is true, move on. If it is false, rewrite it to make it true.**

*Just a Dream*

Walter was always careful not to litter. ________________________________________ Walter thought his neighbor Rose's tree was a dumb present. ________________________________________ Walter visited future worlds in a time machine. ________________________________________ In his dream, the garbage dump covered Walter's street. ________________________________________ In Walter's dream, people vacationed on top of Mount Everest.

________________________________________

When Walter woke up, he rushed downstairs for a jelly doughnut. ________________________________________ Walter learned from his dreams that the earth will be spoiled if we don't take care of it now.

________________________________________

Walter's favorite birthday present was a laser gun set. ________________________________________

Name

# Sum It Up

**Your little sister wants to know what *Just a Dream* is about. Fill in the chart. Then use the information to write a summary.**

**CHARACTER:**

**SETTING:**

**PROBLEM:**

**PLOT:**

**THEME:**

**SUMMARY:**

Name

# Brainstorm for a Book Report

Title:

Author:

Ways to get the reader's attention:

Words that describe the story:

Things to include in the summary:

My opinion of the book:

Facts that support my opinion:

Name

# Green's Plant

**Kyle just read a great book about recycling. Read his conversation with Dad. Circle all the contractions and possessives.**

Dad, here's an ad for a tour of Green's Recycling Plant. Kevin's mom took him, and they learned a lot. Let's go.

I didn't say we wouldn't go. And I can't say we won't. So I'll just say we'll see. Why don't you call and ask about the plant's hours?

**Now write the words that make up each contraction or possessive you circled.**

1 ______________________ 7 ______________________

2 ______________________ 8 ______________________

3 ______________________ 9 ______________________

4 ______________________ 10 ______________________

5 ______________________ 11 ______________________

6 ______________________ 12 ______________________

**Rewrite!** **Can you think of another way of saying these sentences? Rewrite each sentence.**

This is nobody's chair. Nobody's been sitting in it.

______________________________________________

______________________________________________

Name ______________________________

# Dreamy Word Scramble

**Read each clue and unscramble the answer.**

1. Walter's favorite pastry: **LEJYL GOUNTHUD**

   ______________________________

2. What Walter was supposed to sort: **BRAGGAE**

   ______________________________

3. Woodcutters were slicing through the tree where Walter's bed was so that they could make these: **KOTHOPICTS**

   ______________________________

4. Walter's bed was on top of one of these, which was belching foul smoke: **MOSSKATECK**

   ______________________________

5. The name of the enormous building that Walter saw on top of Mount Everest: **LETHO VEERSTE**

   ______________________________

6. When Walter awoke to a shrieking horn, he was in the middle of this: **GIYHAWH**

   ______________________________

7. Walter couldn't see this because of the yellow haze that blocked his view: **DRANG YANNOC**

   ______________________________

8. Walter suspected that the flying ducks might not find this: **CUKD NOPD**

   ______________________________

Name

# Cleanup!

**Vowel Sound in *walk*** Each Spelling Word has the vowel sound you hear in ***walk***. This sound, written as |ô|, is often spelled with the pattern ***a*** before ***l***, ***aw***, ***au***, ***ough***, or ***augh***.

|ô| walk awful because thought caught

**Circle each hidden word. Then write the Spelling Words that match the sound and pattern on each recycling can.**

## Spelling Words

1. walk
2. awful
3. because
4. lawn
5. thought
6. always
7. caught
8. bought
9. fault
10. taught

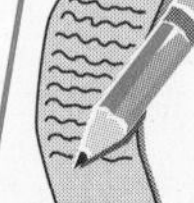

**My Study List**
What other words do you need to study for spelling? Add them to My Study List for *Just a Dream* in the back of this book.

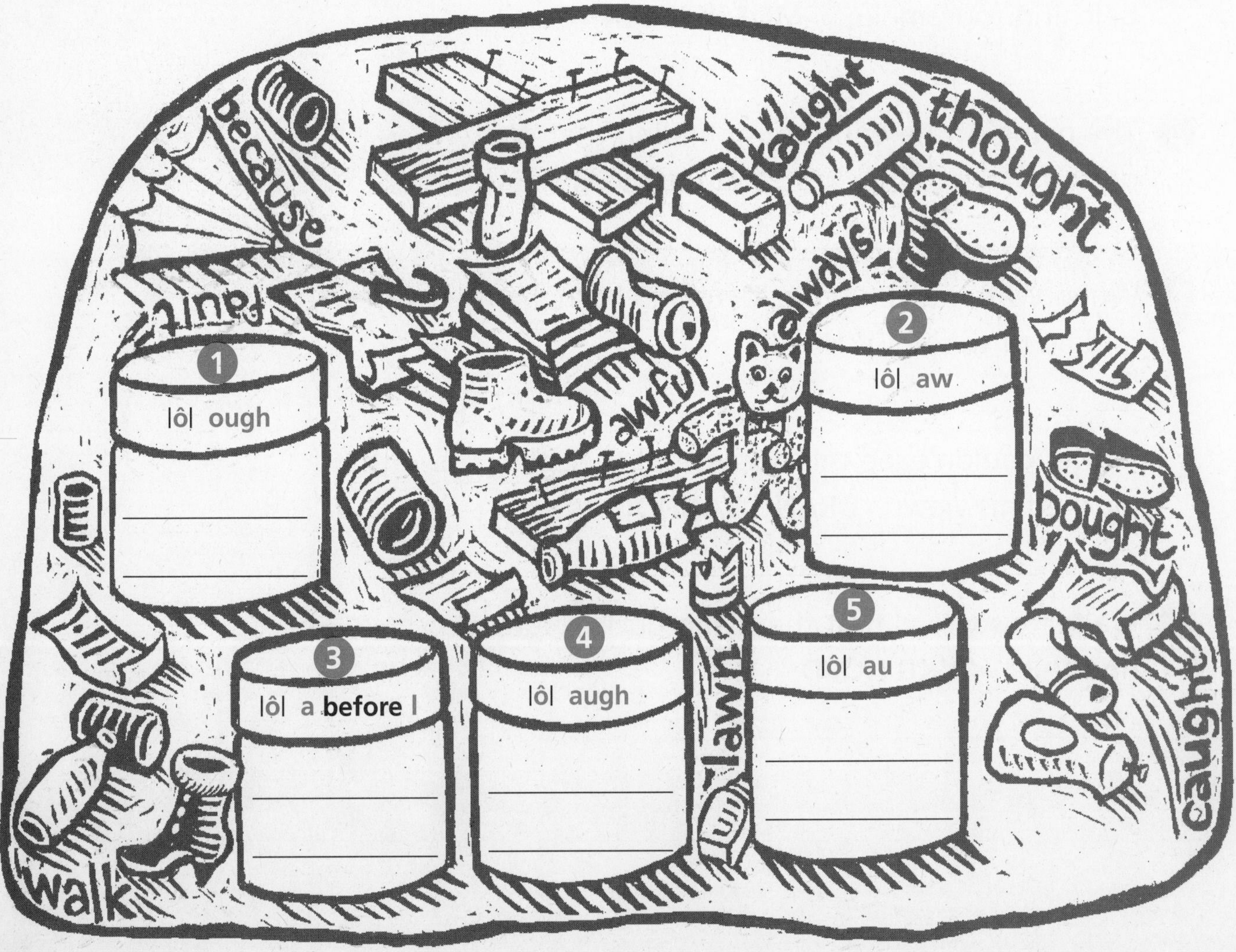

1. |ô| ough
2. |ô| aw
3. |ô| a before l
4. |ô| augh
5. |ô| au

Name

# Spelling Spree

**Spelling Words**

1. walk
2. awful
3. because
4. lawn
5. thought
6. always
7. caught
8. bought
9. fault
10. taught

**Slick Crossword** Complete the puzzle on the oil slick. Write the Spelling Word that fits each clue.

**Across**

1. ground covered with grass
3. stuck
5. for the reason that
6. paid money for

**Down**

2. every time
4. gave a lesson

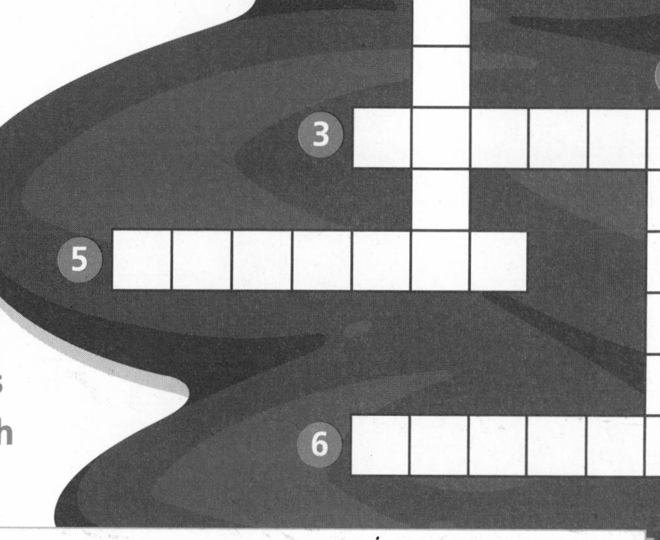


## Proofreading

Circle four misspelled Spelling Words in this letter. Then write each word correctly.

Dear Acme Chemicals:

I am writing about the awfull, smelly smoke coming from your plant. Whenever I wauk by it, my eyes water. I thoght I had an allergy. But then my lawn died. Now I know that your company is at falt.

7 ______________________

9 ______________________

8 ______________________

10 ______________________

**HOPE Happenings** Join HOPE—Help Our Poor Earth. On a separate piece of paper, write five slogans to encourage people to save our planet. Use Spelling Words from the list.

Name

# Don't Pollute!

| Singular | Singular Possessive | Plural | Plural Possessive |
|---|---|---|---|
| rider | rider**'s** | riders | rider**s'** |
| lady | lady**'s** | ladies | ladie**s'** |
| man | man**'s** | men | men**'s** |
| moose | moose**'s** | moose | moose**'s** |

**Possessive Nouns** Help Walter finish the poster. Rewrite each phrase on the poster, using the possessive form of each underlined noun.

1. eggs belonging to <u>birds</u>
2. crops of <u>farmers</u>
3. homes of <u>deer</u>
4. babies of the <u>animals</u>
5. lungs belonging to <u>children</u>
6. catch of the <u>fishermen</u>
7. food belonging to the <u>people</u>
8. forests belonging to our <u>country</u>
9. lakes in the <u>state</u>
10. health of <u>everyone</u>

**STOP POLLUTION NOW!**
**10 Things YOU Can Save**

1. ______________________
2. ______________________
3. ______________________
4. ______________________
5. ______________________
6. ______________________
7. ______________________
8. ______________________
9. ______________________
10. ______________________

Then write these phrases with possessive nouns to complete the sentence below.

poster belonging to <u>Walter</u>    project of the <u>class</u>

This is ______________________ for the ______________________.

Name ................................................................

# It's a Secret!

**Possessive Nouns** Use the pictures from the boy's dream to write secret words. Think of a word. Then write clues telling where to find the letters in the word. Use possessive nouns. (Be sure the clues are in the correct order!)

**Example:** Secret word: ape
**Clues** twins' sign A; octopus's second arm P; fisherman's net E

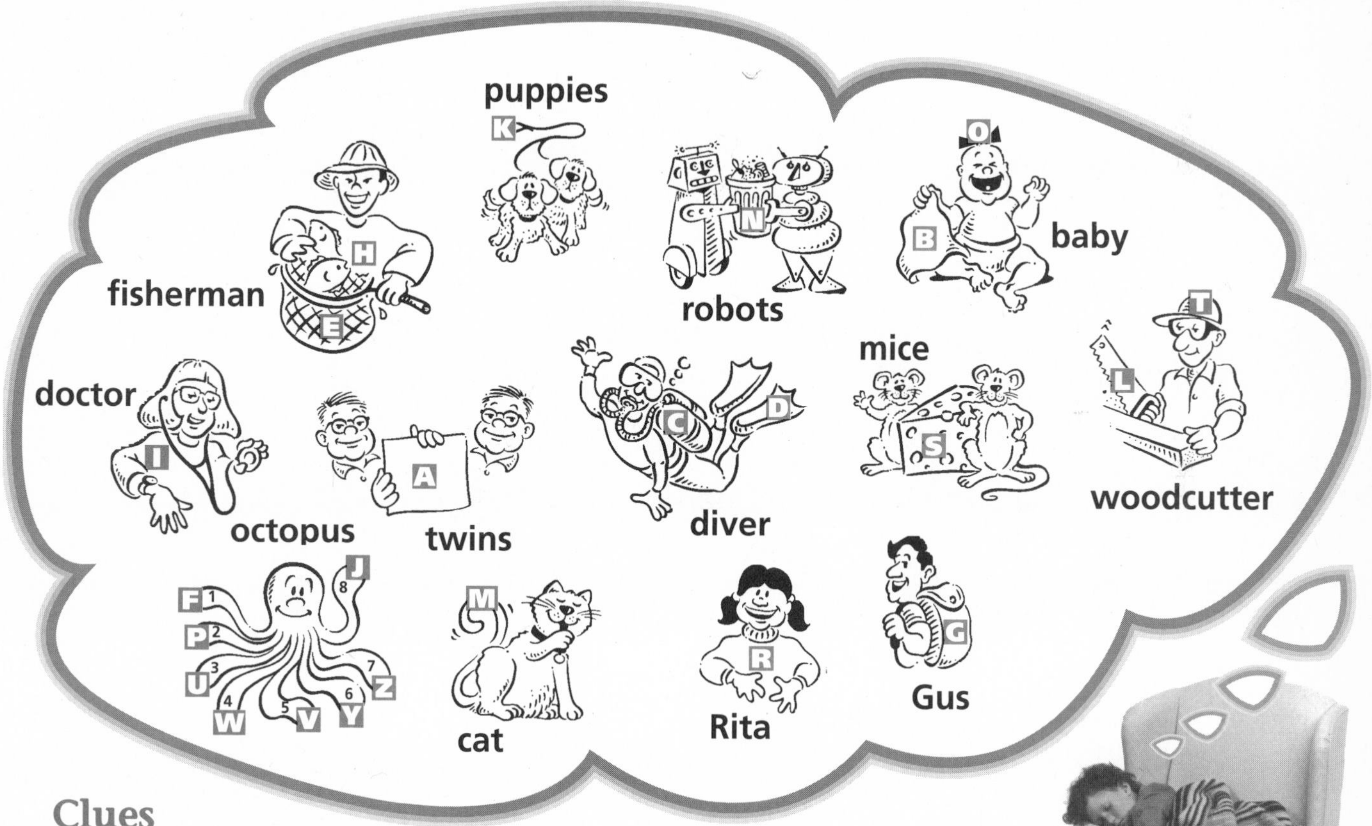

puppies K
fisherman H E
robots N
baby O B
doctor I
twins A
diver C D
mice S
woodcutter T L
octopus F 1 P 2 U 3 W 4 V 5 Y 6 Z 7 J 8
cat M
Rita R
Gus G

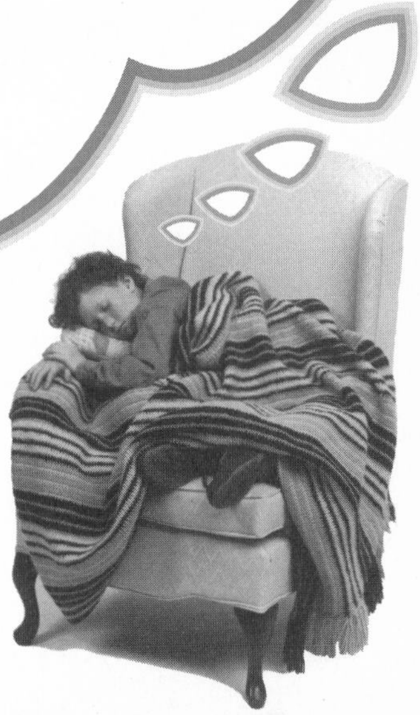

## Clues

______________________________________________

______________________________________________

______________________________________________

______________________________________________

**Extra!** Trade clues with a classmate and figure out each other's secret words.

Name

# Video Announcement

**Study this storyboard for a video announcement.**

|  | <br> |  |
|---|---|---|
| "Stop cutting down the rain forest." | "It is home for many plants and animals." | "They will all become extinct without it." |

**Persuade people to save the environment. Create a storyboard based on your reading in Earth Patrol.**

1. Write the topic of your storyboard. ______________________
2. Use the chart below to draft your ideas for images and script. Include general statements and facts that support your opinions.
3. Practice your announcement. It should last only 30 seconds.
4. Make a final copy of your storyboard.

| | | |
|---|---|---|
| | | |
| | | |

## Checklist

**Before you share your storyboard, use this list to check your work.**

- ☐ My work shows that the world's future is linked to the environment.
- ☐ I can identify both opinions and facts in my storyboard.
- ☐ The opinions I've used are backed by facts.
- ☐ The generalizations I've used are accurate and persuasive.

Name

# Super Sleuths

Hello, Super Sleuth! Chart your progress as you and the Super Sleuths solve each mystery and crack each case.

| | What mystery has to be solved? | What details in the story were important clues? Why? |
|---|---|---|
| Meg Mackintosh and the Case of the Curious Whale Watch | | |
| Julian, Secret Agent | | |
| Encyclopedia Brown and the Case of the Disgusting Sneakers | | |

So far, so good, Super Sleuth! Now continue charting your progress on the next page.

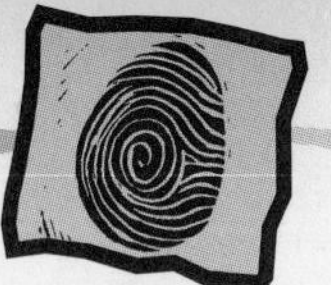

Name

# Super Sleuths

Super Sleuth, continue charting your progress as you and the Super Sleuths solve each mystery and crack each case.

| | How did the Super Sleuth crack the case and solve the mystery? | Were you able to solve the mystery before the Super Sleuth? How? |
|---|---|---|
| Meg Mackintosh and the Case of the Curious Whale Watch | | |
| Julian, Secret Agent | | |
| Encyclopedia Brown and the Case of the Disgusting Sneakers | | |

What did you learn about how Super Sleuths find clues in order to solve a mystery? ______________________________

______________________________

______________________________

Name ______________________________

# How to Cook Up a Mystery Story

Complete the recipe for writing a mystery by writing the correct definitions next to the boldface words.

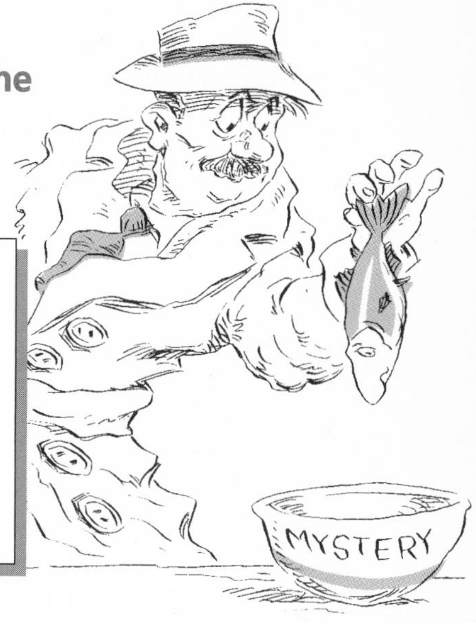


**Definitions You Will Need**

- an opinion or a guess based on a little information
- reach a conclusion about
- a reason for committing a crime
- a claim that a person was not at the scene of a crime
- a false clue that throws a person off the trail
- a person who does something for pleasure, not money
- people who may be guilty

First, find a crime.

To this crime, add two or more **suspects,** ______________________________ ______________________________. Each suspect needs a **motive,** ______________________________, such as a need for money.

To each suspect add an **alibi,** ______________________________ ______________________________, to show that the suspect might not be guilty.

Stir in a detective. A police officer or a smart **amateur,** ______________________________ ______________________________, will do.

Set the detective on the trail of clues until the detective develops a **theory,** ______________________________, about who did the crime.

Spice up your mystery with a **red herring,** ______________________________ ______________________________, to confuse your readers.

When everything is nicely whipped together, let the detective add up all the clues to **deduce**, or ______________________________, who the real criminal is. Pour into a book and allow readers to enjoy!

Name

# Get Meg Organized

Help Meg organize her notes. Write the clues that go with each suspect on his or her notebook page. Draw a line through the clues that turned out to be red herrings, or false clues.

**Clues**

- said his pocket watch was jammed
- personal things found at the crime scene
- doesn't like treasure hunters
- needs money for school
- likes expensive gems
- collects stamps
- needs money to retire
- took photos from the pilothouse
- used the telescope in the pilothouse

Dr. Susan Peck

Mr. Oliver Morley

Mrs. Clarissa Maxwell

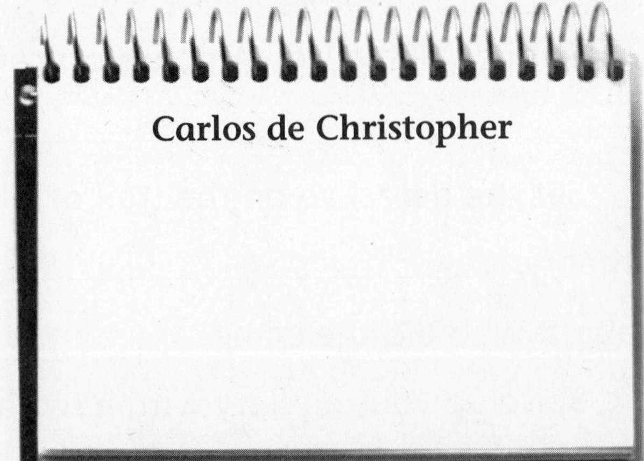

Carlos de Christopher

Explain how the clues you didn't cross out helped Meg solve the mystery.

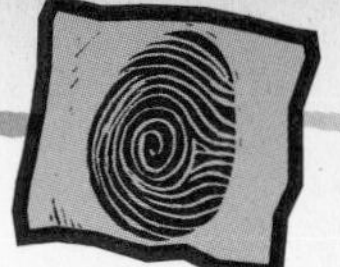

Name

# Souper Sleuthing the Details

**Read the page from the journal of detective Sam Slade and complete the chart. Then solve the mystery.**

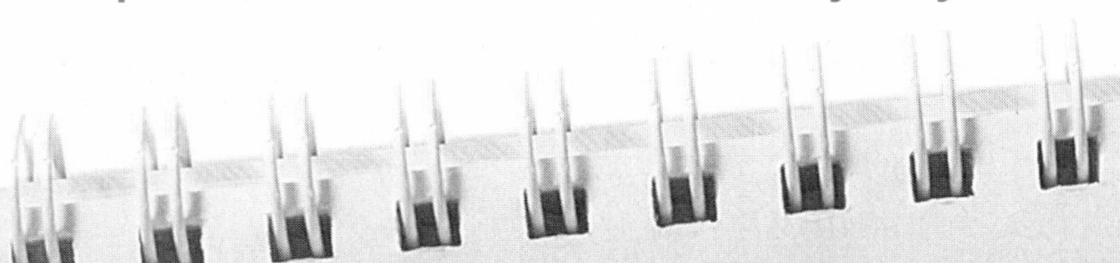

I was on a stakeout with my rival detective, Big Floyd Fink. We were in an alley, watching the old warehouse. It was a cold night, the kind of cold that stings your nose.

I bought some hot soup from Eddie's Diner. I had forgotten to get crackers, so I left the soup at the stakeout and went back to the diner. When I got back to the alley, Big Floyd was eating soup, and my soup was gone.

"What's the big idea? Give me back my soup, you crook!" I said.

"This isn't your soup," gasped Floyd, burning his tongue. "I brought this soup with me four hours ago."

I'm sure Big Floyd took my soup, but I can't prove it.

| Detail | Why Is It an Important Clue? |
|---|---|
| It was a very cold night. | |
| The stakeout was in an alley. | |
| Big Floyd said he had his soup with him for four hours. | |
| Big Floyd burned his tongue. | |

How can you prove that Big Floyd Fink was not telling the truth?

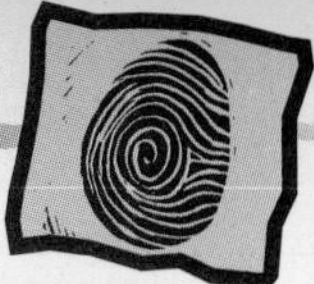

Name

# The Play's the Thing

**Rewrite this story beginning in a play format. Include any necessary stage directions to tell the actors how to speak or what to do. Use a separate sheet of paper if you need more room.**

On Monday, Mr. MacIntyre unlocked the door to his fourth-grade classroom and walked to his desk. As he was straightening papers, he suddenly stopped.

"Oh, no," he muttered, quickly opening and shutting desk drawers. "It can't be."

"Hey, Mr. Mac! We see you hiding!" said two laughing voices together. Jamal and Leticia entered the room just as Mr. MacIntyre was crawling under his desk, searching.

"I can't find my grade book!" Mr. MacIntyre exclaimed. "I know I left it in my desk Friday afternoon."

**Characters** (include only the characters introduced)

**Scene 1**

Name ..............................................

# Telegraphic Messages

Solve the case of the hidden message! Match each clue to one of the words with the root *tele* or *graph.* Write the word on the blanks.

| autobiography | autograph | geography | graphics |
|---|---|---|---|
| graphite | telephoto | telescope | telecommunications |

1. We study ___ ___ ___ ___ ___ ___ ___ ___ (___) to learn about the earth's places and people.
2. Use a ___ ___ ___ ___ ___ ___ (___) ___ ___ to see planets and stars.
3. A fan might ask a basketball player to ___ (___) ___ ___ (___) ___ ___ ___ ___ a picture.
4. Ima Starr wrote the story of her life. Her book is called an ___ ___ ___ (___) ___ ___ ___ ___ ___ ___ ___ ___ ___ ___ ___ ___.
5. The science of sending messages over long distances is called (___) ___ ___ ___ ___ ___ ___ ___ ___ ___ ___ (___) ___ ___ (___) ___ ___ ___ ___.
6. Computer ___ (___) ___ ___ ___ (___) ___ ___ are charts and pictures you can add to text.
7. Pencils need (___) ___ ___ ___ (___) ___ ___ ___ to write.
8. A ___ ___ ___ ___ ___ ___ ___ (___) ___ camera lens makes far-off things seem closer.

To find the hidden message, write the circled letters in order.

___ ___ ___  ___ ___ ___  ___ ___  ___ ___ ___ ___ ___ ___!

Name

# Villainous Vocabulary

Each clue goes with a word on Captain Edword Teach's map. Trace the path to the treasure by drawing a line that follows the clues. Your line must touch the **X** next to each word once. The first one is done for you. Happy treasure hunting!

## Clues

1. Go from the ship's anchor to the word that is something you show to prove you're right.
2. Take five paces to the word that means a guess a detective might make to solve a crime.
3. Go west to the word that tells how you can think to reach a conclusion.
4. Now move to the word that means a story that proves someone was not at a crime.
5. Take a short walk to the word that tells where you might hide jewels.
6. A word talking about a person who is not a professional is your next stop.
7. Be careful not to meet any people who might be guilty of a crime at your next stop.
8. Are you on the right track? This next word might be false evidence that could make you lose your way!
9. Why are you doing this? You must have a reason, and that word is your next stop.
10. Now, find the treasure! Go to the word that means something that you want to solve!



If you found the treasure, you also discovered a clue to the name of Captain Teach's ship. What do you think it is? ____________________

Name

# Whale Words

**Unusual Vowel Spellings** Each Spelling Word has an unusual spelling pattern for the long *a*, short *u*, or short *e* sound. Some Spelling Words have the long *a* sound spelled with the pattern *ea*.

|ā| great

Other Spelling Words have the short *u* sound spelled with the pattern *ou* or *o*.

|ŭ| touch nothing

The other Spelling Words have the short *e* sound spelled with the pattern *ea*.

|ĕ| meant

**Write each Spelling Word beneath the correct pattern.**

## Spelling Words

1. great
2. touch
3. meant
4. break
5. nothing
6. young
7. weather
8. money
9. ton
10. breath

**My Study List**
What other words do you need to study for spelling? Add them to My Study List for Meg Mackintosh and the Case of the Curious Whale Watch in the back of this book.

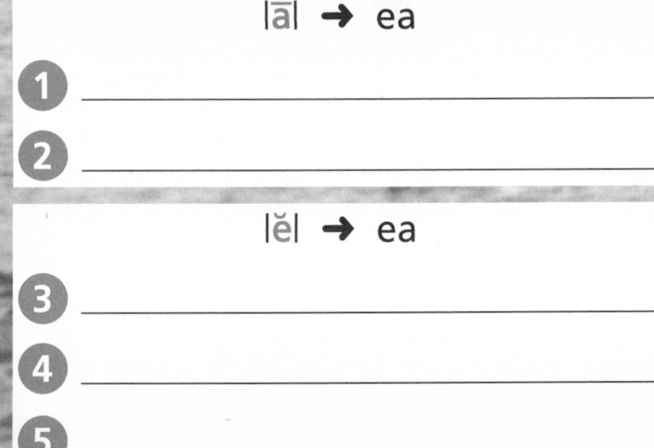


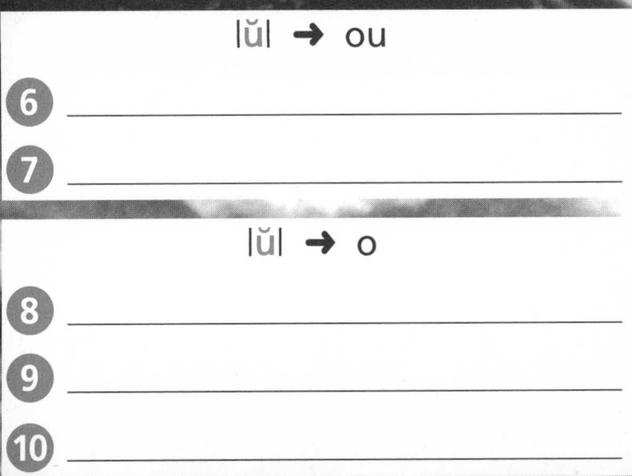

Name

# Spelling Spree

**Spelling Words**

1. great
2. touch
3. meant
4. break
5. nothing
6. young
7. weather
8. money
9. ton
10. breath

**Proofreading** Circle five misspelled Spelling Words in this ship captain's log. Then write each word correctly.

*August 6 Today's whale watching trip was nouthing but trouble. First, the wether turned stormy. Then a passenger decided to brake into my strongbox. There was no mony there, but the man did steal a valuable stamp. A yung girl onboard deserves a ton of praise for catching the thief.*

1 ______
2 ______
3 ______
4 ______
5 ______

**Treasure Hunt** Start at the first point and follow each set of directions, picking up a letter at each point. Then unscramble the letters to write a Spelling Word.

6. southern tip ➜ palm tree ➜ top of mountain ➜ small lake ➜ sandy beach
7. large lake ➜ palm tree ➜ sandy beach
8. small lake ➜ northern tip ➜ southern tip ➜ sailboat ➜ shack ➜ palm tree
9. large lake ➜ bottom of mountain ➜ palm tree ➜ campfire ➜ northern tip
10. sailboat ➜ southern tip ➜ palm tree ➜ flag ➜ small lake

6 ______
7 ______
8 ______
9 ______
10 ______

**A Sailor's Song** The sailor who made Captain Quinn's treasure map may have been a pirate. What kind of song might he have sung? Write it on a separate sheet of paper. Use Spelling Words from the list.

Name

# Good Detective Work!

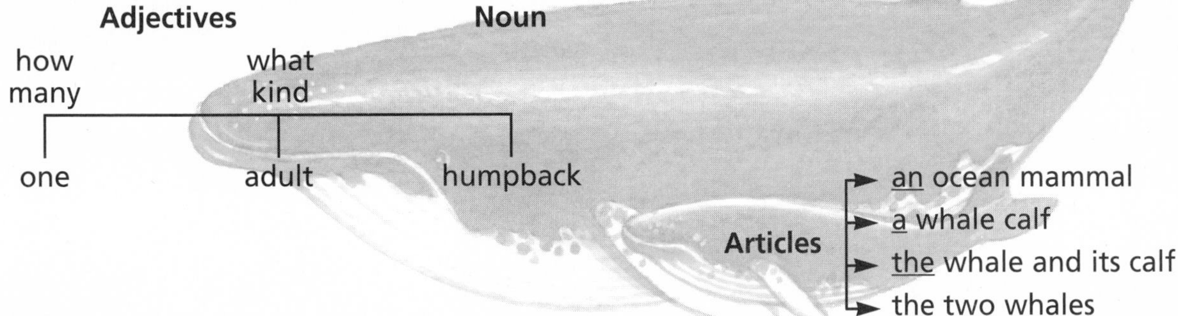


**Adjectives** Complete each sentence with the adjective that fits best. Use each adjective only once. Underline the noun each adjective modifies. Write whether the adjective tells *what kind* or *how many*.

**all six puzzling color one**

1. Meg had **o**nly __________ goal. __________
2. She would crack **t**his __________ case. __________
3. There were __________ p**o**ssible suspects. __________
4. She studied __________ her c**l**ues. __________
5. Her __________ photo**g**raphs were useful. __________

Complete each sentence by choosing the correct article in ( ). Then write your choice in the blank.

6. Every **s**uspect had ______ motive. (a, an)
7. She needed to find o**u**t who did not have ______ alibi. (a, an)
8. Meg looke**d** at ______ drawings she had made. (a, the)
9. Finally, she had ______ answ**e**r. (a, the)
10. Mr. Morley was ______ one who stole t**h**e treasure map! (an, the)

Now write the letters in dark type in the spaces that match the sentence numbers.

Meg is a ___ ___ ___ ___ (5 1 3 8) ___ ___ ___ ___ ___ ___ (6 4 9 7 2 10).

Name

# Suspect Lineup

**Adjectives** Here are three possible suspects for Meg's next adventure. Write a brief description of each one. Use adjectives that tell what kind and how many, and the articles *a, an*, and *the.*

Name

# The Mystery of the Missing Polar Bear

**Use the vocabulary words to complete these storyboards for a new mystery movie. Write captions for the first four scenes. Then draw the last two scenes and write the captions.**

| investigate | mischievous | mighty | glared |
|---|---|---|---|

Name ______________________________

# Neighborhood Children Save Dog

**A newspaper reporter is interviewing the characters from *Julian, Secret Agent*. Write Y if the answer to each question is yes. Write N if the answer is no. If the answer is no, write the correct answer.**

_____ **Gloria,** did you, Julian, and Huey go to the supermarket to buy groceries?

______________________________

_____ **Julian,** did you and your friends find a dog locked in a car in a parking lot?

______________________________

_____ **Huey,** did Gloria want to leave the dog and find another crime to investigate?

______________________________

_____ **Gloria,** did the license plate on the car read "MIGHTY-1"?

______________________________

_____ **Julian,** is it true that the store manager was not worried about the dog because it was cold outside?

______________________________

Now, tell the reporter how Julian, Gloria, and Huey solved the case.

______________________________

______________________________

______________________________

______________________________

Name

# Dear Problem-Solver

This letter is from the advice column in a newspaper. Read the letter. Then fill in the problem-solving chart.

Dear Problem-Solver,

A new girl just moved to our neighborhood. She has a huge, shaggy dog that barks fiercely at me when I pass by her house. I don't want to walk all the way around the block on my way to school. What should I do?

Not Really Scared

**Problem:**

| Possible Solutions | Advantages | Disadvantages |
|---|---|---|
| 1. talk to girl about dog | | |
| 2. | | |
| 3. | | |

**On another sheet of paper, write a letter from Problem-Solver to Not Really Scared suggesting the solution you think is best.**

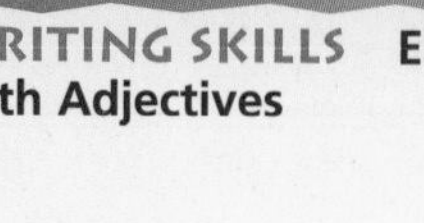

Name

# Dog Catalog

**The pictures show items in a catalog for dog owners. Write a caption for each picture, describing the item. Use adjectives to tell what kind and how many. Color the pictures to show what they look like and to help you describe them.**

**Dog Beds**

**Dog Collar**

**Dog Dishes**

**Our Best Dog Food**

Name

# Hot Dog!

Find antonyms from the box that fit in the sentences. Your antonyms must also fit in the crisscross puzzle.

long
open
happy
fast
early
hot
late
short
slow
closed
sad
cold

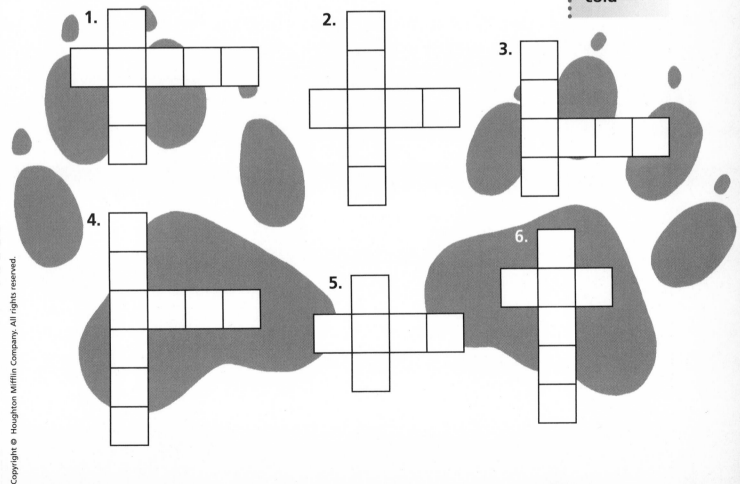

1. It was ____ in the afternoon.
2. We rode bikes around for a ____ time looking for crimes to solve.
3. I like to ride ____ when I'm on the job!
4. We spotted a dog in a car with the windows ____.
5. The temperature was very ____ that day.
6. The story had a ____ ending.

1.

2.

3.

4.

5.

6.

Name ______________________

# Join Super Sleuths, Inc.

Fill out this application to become a super sleuth.

1. A broken cookie jar is on the floor. Who did it, a **mischievous** child or a dangerous **criminal**? ______________________
   Why? ______________________
   ______________________

2. Strange cries of "Help!" come from a shut closet. The door is stuck! Why might someone called **Mighty** Mo be helpful?
   ______________________
   ______________________

3. Desserts have been disappearing from the school lunchroom. You have been asked to **investigate**. What should you do?
   ______________________
   ______________________

4. Your first suspect looked **nervous**, the second **glared** at you, and the third gave a **sigh**. Explain why each might be showing signs of guilt.
   First: ______________________
   ______________________
   Second: ______________________
   ______________________
   Third: ______________________
   ______________________

Name

# Worth Barking For

**Vowel + *r* Sounds** Each Spelling Word has a vowel sound + *r*. The vowel sound + *r* in ***park*** is written as |är|. It is often spelled with the pattern ***ar***.

|är| park

The vowel sound + *r* in ***care*** is written as |âr|. It is often spelled with the pattern ***are*** or ***air***.

|âr| care air

The vowel sound + *r* in ***ear*** is written as |îr|. It is often spelled with the pattern ***ear*** or ***eer***.

|îr| ear peer

## Spelling Words

1. park
2. care
3. cart
4. glare
5. ear
6. peer
7. air
8. chair
9. beard
10. cheer

**My Study List**
What other words do you need to study for spelling? Add them to My Study List for *Julian, Secret Agent* in the back of this book.

**Write each Spelling Word on the bone that has the same pattern for the |är|, |âr|, or |îr| sound.**

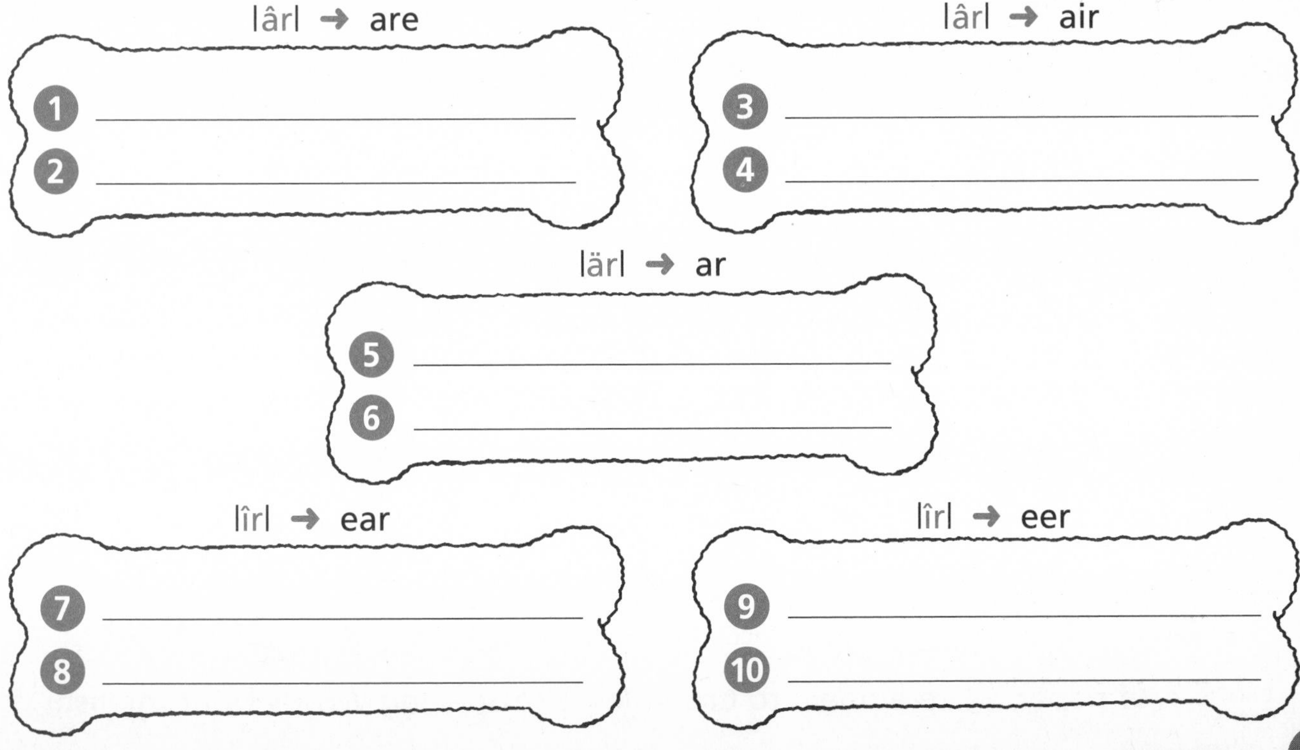

Name

# Spelling Spree

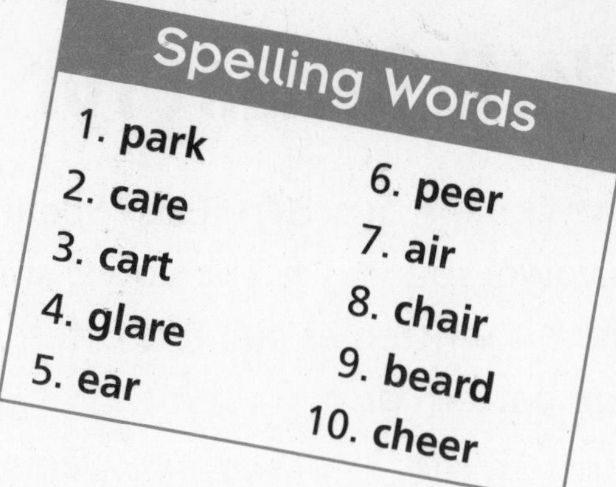

**Spelling Words**
1. park
2. care
3. cart
4. glare
5. ear
6. peer
7. air
8. chair
9. beard
10. cheer

**Write the Spelling Word that best completes each photo caption.**

1 
This dog trims its own ______________.

2 
This dog pushes its own grocery ______________.

3 
This dog can wiggle one ______________ at a time.

4 
This dog sits in its own ______________.

5 
This dog can ______________ its own car.

6 
This dog loves to ______________.

**Proofreading** **Circle four misspelled Spelling Words in this note. Then write each word correctly.**

*Dear Crimebusters,*

*Thanks for saving Crumbles. He is alive today because you decided to pere into my car. I'm taking good caire of him now. I always park my car in the shade and make sure he has fresh are. I don't ever want my little dog to glaer at me again!*

*Your friend,*

*MIGHTY-1*

7 ______________

8 ______________

9 ______________

10 ______________

**Puppy Love** Pretend that you are MIGHTY-1. On a separate sheet of paper, write a poem to Crumbles. Use Spelling Words from the list.

Name

# Puzzle It Out

**Comparing with Adjectives** Use the sentence clues to write the correct form of the adjective with *-er* or *-est* on the puzzle. The letters in the shaded column tell something that all good detectives must be.

Adjective
young
fine
happy
flat
Comparing two
younger
finer
happier
flatter
Comparing three or more
youngest
finest
happiest
flattest


1. A car was the ____ of all places that day. (**hot**)
2. It would be ____ to stay in the shade than in a car. (**healthy**)
3. MIGHTY-1 was the ____ of them all when his dog fainted. (**sorry**)
4. That supermarket aisle needs to be much ____ for carts to pass. (**wide**)
5. The rawhide bone was the ____ toy of all to chew. (**tough**)
6. Someone answered in a ____ voice than his. (**rude**)
7. He gave them the ____ look they had ever seen. (**angry**)
8. The heat made them ____ than before. (**thirsty**)

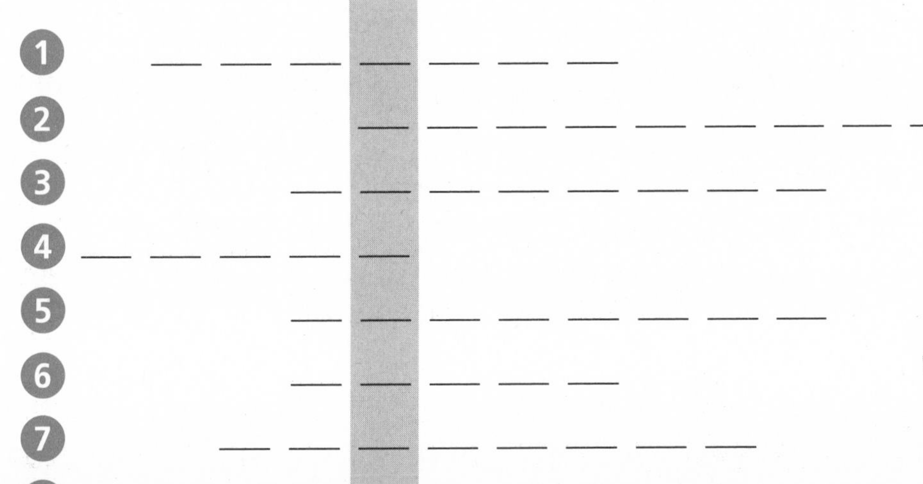

Name

# The Most Difficult Choice

### Comparing with *more* and *most*

| Adjective | Comparing Two | Comparing Three or More |
|---|---|---|
| enormous | more enormous | most enormous |

**Comparing with Adjectives** **Suppose that MIGHTY-1 invites Julian, Huey, Gloria, and their parents on an outing. The children are trying to decide where to go. Complete the letter with *more* or *most*. On the last blank, write the choice you would make!**

Dear MIGHTY-1,

We have been thinking about whether to go to the dog show, the zoo, or the carnival on Saturday. We think the dog show would be the __________ informative. The carnival would be __________ entertaining than the dog show, but it is also the __________ expensive of the three choices. The zoo is a good choice too, because we think it is __________ informative than the carnival and __________ entertaining than the dog show.

Choosing where to go seems even __________ difficult than fighting crime! We are not sure which idea is the __________ appealing. We finally decided to choose what we thought would be the __________ enjoyable for you and Crumbles. Our choice is the ____________________! We'll see you on Saturday.

Sincerely,
Julian, Gloria, and Huey

**Extra!** On a separate sheet of paper, write two sentences using adjectives with *more* and *most* to tell why you made the choice you did.

Name

# Search for a Topic

## Description Ideas

**Do these ideas suggest any topics?**

- your favorite food
- the food you like least
- your favorite person
- a family "treasure"
- your favorite place
- something old that you love
- the ugliest place in your neighborhood
- the oldest or newest building in your area
- something in nature: rain, a tree, a flower, an insect

**List your five best topics for a description.**

1. ______________________
2. ______________________
3. ______________________
4. ______________________
5. ______________________

**Think about each idea you wrote. Ask yourself . . .**

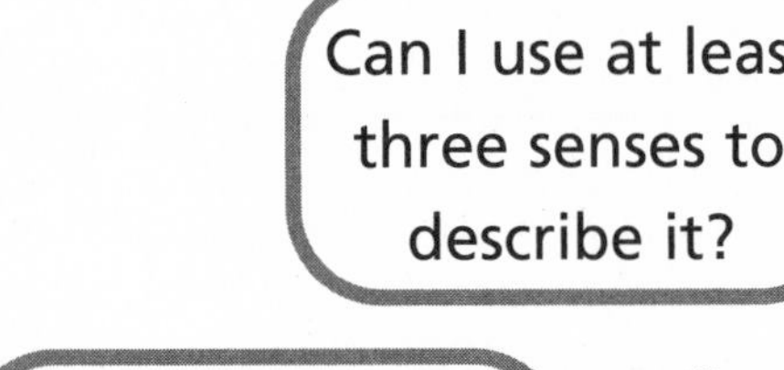

Can I use at least three senses to describe it?
Would I enjoy writing about this?
Is this something I can look at while I write about it?

**Circle the topic you would like to write about.**

Name

# Tune in to Your Five Senses

Explore your topic. First, write your topic. Fill in the rest of the chart when you are observing the object, place, or person you are describing. Think about how it looks, sounds, tastes, smells, and feels to touch.

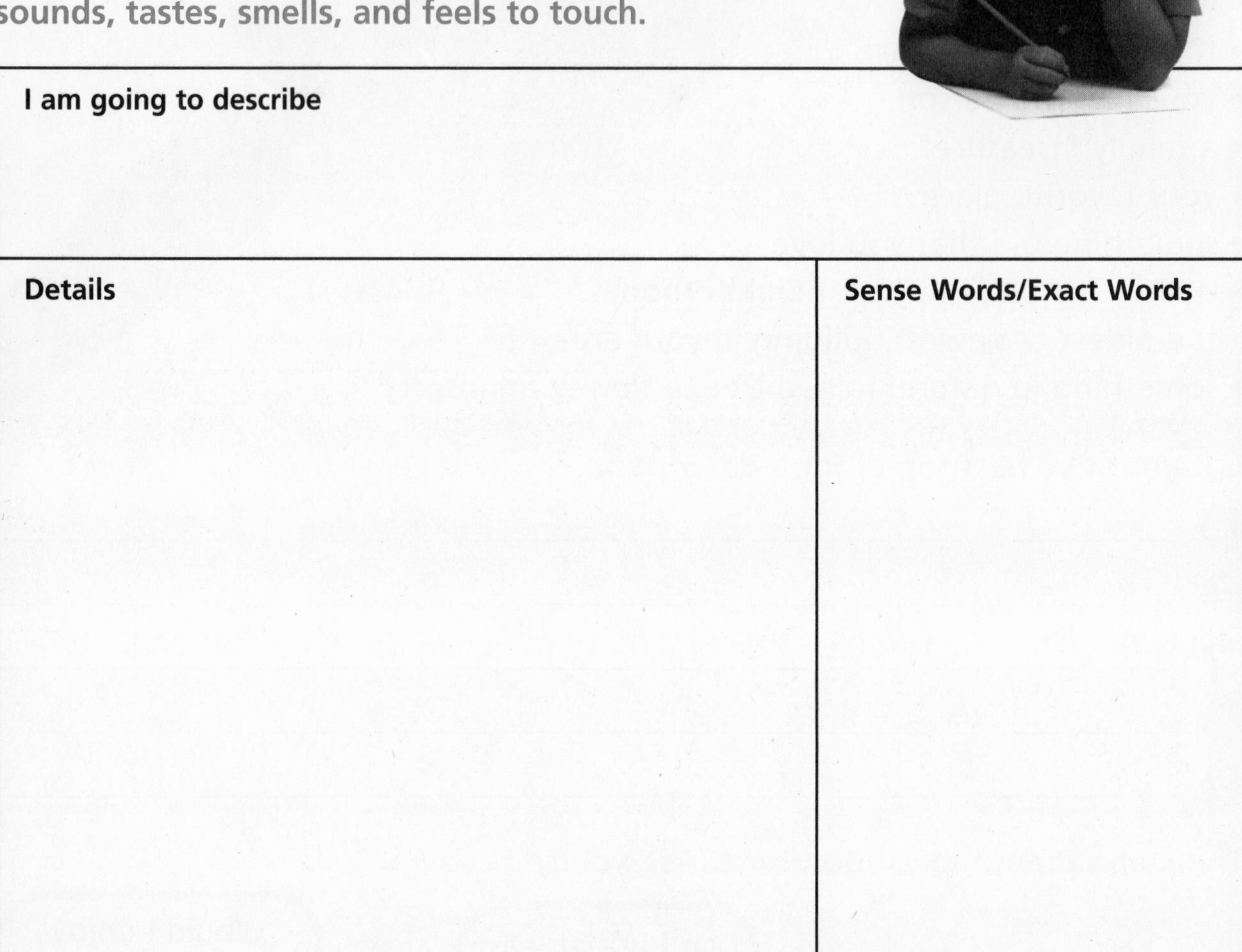

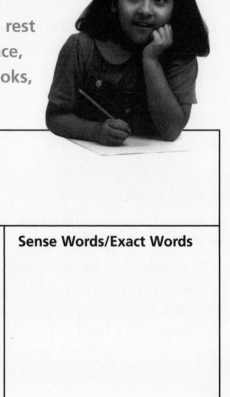

| I am going to describe | |
|---|---|
| **Details** | **Sense Words/Exact Words** |
| | |

**Comparisons**

Its ________________ is as ________________ as ________________

______________________________________________.

Its ________________ is like ______________________________

______________________________________________.

Name

# Make It Better!

## Revising Checklist

Ask yourself these questions about your description.

- ☐ Does my topic sentence state my point of view?
- ☐ Did I choose details that support my point of view?
- ☐ Did I use several senses?
- ☐ Have I used sense words, exact words, and comparisons?
- ☐ Is the order easy to understand?

## Questions for a Writing Conference

Use these questions to help you discuss your description with a classmate.

- What do you like about this description?
- What details are given? What other details are needed?
- Where could more exact words or sense words be used?
- What comparisons are used? Are they clear? Where could more comparisons be used?
- What parts are unclear?
- How could the description be made even clearer?

Write notes to remember ideas from your writing conference.

### My Notes

Name

# Smelly Selling Words

**Complete the text for the advertising poster. Then add illustrations to the poster.**

## COME TO THIS YEAR'S DISGUSTING SNEAKER CONTEST!

Thanks to our generous sponsors, this year's contest will ____________

____________

____________

Last year's champion, who ____________

____________

____________, is back!

Can anyone defeat her, or will she

____________

____________

Watch her rival from last year

____________

____________

____________

Watch the judges hold their noses as they ____________

____________

____________

Name ______________________________

# Case Closed!

**Finish filling out this case report for *The Case of the Disgusting Sneakers.***

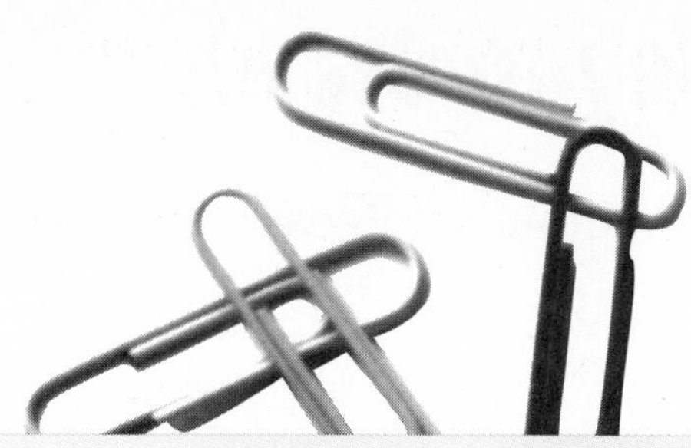

CASE CLOSED

**Client:** Phoebe

**Problem:** ______________________________

______________________________

**Important Clues:**

Phoebe spotted the thief when she was ______________________________

______________________________

The thief had to be someone who had entered the contest, because ______________________________

______________________________

Tessie was a likely suspect because ______________________________

______________________________

Phoebe thought that Stinky did it because ______________________________

______________________________

**Solution:**

______________ was guilty because ______________________________

______________________________

______________________________

Disgusting Sneakers

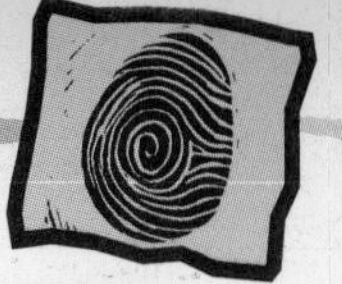

Name

# The Key to Drawing Conclusions

**You are a detective. Read the statement of your client, Susan, and fill in the chart with the details and the conclusion you reach about the case.**

## Crime Report: Victim Statement

**Name of Victim** Susan

The last time I saw my bicycle was at the school bike rack. I locked it to the rack with my key. But at the end of the day, my bike was gone.

Feeling upset, I walked home. My brother was already there. "He's home early," I thought. I told him about the bicycle. He just laughed and said, "Why don't you look in the garage?"

Sure enough, that's where the bicycle was. "How strange," I thought. I went to put my bicycle key in my dresser. Then I saw that the spare key I keep there was gone. What happened to my bike?

**Detail**
What did Susan notice as soon as she got home?

**Detail**
What did Susan's brother know?

**Detail**
Besides the bicycle, what else was missing?

**Conclusion**
Who did it, and how?

Draw another conclusion: Why do you think this person did it?

Name

# An Explanation, Please

There are many things you can explain to someone else. Do these suggestions give you any ideas?

- why things fall instead of float in the air
- why fog forms
- how a caterpillar becomes a butterfly
- how a crop is planted and harvested
- how cheese, maple syrup, ice cream, or other food is made
- why it rains

Write your topic.

I will explain ______________________________

______________________________.

In each box, list facts or details that you will use in your explanation.

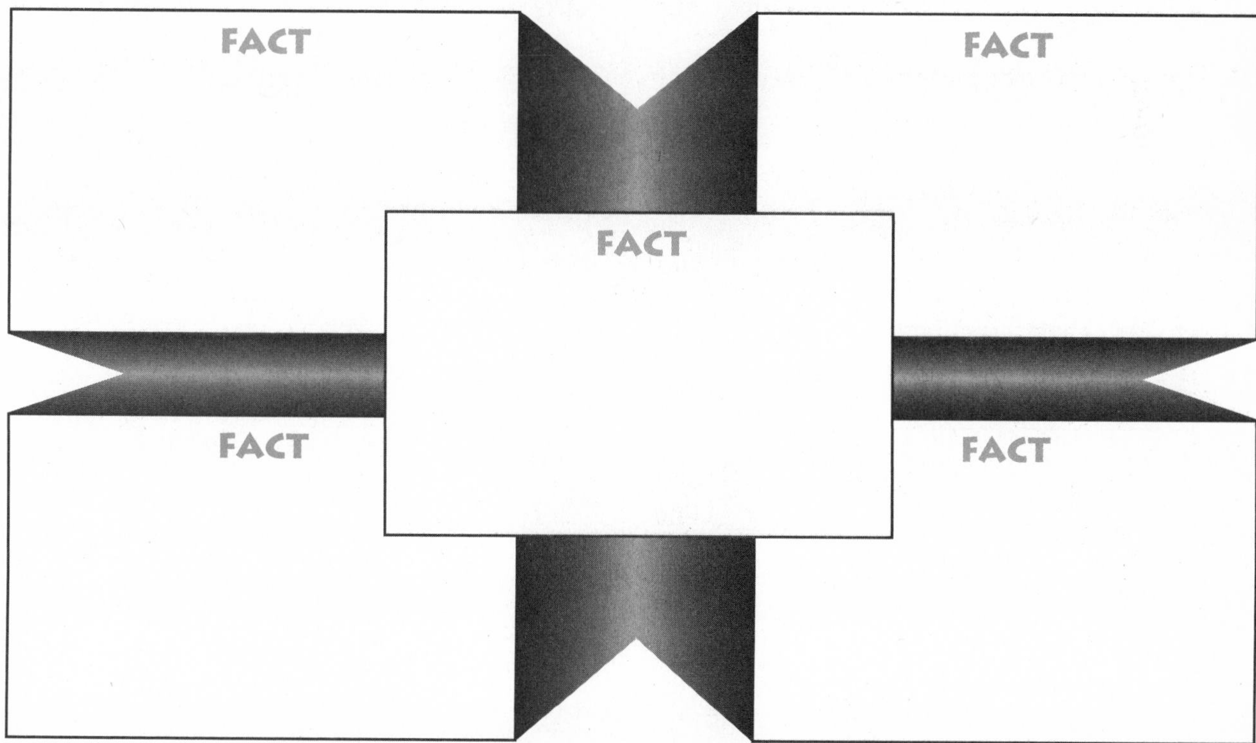


Now write your explanation on another sheet of paper.

Name ______________________

# Dirty Sneak!

**Each word in the box has more than one meaning. Use each word twice to complete the newspaper article.**

| faint | back | spot | turn |
|---|---|---|---|
| nails | can | right | beat |

## Sneaker Contest Won Fair and Square

Some kids would do anything to win the annual Disgusting Sneaker Contest: steal, cheat, poke holes in their sneakers with ______________.

One unlucky contestant was clipping her ______________ and had her ______________ sneaker stolen to keep her from entering the contest. "It's just not ______________!" she complained.

Another tricky contestant ______________ up his sneakers with a weed cutter. "I really wanted to ______________ the other contestants!" he whispered to reporters behind the judge's ______________. The judge wasn't fooled. He disqualified the boy and told him not to come ______________ next year.

One pair of sneakers was especially disgusting. "Come on, it's my ______________!" said their owner, tugging the judge's sleeve. But the judge had to ______________ away a moment to catch his breath. This was no ordinary pair of sneakers. The smell was anything but ______________!

"I thought I'd ______________ after leaning too close," explained the judge. The sneaker owner handed the judge a ______________ of air freshener and boasted, "I ______________ see I'm going to win!"

He did win, and took his ______________ up on the winner's podium. Runners-up received foot powder, soap, and bottles of ______________ remover.

Name

# And Now a Word from Our Sponsor

You won the Disgusting Sneaker Contest and are being interviewed by a television reporter. Write a sentence or two to answer each question. Use the words in ( ).

"Hello, folks. This is Nick Nicehair for station WXYZ. Well, it's time to meet this year's winner of the Disgusting Sneaker Contest."

**Q:** How did you beat last year's winner?

(defeat, rival)

**A:**

**Q:** Now that the contest is over, how do you feel?

(champion)

**A:**

**Q:** Is there anyone that you want to say thank you to?

(sponsors)

**A:**

**Q:** Tessie Bottoms looked strong early in the contest. Were you worried?

(lead, judges)

**A:**

**Q:** Will you be in next year's contest?

(title)

**A:**

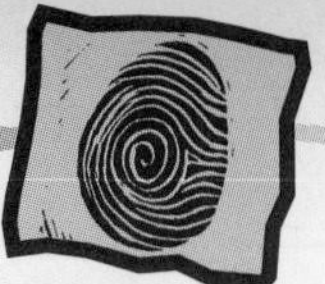

Name

# Sneaker Scrawls

**More Vowel + *r* Sounds** Some Spelling Words have the vowel sound + ***r*** that you hear in ***wore***. These sounds, written as |ô**r**|, can be spelled ***ore*** or ***or***.

|ô**r**| wo**re** to**r**n

The other Spelling Words have the vowel sound + ***r*** that you hear in ***third***. These sounds, written as |û**r**|, can be spelled with the patterns ***ir***, ***or***, and ***ur***.

|û**r**| thi**r**d wo**r**se tu**r**n

## Spelling Words

1. third
2. wore
3. girl
4. worse
5. turn
6. urge
7. torn
8. score
9. storm
10. worm

**My Study List**
What other words do you need to study for spelling? Add them to My Study List for *Encyclopedia Brown and the Case of the Disgusting Sneakers* in the back of this book.

**Write each Spelling Word on the correct pair of sneakers.**

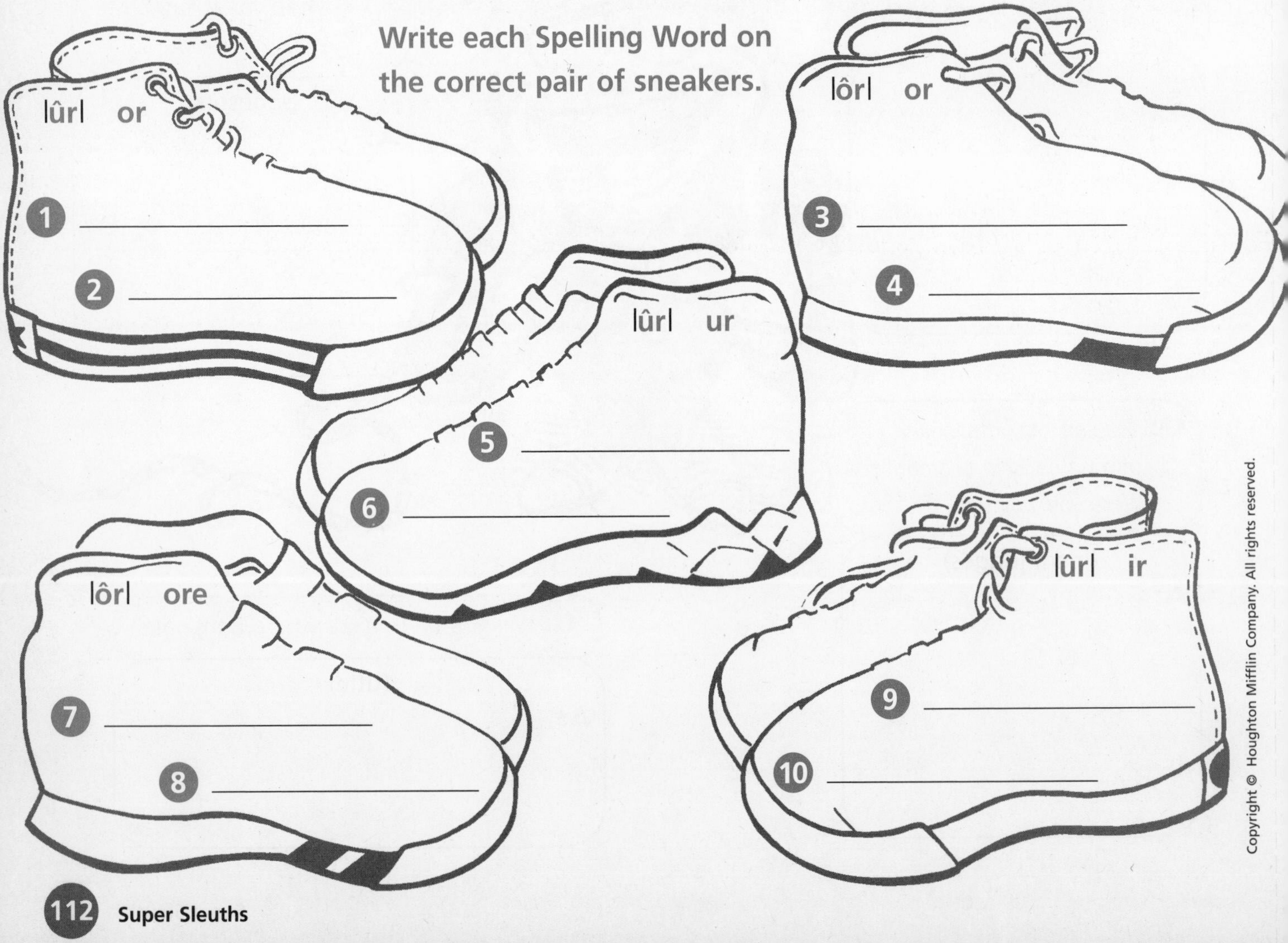

|ûr| or
1. ____________________
2. ____________________

|ôr| or
3. ____________________
4. ____________________

|ûr| ur
5. ____________________
6. ____________________

|ôr| ore
7. ____________________
8. ____________________

|ûr| ir
9. ____________________
10. ____________________

Name

# Spelling Spree

**Proofreading** Find and circle four misspelled Spelling Words in this ad. Then write each word correctly.

**Spelling Words**

1. third
2. wore
3. girl
4. worse
5. turn
6. urge
7. torn
8. score
9. storm
10. worm

## Super Snazzy Sneakers

Are your old sneakers so toren that your toes are sunburned? Are your socks soaked in every starm? Do your blisters keep getting worce? If so, give Super Snazzies a turn on your poor, suffering feet. We erge you to try them soon!

1. ______
2. ______
3. ______
4. ______

**Sentence Sense** Write the Spelling Word that means the same as the underlined words in each sentence.

5. Who do you think will get the highest number of points in the contest?

6. I'm not sure, but if I don't finish in second place, I should certainly get the number after second.

7. My mom said she would ground me if I had these sneakers on my body in public.

8. Yeah, well, my dad says these sneakers upset his stomach.

9. My sneakers are so disgusting that I found a crawling animal living in them.

10. That young female says that her sneakers have fleas!

5. ______
6. ______
7. ______
8. ______
9. ______
10. ______

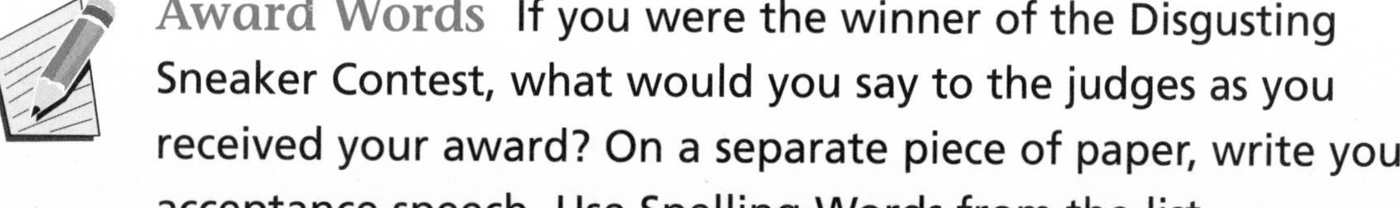

**Award Words** If you were the winner of the Disgusting Sneaker Contest, what would you say to the judges as you received your award? On a separate piece of paper, write your acceptance speech. Use Spelling Words from the list.

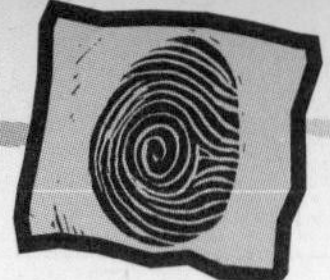

Name

# You Choose the Shoes

| **Comparing with *good*** | **Comparing with *bad*** |
|---|---|
| Third prize is **good.** | The baby's shoes are **bad.** |
| Second prize is **better** than third prize. | Mom's shoes are **worse** than the baby's. |
| First prize is the **best.** | Dad's shoes are the **worst** ones of all. |

**Comparing with *good* and *bad*** Use *good, better, best, bad, worse,* or *worst* to describe whether the shoes are suitable for the occasions.

**Phoebe's Shoes**

These are the ____________ shoes for a Disgusting Sneaker Contest.

They are the ____________ shoes for a fancy party.

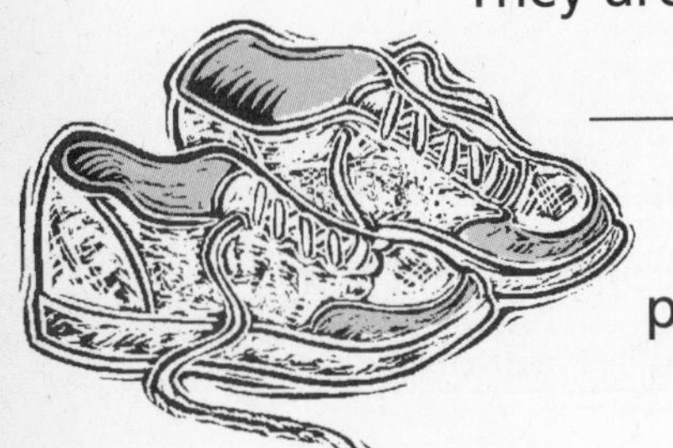

**Stinky's Shoes**

This is a ____________ pair of shoes for basketball.

These high-tops are ____________ than Bugs's boots for climbing a mountain.

**Bugs's Shoes**

These are the ____________ shoes of all for hiking.

This footwear is a ____________ choice for a wedding.

**Encyclopedia's Shoes**

These shoes are ____________ than Bugs's for going to a wedding.

This style is the ____________ of all for meeting the mayor.

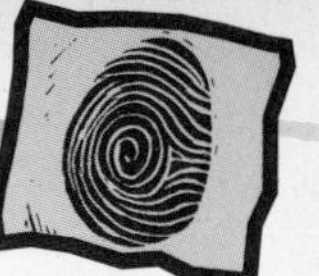

Name ______________________________

# Helpful Hints for a Secret Messenger

**Comparing with *good* and *bad*** A secret messenger has a note for Phoebe about someone who is after her prize sneakers. Study the schedule and fill in the blank in each question with the word *good, better, best, bad, worse,* or *worst.* Then answer each question, writing one of the adjective forms in a sentence of your own.

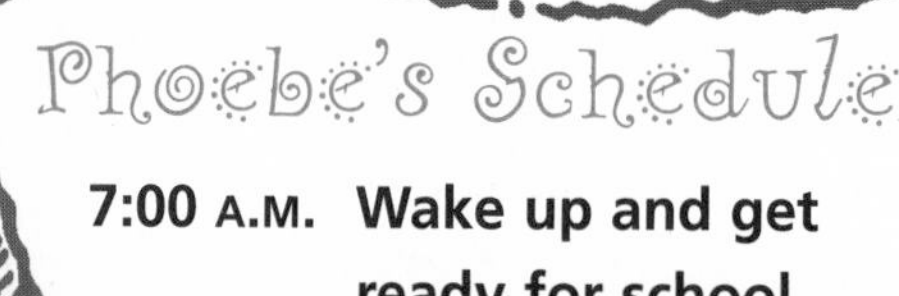


| Time | Activity |
|---|---|
| 7:00 A.M. | Wake up and get ready for school. |
| 7:30 | Have breakfast. |
| 7:45 | Ride bike to school. |
| 8:00 | Start school. |
| 10:30 | Recess—Meet Sally at the track. |
| 11:00 | Back to class |
| 11:45 | Lunch—Meet Ann at the cafeteria. |
| 12:15 P.M. | Back to class |
| 3:00 | Go to locker; then leave school. |
| 3:30 | Gymnastics class at the community center |
| 4:30 | Ride home. |
| 5:00 | Do homework. |
| 6:00 | Set table for supper. |

1. Would it be ____________ to slip Phoebe a note at 3:30 than at 7:30? ____________

   ______________________________________________

2. Is 2:00 a ____________ time to leave a message in Phoebe's locker? ____________

   ______________________________________________

3. Why would 10:30 be a ____________ time to look for Phoebe in her classroom? ________

   ______________________________________________

4. Is 7:00 the ____________ time of all to meet Phoebe on her bike? ____________

   ______________________________________________

5. Why is 11:45 a ____________ time than 10:30 to give Phoebe a note at the track?

   ______________________________________________

   ______________________________________________

Name

# Making a Wanted Poster

**A burglary has occurred. The picture on the left shows the room before it was burglarized. The picture on the right shows the same room afterwards. Find and list at least four clues in the chart.**

| Clues | Conclusions<br>What does this clue tell you about the burglary or the burglar? |
|---|---|
| | |
| | |
| | |
| | |

**Use your conclusions to make a wanted poster that describes the burglary and the burglar. Give as much information as possible. Draw pictures of some of the clues to give more information.**

**Checklist**

**Use the checklist to make sure you're ready to share your work.**

- ❑ My poster gives information about the burglar and the burglary.
- ❑ My poster uses at least four clues from the pictures.
- ❑ I can describe the observations and conclusions I made.

Name

# American Snapshots

Record your explorations on the chart below and on the next page as you visit some of the people and places contributing to the heritage of the United States.

| | Grandfather's Journey | All for the Better |
|---|---|---|
| What is the selection about? | | |
| Where do the characters start out? | | |
| Where do they go? | | |
| How do the characters feel about leaving their homes and going to new places? | | |
| What does the selection tell you about the United States? | | |

Name

# American Snapshots

Record your explorations on the chart below as you visit some of the people and places contributing to the heritage of the United States.

| | Sarah, Plain and Tall | The Seminoles |
|---|---|---|
| What is the selection about? | | |
| Where do the characters start out? | | |
| Where do they go? | | |
| How do the characters feel about leaving their homes and going to new places? | | |
| What does the selection tell you about the United States? | | |

Name

# Beckoning Brochure

Make a travel brochure about a travel destination. Draw things that visitors might see, and write captions for the pictures. Write a short paragraph about the region. Use each vocabulary word at least once.

astonished marveled bewildered homesick excited amazed longed

N W E S

WORTH ★ A ★ VISIT

Name

# Interview with Grandfather

The grandfather in the story is being interviewed for a film about his life. Help him answer the questions.

| Interviewer: | Grandfather: |
|---|---|
| 1 Why and how did you leave Japan? | |
| 2 Where did you travel in North America? | |
| 3 Where did you settle, and what happened while you lived there? | |
| 4 Why did you return to Japan? | |
| 5 What happened to your daughter? | |
| 6 Why didn't you ever return to California for a visit? | |

Name

# The Case of the Missing Bird

**One of Grandfather's birds escaped. Study the causes. Fill in the effects to find the bird.**

**Cause:** Food is put in the cage.

**Effect:** ______________________

**Cause:** The hungry bird sees more food in the cabinet.

**Effect:** ______________________

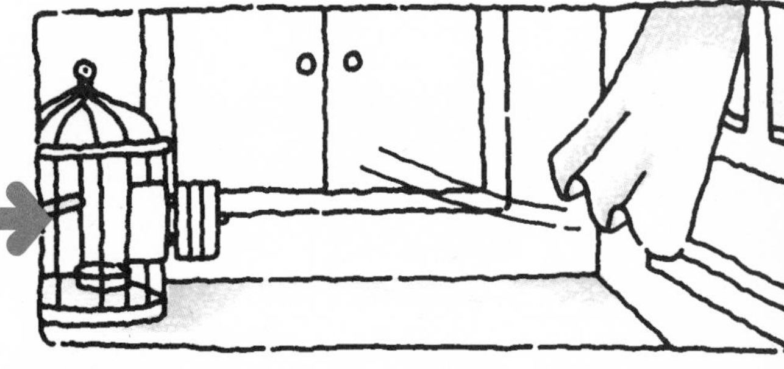

**Cause:** The wind is coming through an open window.

**Effect:** ______________________

Where is the bird? ______________________

Name

# Wish You Were Here

**This letter has many short, choppy sentences. Rewrite the body of the letter. Combine related sentences into compound sentences using *and, or,* or *but.***

Dear Anna,

I'm in Japan again. I'm having a good time. I'm already homesick for California. Whenever I'm in one country, I seem to miss the other. Yesterday I visited the mountains of my childhood. I hiked around for hours. I listened to the birds sing. It was a wonderful day.

Tomorrow I might meet some old friends for lunch. I might visit Grandfather's village. It depends on the weather. I want to visit the village one day this week to take some pictures for you. It's a beautiful place. I'd like you to see it. Someday I'll take you there.

Love,

Karen

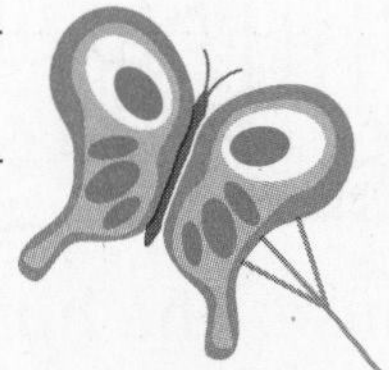

Name

# Syllable Seas

Read the words in Grandfather's boat and decide how many syllables each word has. Match the number of syllables in each word to the number on one of the fish. Then write each word under the wave next to the fish.

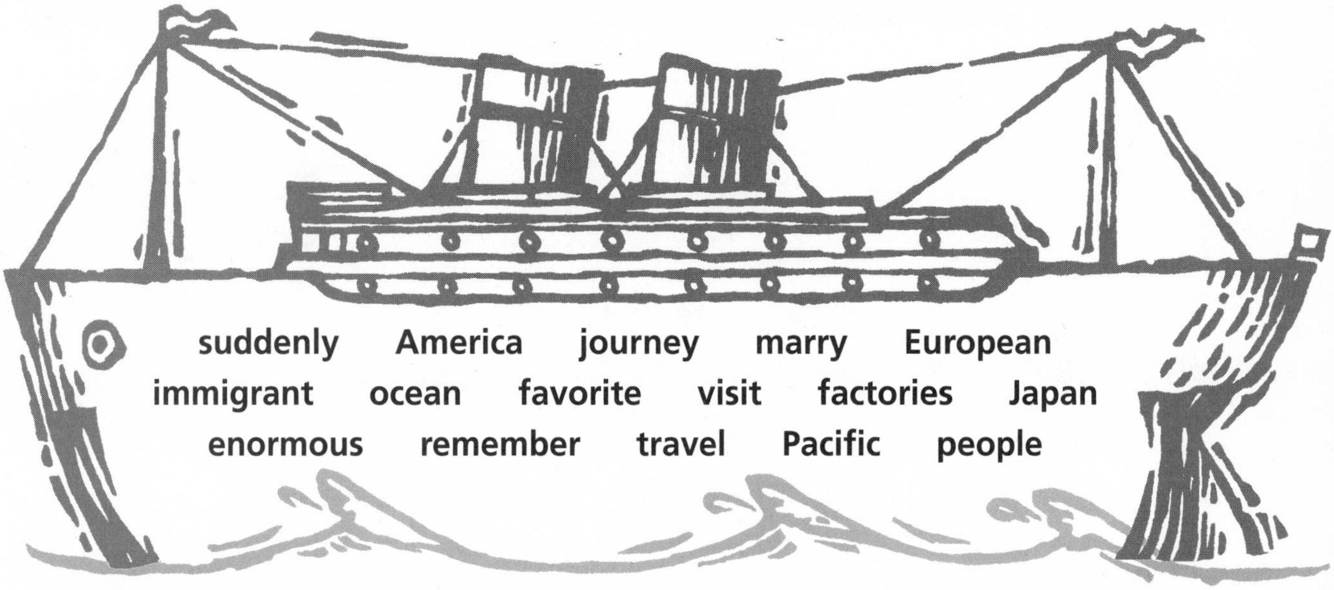

suddenly America journey marry European
immigrant ocean favorite visit factories Japan
enormous remember travel Pacific people

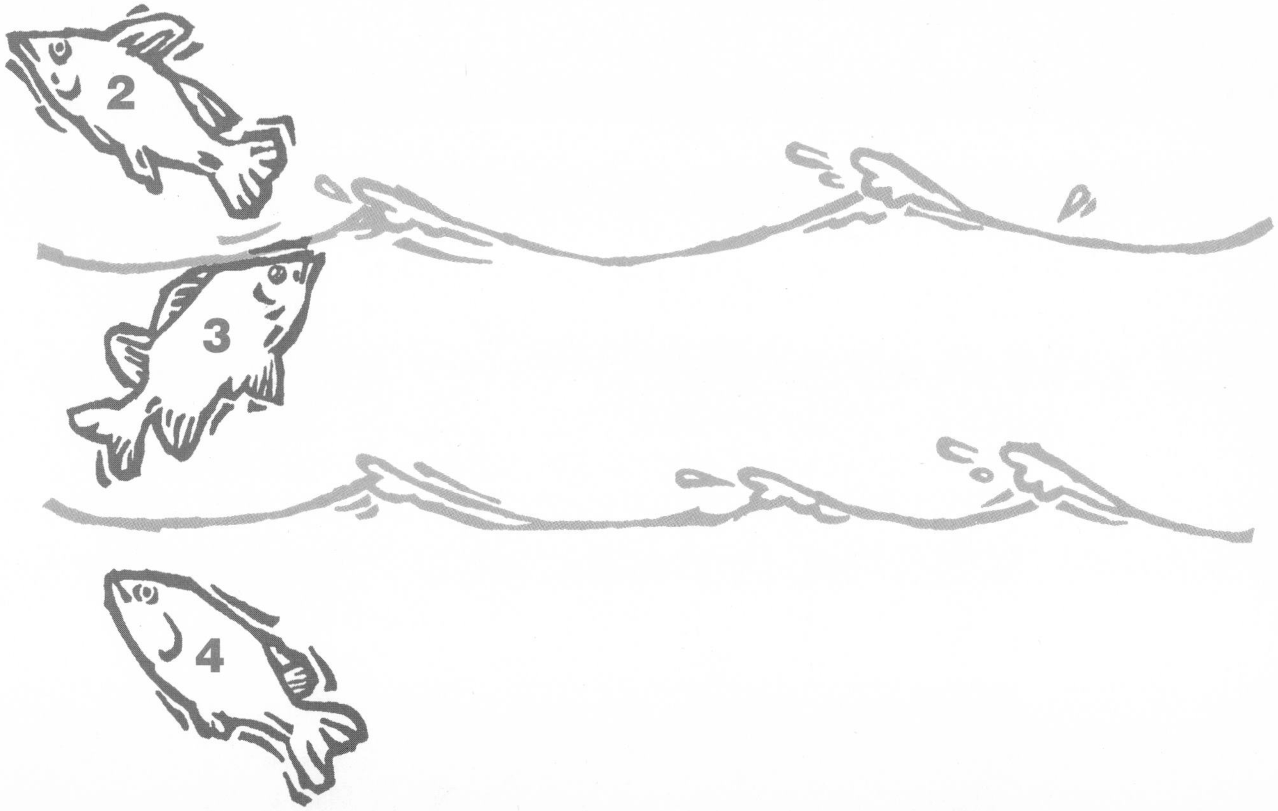

2

3

4

Name

# A Traveler's Post Card

**This is a post card from an American student visiting Japan. The student was so sleepy from traveling that the words in the post card got mixed up! If an underlined word does not make sense, draw a circle around it. Then choose another underlined word that does make sense, and write it above the circled word. The first one is done for you.**

Dear friends,

I am so <u>towering</u> (excited) by the places I've seen. I have not had time to be <u>surrounded</u>, and I have not once <u>astonished</u> for the United States. I am <u>homesick</u> by beauty! I have marveled at the temples and farm fields. In addition, I have been <u>enormous</u> by the <u>bewildered</u> mountains and long rivers. At first, I was afraid of the crowded cities, but now I am simply <u>longed</u> by them. I am amazed at the <u>excited</u> buildings in the city of Tokyo!

Name

# Traveling Words

**Compound Words** Each Spelling Word is a **compound word** made up of two or more smaller words. A compound word may be written as one word, two words joined by a hyphen, or two separate words.

| | | | | |
|---|---|---|---|---|
| **grand** | + | **parents** | = | grandparents |
| **great** | + | **aunt** | = | great-aunt |
| **post** | + | **office** | = | post office |

## Spelling Words

1. **grandparents**
2. **homesick**
3. **sweetheart**
4. **weekend**
5. **sunlight**
6. **post office**
7. **great-aunt**
8. **breakfast**
9. **pen pal**
10. **make-believe**

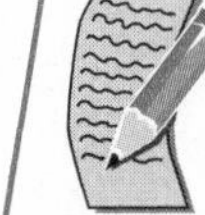

**My Study List**
What other words do you need to study for spelling? Add them to My Study List for *Grandfather's Journey* in the back of this book.

**Write each Spelling Word under the correct heading.**

*Pacific Ocean*

*Japan*

*North America*

**Two Words with a Hyphen**

1. ____________________
2. ____________________

**One Word**

3. ____________________
4. ____________________
5. ____________________
6. ____________________
7. ____________________
8. ____________________

**Two Separate Words**

9. ____________________
10. ____________________

Name

# Spelling Spree

**Spelling Words**

1. grandparents
2. homesick
3. sweetheart
4. weekend
5. sunlight
6. post office
7. great-aunt
8. breakfast
9. pen pal
10. make-believe

**Proofreading** Circle four misspelled Spelling Words. Then write each word correctly.

Dear Hiroko (my favorite penpal),

I'm so happy that I will finally get to meet you in California next week end! I have dreamed about this trip for so long that it seems almost make-beleave to me. Is the sunlight really different there? I'd better go eat breakfist, but I'll see you soon. California, here I come!

Love,

*Jessie*

1. ______
2. ______
3. ______
4. ______

**A Compound Puzzle** Write the Spelling Word that fits each clue. Then arrange the letters 1–9 to make a compound word that tells how Grandfather traveled.

5. a star's energy that lets us see — ___ ___ ___ ___ ___(8) ___ ___ ___
6. longing for home and family — ___(7) ___ ___(5) ___ ___ ___ ___ ___
7. the sister of one's grandparent — ___ ___ ___ ___(4) ___ ___ ___ ___ ___
8. a person whom one loves — ___(6) ___ ___ ___ ___ ___ ___ ___ ___ ___
9. a place where mail is sorted and sent out — ___ ___ ___(1) ___ ___ ___ ___ ___ ___ ___(3)
10. the father and mother of one's father or mother — ___ ___ ___ ___ ___ ___(9) ___ ___ ___ ___ ___(2) ___

___ ___ ___ ___ ___ ___ ___ ___ ___
1 2 3 4 5 6 7 8 9

**Captioning the Moment** Imagine that you are making an album of family photos. On a separate sheet of paper, use Spelling Words from the list to write captions for your photos.

Name

# Travel Plans

**Verb Tenses** Help organize this traveler's notes. Underline the verb in each sentence. Then write each verb under *Present Tense, Past Tense,* or *Future Tense.*

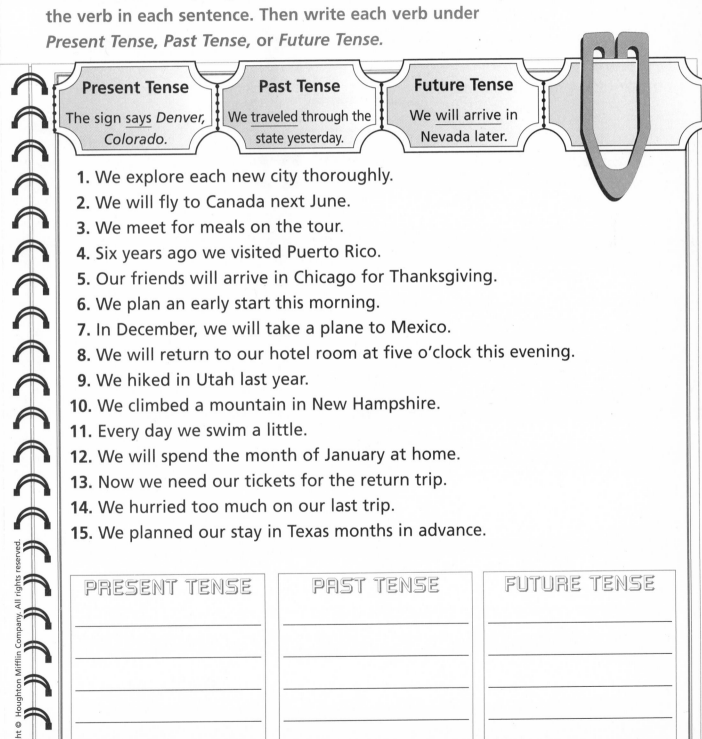

| Present Tense | Past Tense | Future Tense |
|---|---|---|
| The sign says *Denver, Colorado.* | We traveled through the state yesterday. | We will arrive in Nevada later. |

1. We explore each new city thoroughly.
2. We will fly to Canada next June.
3. We meet for meals on the tour.
4. Six years ago we visited Puerto Rico.
5. Our friends will arrive in Chicago for Thanksgiving.
6. We plan an early start this morning.
7. In December, we will take a plane to Mexico.
8. We will return to our hotel room at five o'clock this evening.
9. We hiked in Utah last year.
10. We climbed a mountain in New Hampshire.
11. Every day we swim a little.
12. We will spend the month of January at home.
13. Now we need our tickets for the return trip.
14. We hurried too much on our last trip.
15. We planned our stay in Texas months in advance.

| PRESENT TENSE | PAST TENSE | FUTURE TENSE |
|---|---|---|
| | | |
| | | |
| | | |
| | | |
| | | |

Name

# A Trip Home

**Verb Tenses** **In the puzzle, write the past tense form of the verb that completes each numbered sentence. Use all capital letters. Find in the puzzle the name of a place loved by the author of *Grandfather's Journey*.**

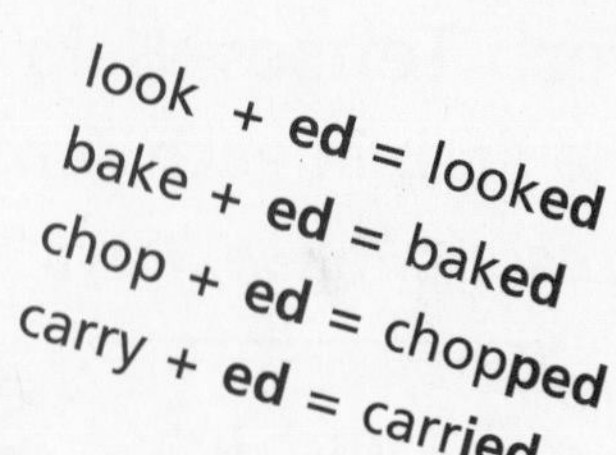


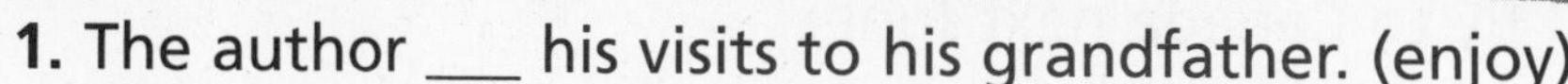

1. The author ___ his visits to his grandfather. (enjoy)
2. He ___ his stories of another land. (recall)
3. Many places ___ wonderful to him. (appear)
4. The California coast ___ him. (amaze)
5. He always ___ to return to California. (plan)
6. He ___ about all his old friends. (worry)

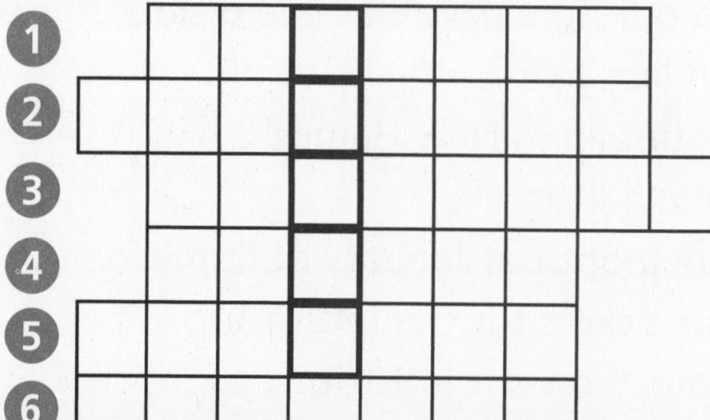

**Write four sentences about a place or places you have enjoyed visiting. Use a verb in the past tense in each sentence.**

7 ______________________________

8 ______________________________

9 ______________________________

10 ______________________________

Name

# Scrambled Suitcases

| | |
|---|---|
| bustled | community |
| dreary | forbidding |
| loomed | scurried |
| uptown | |

Help the passengers locate their mixed-up baggage. Unscramble each word. Then draw a line connecting each suitcase with the claim ticket that contains its meaning.

1. mcutynimo ____________
2. eyrdar ____________
3. tslbued ____________
4. moodel ____________
5. wonput ____________
6. rdieurcs ____________
7. dngbfiordi ____________

- hurried busily
- a place where a group of people live
- gray and depressing
- unfriendly or frightening
- toward the upper part of a city
- rushed about
- seemed huge and threatening

On a separate sheet of paper, write a short letter to the owners of the ship *El Ponce* complaining about their poor baggage handling. Use at least three of the vocabulary words.

Name

# Evelina's Jumbled Journey

The map shows Evelina's journey. Write the events in the order in which they occurred. Use the map to help you.

- **Doña Clara became seasick.**
- **Evelina said good-bye to her mother and sisters.**
- **Tía Vicenta and Tío Godreau met Evelina at the dock.**
- **Evelina made friends with others on the ship.**
- **Her first sight of New York City made Evelina's heart sink.**

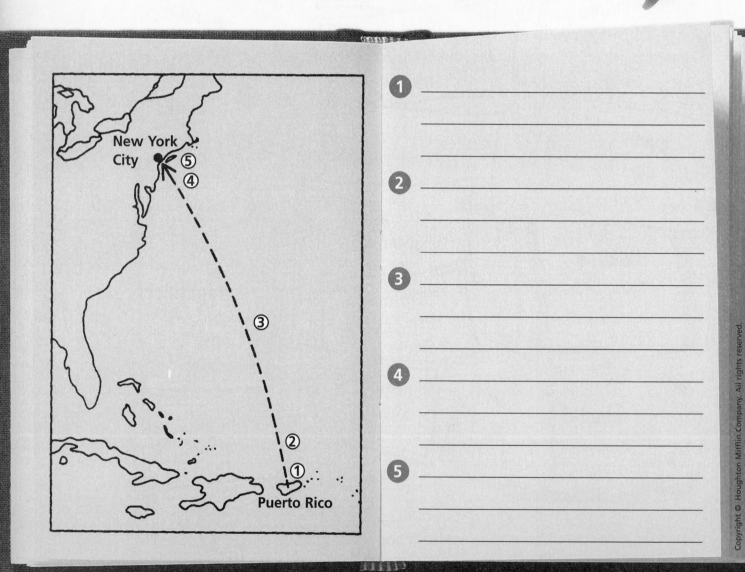

New York City
⑤
④
③
②
①
Puerto Rico

1 ____________________

2 ____________________

3 ____________________

4 ____________________

5 ____________________

Name

# Moving Away

In the left column, write what each picture shows. In the right column, write an inference. The first item has been completed for you.

| | What the Picture Shows: | Inference from Picture: |
|---|---|---|
| 1 | A boy and his family stand in front of a house with boxes and a truck. | The boy and his family are moving. |
| 2 | | |
| 3 | | |
| 4 | | |

Name

# Same or Different?

Plan your paragraphs of comparison and contrast. Write the two topics that you are comparing and contrasting. In the middle section, list the ways your topics are alike. In the outer sections, list the ways they are different.

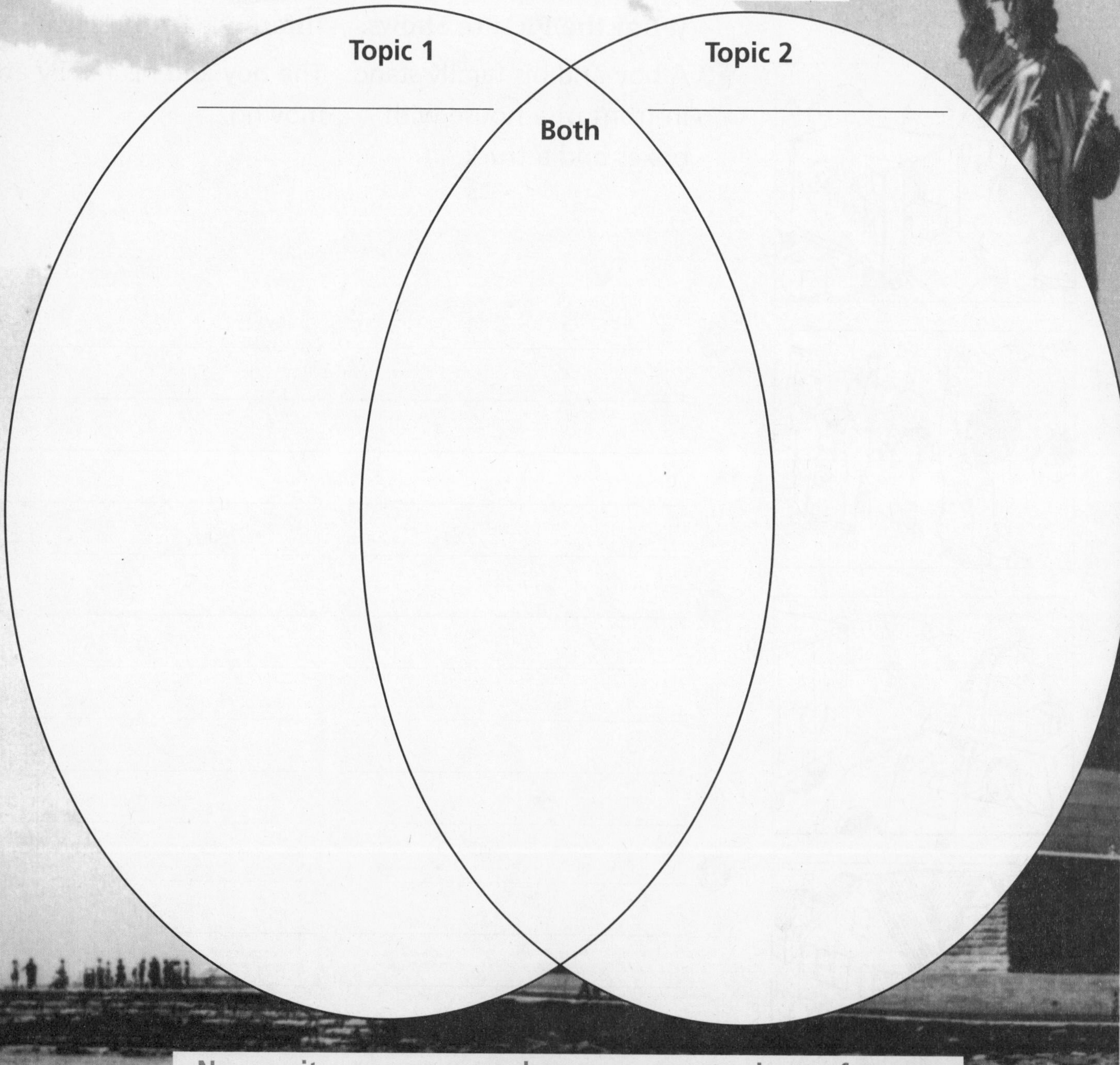

Topic 1

Topic 2

Both

Now write your paragraphs on a separate sheet of paper.

Name

# New Kids on the Block

| hopeless | simple |
|---|---|
| hardships | homesick |
| work | brave |
| continue | unsure |
| enough | hopes |

**Replace the underlined words in the essay with words from the box that mean the same thing. Figure out the meanings of the unfamiliar words by paying attention to their context.**

## A Fresh Start

People choose to come to the United States because they have aspirations (1) for a better life. They may want to escape adversities (2) such as war or hunger. They may be looking for a chance to earn sufficient (3) money to care for their families.

Newcomers must figure out how to get around even if they can speak only rudimentary (4) English. Adults need to find employment (5) and a place to live. A child must overcome feeling shy and tentative (6) about joining in games with other children.

Newcomers are spirited, hopeful, and intrepid (7) people. Success does not always come easily to them, but newcomers have to persevere (8), even when things go wrong. When newcomers remember the familiar sights, sounds, and tastes of their homeland, they often feel nostalgic (9) but must maintain positive attitudes and try not to feel despondent (10).

1 ______________________  6 ______________________

2 ______________________  7 ______________________

3 ______________________  8 ______________________

4 ______________________  9 ______________________

5 ______________________  10 ______________________

Name

# American Scrapbook

**Help Evelina make a scrapbook of her new life in America. Use each pair of words to write a caption. Then draw a picture that shows what the caption describes.**

**1 dreary/forbidding**

**2 shrill/eagerly**

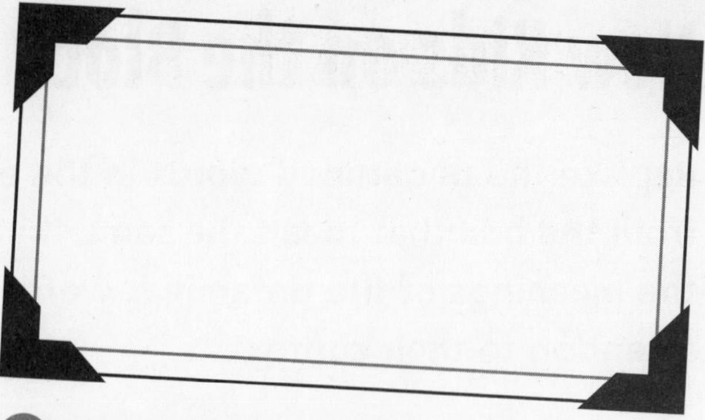

**3 bustled/community**

**4 struggled/scurried**

**5 uptown/loomed**

Name

# Silent Sendoff

**Silent Consonants** Each Spelling Word has a consonant that is "silent," or not pronounced.

| | | | | |
|---|---|---|---|---|
| island | climb | answer | often | honest |
| palm | knew | wrong | half | knee |

**Connect each Spelling Word with its missing silent consonant by drawing a line from each banner to the correct person on the dock. Then write the Spelling Words on the suitcases.**

## Spelling Words

1. island
2. palm
3. climb
4. knew
5. answer
6. wrong
7. often
8. half
9. honest
10. knee

**My Study List**
What other words do you need to study for spelling? Add them to My Study List for *All for the Better* in the back of this book.

Name

# Spelling Spree

| Spelling Words | |
|---|---|
| 1. island | 6. wrong |
| 2. palm | 7. often |
| 3. climb | 8. half |
| 4. knew | 9. honest |
| 5. answer | 10. knee |

**Subway Signs** Write a Spelling Word to complete each message from a subway sign.

1. Never use an arm or a ______________ to hold a door open!
2. Do you ride the subway ______________? Save money with a monthly pass!
3. Does the person next to you look ______________? Guard your belongings!
4. Be alert! You might get off at the ______________ stop!
5. Questions? Let our friendly Rider Rangers ______________ them.
6. Isn't it time you ______________ about your subway system? Pick up a free subway map today!

**Proofreading** Circle four misspelled Spelling Words in this description. Then write each word correctly.

Puerto Rico is an iland about a thousand miles southeast of Florida. Its northern haff is on the Atlantic Ocean, while its southern shore is on the Caribbean Sea. Because Puerto Rico is in the tropics, the temperature there does not clime or fall much more than ten degrees a year. Tourists often enjoy the warm, sandy beaches lined with plam trees.

7. ______________
8. ______________
9. ______________
10. ______________

**Dear Diary** What might Evelina have written in her diary on her first night in *El Barrio*? On a separate sheet of paper, write Evelina's diary entry. Use Spelling Words from the list.

Name ______________________________

# A Letter Home

**Present Tense Verbs** Complete Evelina's letter to Mami by writing the correct form of the present tense verb.

*They reach* New York.

*She reaches* home in her thoughts.

Dear Mami,

I ______________ (miss, misses) you and my sisters very much already. Tía Vicenta ______________ (miss, misses) you too. New York ______________ (seem, seems) very unusual. It does not look like Puerto Rico at all. Tía Vicenta ______________ (guide, guides) me around the city. I ______________ (know, knows) some English already. Tío Godreau helps me.

It ______________ (take, takes) ten minutes to get to school. My new best friend ______________ (walk, walks) with me there every morning.

I ______________ (hope, hopes) to see you here one day.

Love,

*Evelina*

Name

# The Voyage of *El Ponce*

**Present Tense Verbs** *El Ponce* sailed from Puerto Rico to New York. Complete the passenger's notes with the correct form of the verb in parentheses. Then write three sentences about the voyage using present tense verbs. Be sure all verbs agree with their subjects.

The ship ______________ (leave) the dock on time. Once at sea, the ship ______________ (turn) west. Soon the coast of Haiti ______________ (appear). A storm ______________ (arrive) our first night out. The captain ______________ (try) a turn to the northwest. He ______________ (avoid) the worst part of the storm. The first officer ______________ (steer) the ship through the Bahamas.

The next morning we ______________ (catch) our first glimpse of Florida. Each new day ______________ (pass) uneventfully. At night, the lights of Washington, D.C., ______________ (appear) on the horizon. At last the Statue of Liberty ______________ (come) into view! She ______________ (carry) her torch high for *El Ponce.*

______________________________________________

______________________________________________

______________________________________________

______________________________________________

______________________________________________

______________________________________________

______________________________________________

Name

# Plain Speaking

Help the printer fix this advertisement. Write the vocabulary words to fill in the blanks.

- alarmed
- pesky
- perfect
- greetings
- prefer

## Come Live on the GREAT PLAINS!

______________ from the GREAT PLAINS! The GREAT PLAINS are ______________ for farming! Do not be ______________ because the GREAT PLAINS are far away. You will ______________ the GREAT PLAINS once you come. Leave the ______________, noisy city and come today!

Write a letter of inquiry asking the advertisers for more information. Use at least three of the vocabulary words.

*Dear Advertiser,*

______________________________________________

______________________________________________

______________________________________________

______________________________________________

______________________________________________

Name

# Anna's Prairie Diary

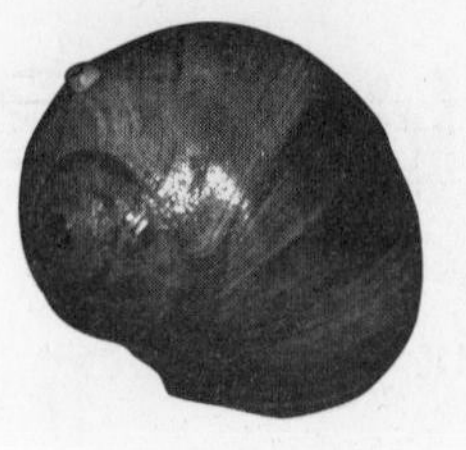

**Help Anna finish this page in her diary by completing the sentences.**

Sarah came today. She came from her home in Maine. Her home is very different from ours because ______________________________________________.

Papa went to ______________________________. Sarah wrote that he would recognize her because ______________________________.

Caleb was afraid that ______________________________. Sarah is very nice. As presents, she brought ______________________________.

I think that she is sad because ______________________________. In a month, a preacher may come to ______________________________.
But I am afraid that ______________________________.

I like her, and I hope ______________________________.

Name

# Colorful Correspondence

**Read the letters to find out how Sarah's and Caleb's homes are alike and different. Then fill in the chart with comparisons and contrasts.**

Dear Caleb,

You asked me what the seasons are like here. The spring is usually rainy and cool, and the summer is usually warm and pleasant. There are many trees here, and in the fall they change color to red, orange, and yellow. In the winter, it snows a lot, and the sea sometimes turns very rough. What are the seasons like where you live?

Very truly yours,
Sarah Elisabeth

Dear Sarah,

We also get lots of snow in the winter, and it's very cold. We hardly have any trees here, and in the fall the grass turns brown. In the spring, it can be rainy and cool. The summer is often very hot.

Very truly yours,
Caleb

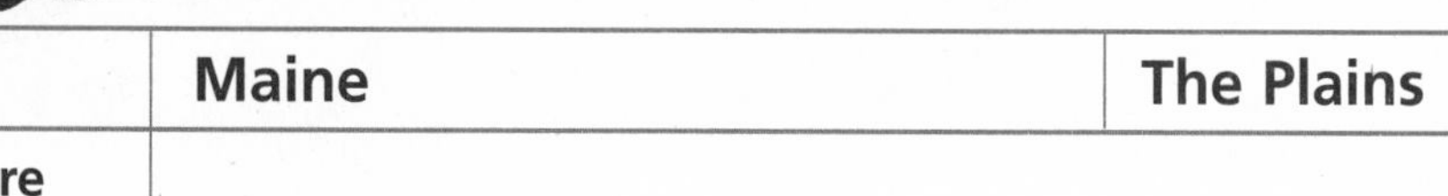

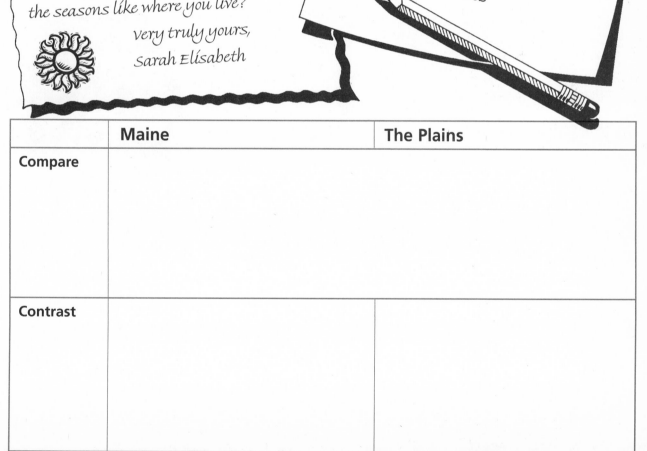

| | Maine | The Plains |
|---|---|---|
| **Compare** | | |
| **Contrast** | | |

Name

# Write Back Soon

**An envelope has two parts:**

- The *return address* is the sender's name and address.
- The *address* is the name and address of the person receiving the letter.

Susan Brown
52-A Parker Towers
Columbus, OH 43215
**(return address)**

**(address)**
Melissa Powers
325 Milton Drive
Little Rock, AR 72201

**On these labels, write your return address and the names and addresses of some friends or relatives.**

Name

# Homophone Stew!

Sarah tells Caleb she can make stew. Help her add the ingredients to the pot by using the homophones to complete the sentences.

| red | cents | tales | sails | patients | pains |
|---|---|---|---|---|---|
| tails | panes | patience | scents | sales | read |

1. Discount stores have ______________________.

   Boats have ______________________.

2. An apple can be ______________________.

   A book can be ______________________.

3. Perfume shops carry ______________________.

   Change purses carry ______________________.

4. Dogs have ______________________.

   Storybooks have ______________________.

5. Windows have ______________________.

   People with toothaches have ______________________.

6. Doctors have ______________________.

   People waiting must have ______________________.

Name

# Prairie Word Puzzle

Cut out and match each puzzle piece with its definition. Fit the puzzle pieces together and glue them into place. Then look at the picture on the completed puzzle and answer this question:

What did Caleb find that belonged to Jack? ____________________

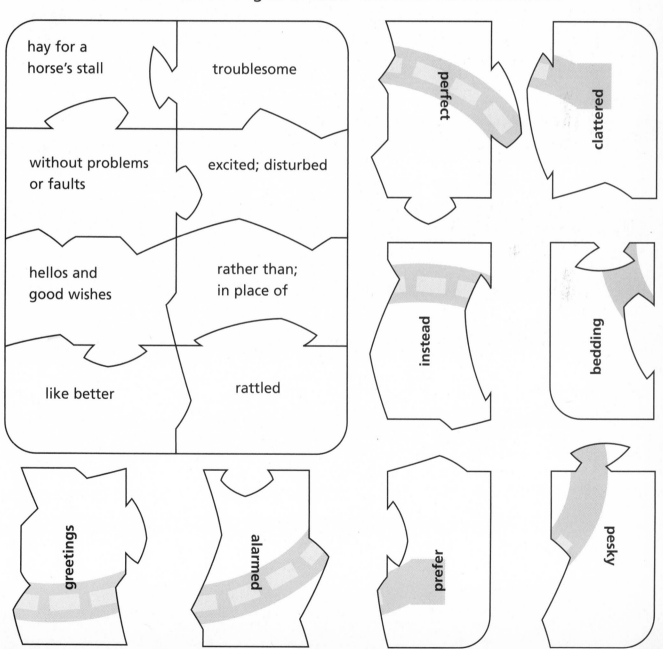

| | |
|---|---|
| hay for a horse's stall | troublesome |
| without problems or faults | excited; disturbed |
| hellos and good wishes | rather than; in place of |
| like better | rattled |

perfect

clattered

instead

bedding

greetings

alarmed

prefer

pesky

Name

# Maine and Plains Quilt

**Homophones** Each Spelling Word is a homophone of another Spelling Word. **Homophones** are words that sound alike but have different meanings and spellings.

|plān| plain "not beautiful or handsome"
|plān| plane "a winged vehicle that can fly"

**Each row on the quilt has three boxes. The meanings of two homophones are given in two boxes. Write the matching Spelling Words in the third box.**

**Spelling Words**

1. plain
2. plane
3. would
4. wood
5. dear
6. deer
7. mail
8. male
9. fourth
10. forth

**My Study List**
What other words do you need to study for spelling? Add them to My Study List for *Sarah, Plain and Tall* in the back of this book.

| | | |
|---|---|---|
| (1) the past tense of *will* | 1 ________ 2 ________ | (2) the hard material of trees |
| 3 ________ 4 ________ | (3) a man or boy | (4) to send by a postal system |
| (5) a winged vehicle that can fly | 5 ________ 6 ________ | (6) not beautiful or handsome |
| (7) coming after the third | (8) forward; onward | 7 ________ 8 ________ |
| (9) a greeting used in letters | 9 ________ 10 ________ | (10) forest animals with antlers |

Name

# Spelling Spree

**Proofreading** Find and circle five misspelled Spelling Words in this letter. Then write each word correctly.

| Spelling Words | |
|---|---|
| 1. plain | 6. deer |
| 2. plane | 7. mail |
| 3. would | 8. male |
| 4. wood | 9. fourth |
| 5. dear | 10. forth |

My dere Sarah,

Your letter just arrived. You seem to like the children, as I had hoped you wold. You might like to know that the deer have not yet eaten our vegetables. Also, the maile seals, the bulls, have returned to our beach. One is wandering back and fourth, bellowing like mad. It is plan that he misses you almost as much as I do!

Your loving brother,

***William***

1 ______

2 ______

3 ______

4 ______

5 ______

**What's Wrong?** Five things are wrong with the picture. Tell what those things are by writing the correct Spelling Word to complete each sentence.

6 The ______ cow has antlers.

7 Caleb would never drop pieces of ______ into the well.

8 There would not be a ______ in the sky in Sarah's time.

9 A ______ does not have flippers.

10 A truck would not have delivered Anna and Caleb's ______.

**Ad Appeal** Sarah must have liked Jacob's advertisement for a wife. What do you think it said? On a separate sheet, write an ad that Jacob might have placed. Use Spelling Words from the list.

Name

# Special Delivery

**The Past with Helping Verbs** Sarah has written her brother, William, a letter sharing her new impressions. Write *has, have,* or *had* in each blank to complete the sentence. Make sure the subjects and verbs agree.

**They have** placed an advertisement in the newspaper.

**Jacob has** placed an advertisement in the newspaper.

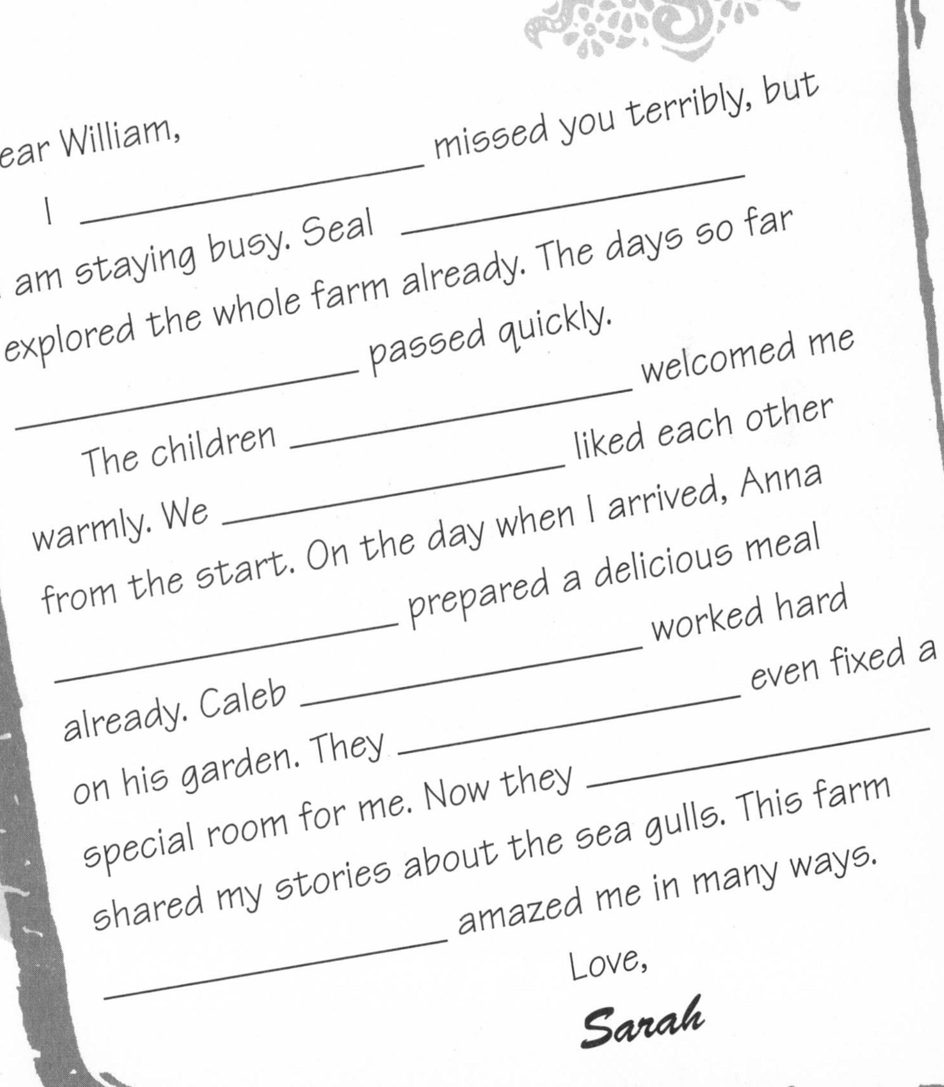

Dear William,

I ______________ missed you terribly, but I am staying busy. Seal ______________ explored the whole farm already. The days so far ______________ passed quickly.

The children ______________ welcomed me warmly. We ______________ liked each other from the start. On the day when I arrived, Anna ______________ prepared a delicious meal already. Caleb ______________ worked hard on his garden. They ______________ even fixed a special room for me. Now they ______________ shared my stories about the sea gulls. This farm ______________ amazed me in many ways.

Love,

*Sarah*

Name

# Questions and Answers

**The Past with Helping Verbs** Caleb and Anna asked Sarah many questions. Complete the answer to each question with *has* or *have.*

1. **Question:** Have you ever baked bread?

   **Answer:** I ____________________ baked bread many times.

2. **Question:** Has your brother ever fished in a stream?

   **Answer:** He ____________________ fished in the ocean only.

3. **Question:** Have you and your brother ever lived on a farm?

   **Answer:** We ____________________ never lived on a farm.

4. **Question:** Has your cat played with dogs?

   **Answer:** Seal ____________________ played with dogs before.

Now write a sentence of your own to answer each question. Use *have, had,* or *has* as a helping verb with the past form of a verb in each sentence.

5. **Question:** Had you decided right away to answer Papa's letter?

   **Answer:** ________________________________________

6. **Question:** Have we convinced you to stay?

   **Answer:** ________________________________________

7. **Question:** Has the story ended happily?

   **Answer:** ________________________________________

Name

# Seminole Crossword

Complete the crossword puzzle using the words from the box.

territory adapted sacred treaty reservation

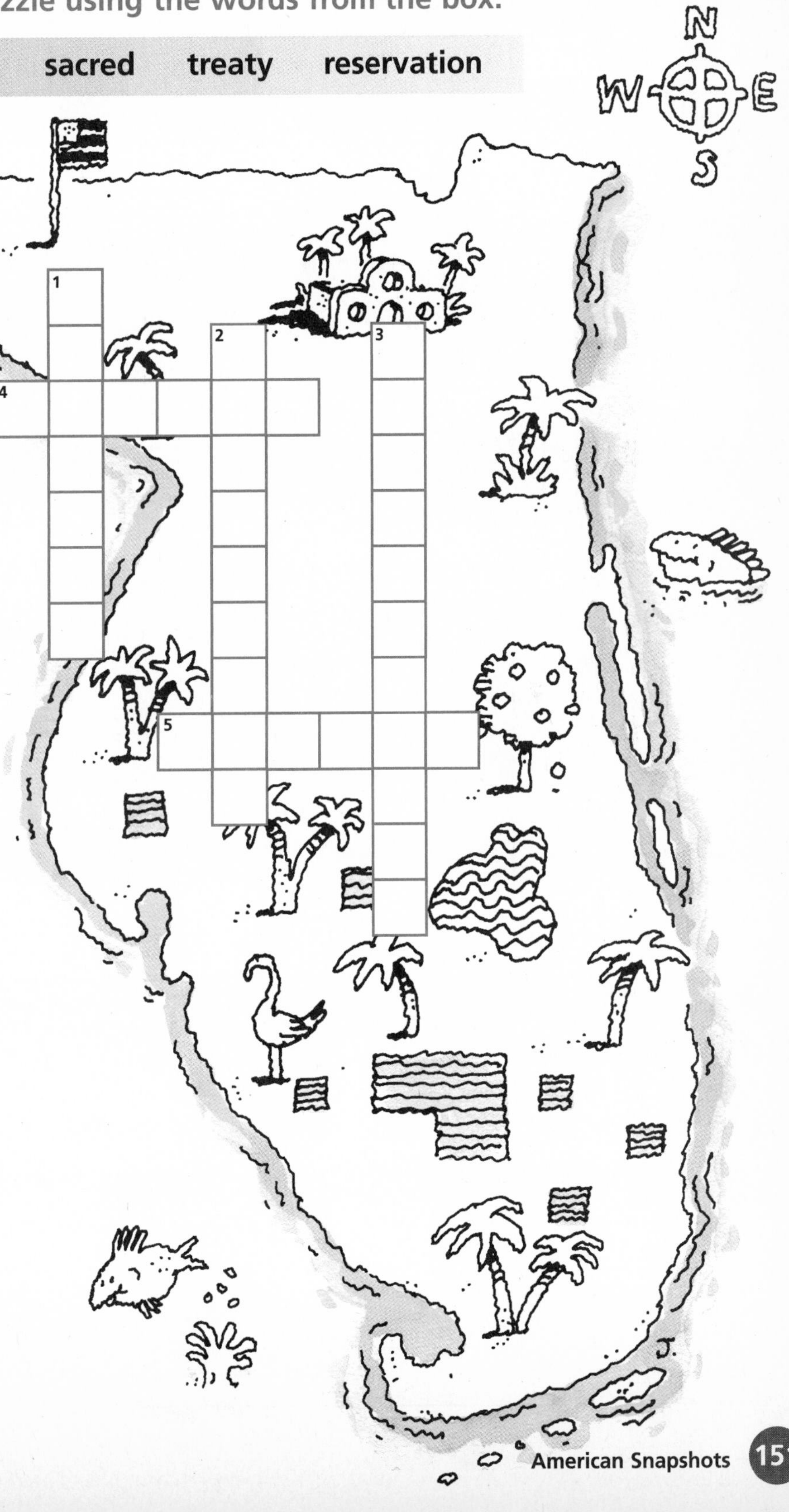

N W E S

1 2 3 4 5

**Down**

1. adjusted
2. an area owned by a government
3. land set aside for Native Americans

**Across**

4. holy
5. an agreement between two or more groups

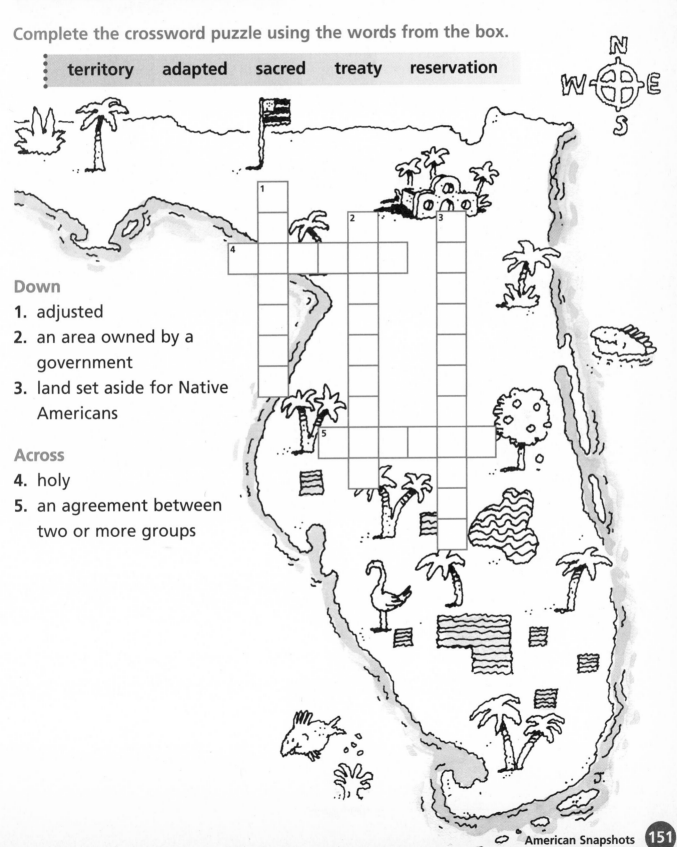

Name ______________________________

# Time After Time

Complete the sentences in the time line. Then answer the question.

A.D. 1500
A.D. 1600
A.D. 1700
A.D. 1800
A.D. 1900
A.D. 2000

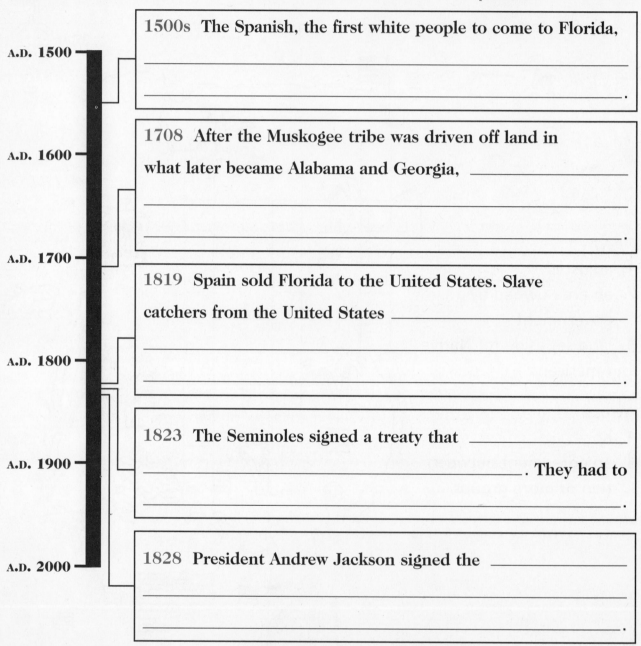

**1500s** The Spanish, the first white people to come to Florida, ______________________________
______________________________.

**1708** After the Muskogee tribe was driven off land in what later became Alabama and Georgia, ______________________________
______________________________
______________________________.

**1819** Spain sold Florida to the United States. Slave catchers from the United States ______________________________
______________________________
______________________________.

**1823** The Seminoles signed a treaty that ______________________________
______________________________. They had to
______________________________.

**1828** President Andrew Jackson signed the ______________________________
______________________________
______________________________.

How has the Seminole way of life changed since the 1920s?

______________________________
______________________________
______________________________

Name

# Get the Idea?

**Read the encyclopedia article and answer the questions.**

Native American

1 **Title:** ______________________

2 **Heading:** ______________________

Before the Europeans came to North America, the Plains Indians did not have horses. When they traveled, they used dogs to help haul their possessions. They raised some of their food by farming. The buffalo, however, was the most important food source, and it provided clothing and shelter as well.

3 **Heading:** ______________________

Hunting buffalo without horses required great skill because the buffalo, even very young ones, can run faster than humans. The Plains Indians developed several ways of hunting buffalo. One method required the Indians to surround a small herd and drive them over a cliff. Falling off the cliff injured or killed the buffalo, and then the Plains Indians would have meat for the winter.

1. What is the topic of this article? Write the topic as a title.
2. What is the main idea of the first paragraph? Write the main idea as a heading for the first paragraph.
3. What is the main idea of the second paragraph? Write the main idea as a heading for the second paragraph.

Name

**The manatee is a rare animal that is protected in the Everglades National Park. Rewrite each paragraph in your own words. You may want to use a dictionary or a thesaurus.**

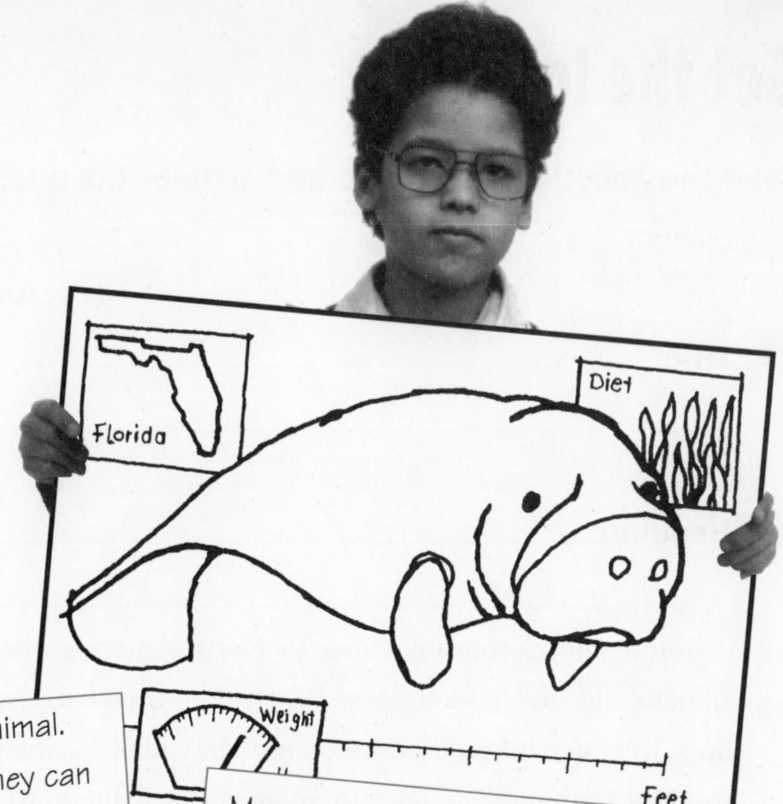


The manatee is a large aquatic animal. Three types of manatees exist. They can grow as long as thirteen feet. They may weigh as much as thirty-five hundred pounds.

Manatees graze on water vegetation. They can consume more than one hundred pounds daily. Their mouths are ideal for harvesting these plants. A manatee's upper lip is divided in half and is suited for grasping and shredding plants.

Name

# Seminole Synonyms

The name *Seminoles* has been **translated** as "runaways" but has also been **interpreted** to mean "lovers of freedom." **Translated** and **interpreted** are used as synonyms in the first sentence. Complete the puzzle by writing a synonym for each clue. Choose synonyms from the words in the trees below.

dense
guide
vanish

guard
escape
leave

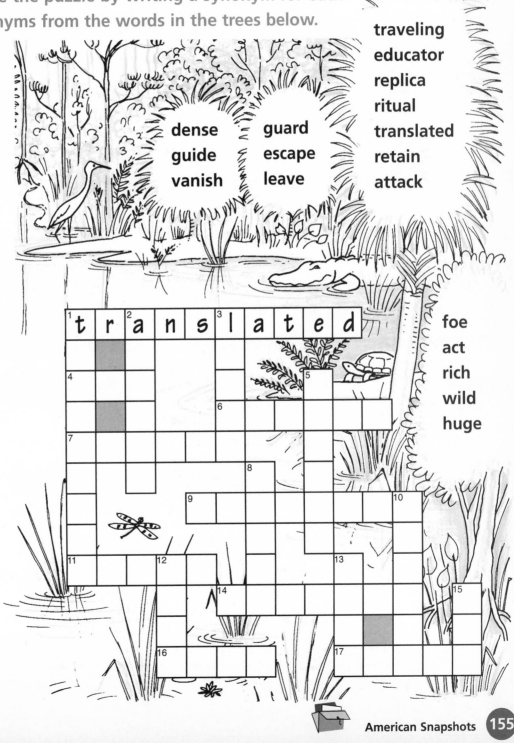

traveling
educator
replica
ritual
translated
retain
attack

foe
act
rich
wild
huge

**Across**

1. interpreted
4. do
6. disappear
7. flee
9. teacher
11. protect
14. copy
16. large
17. thick

**Down**

1. journeying
2. strike
3. depart
5. ceremony
8. lead
10. keep
12. fertile
13. untamed
15. enemy

t r a n s l a t e d

Name ..................................................

# Secret Vocabulary

**Write the word that matches each description. Then find and darken the letters from the circles in the boxes. What is the secret word in the white boxes?**

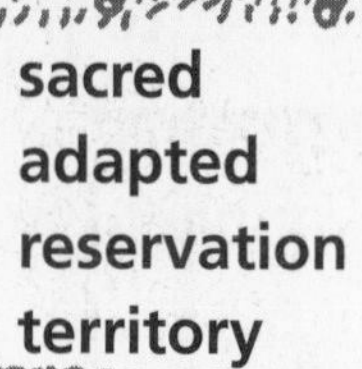

| | |
|---|---|
| sacred | treaty |
| adapted | burial mounds |
| reservation | moccasins |
| territory | canoes |

1. This public land was set aside for Native Americans.
___ ___ ___ ___ ___ (___) ___ ___ ___ ___ ___

2. This is used to describe something or someone who is holy and deserving of great respect. ___ ___ ___ (___) ___ ___

3. These long, narrow boats were often made from hollowed-out trees. (___) ___ ___ ___ ___ ___

4. If someone has adjusted to changing conditions, that person has done this. ___ ___ ___ (___) ___ ___ ___

5. When two or more groups at war make an agreement for peace, they sign one of these. ___ ___ ___ ___ ___ (___)

6. This footwear is made from animal hides.
___ ___ ___ ___ (___) ___ ___ ___ ___

7. The Seminoles buried their dead here.
___ ___ ___ ___ ___ ___ ___ ___ ___ ___ (___) ___

8. This is a geographical area owned by a government.
___ ___ ___ ___ ___ (___) ___ ___ ___

| A | S | P | V | E | R | M | I | C | N | T | O | D | L | Y | E |
|---|---|---|---|---|---|---|---|---|---|---|---|---|---|---|---|

Name

# Exploring the Everglades

## The Final Sounds in *place* and *edge*

Some Spelling Words have the final sound you hear in ***place***. This sound, written as |**s**|, is often spelled with the pattern ***ce***.

|s| place

The other Spelling Words have the final sound you hear in ***edge***. This sound, written as |**j**|, can be spelled with the pattern ***dge*** or ***ge***.

|j| edge large

**Spelling Words**

1. place
2. edge
3. peace
4. once
5. large
6. dance
7. village
8. change
9. choice
10. judge

**My Study List**
What other words do you need to study for spelling? Add them to My Study List for *The Seminoles* in the back of this book.

**As you explore the Everglades, draw a line to connect the first part of each Spelling Word to the pattern that spells its final |s| or |j| sound. Then write each Spelling Word under the correct pattern.**

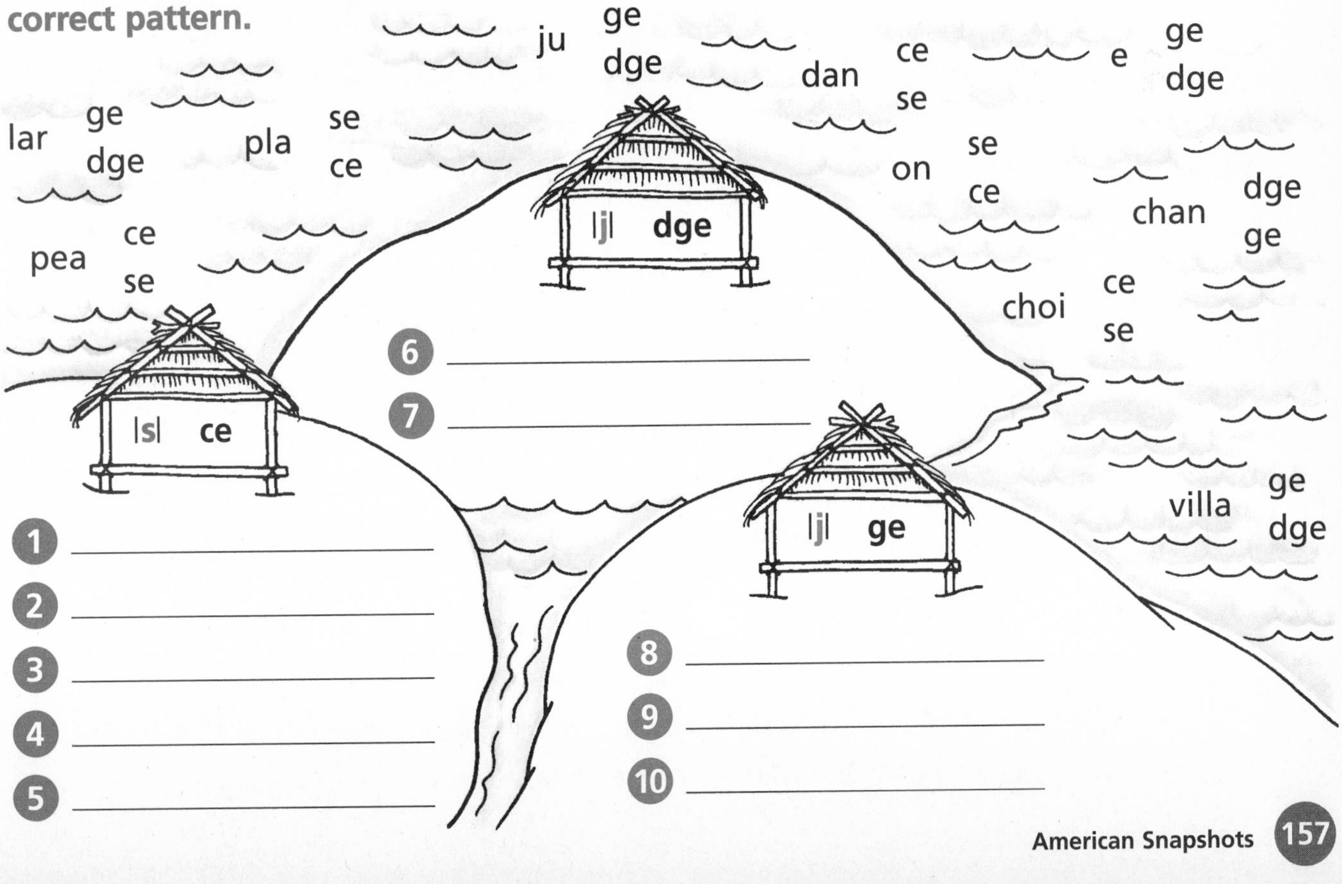

ju ge dge
dan ce se
e ge dge
lar ge dge
pla se ce
on se ce
pea ce se
chan dge ge
choi ce se
villa ge dge

|j| **dge**

6 ______________________
7 ______________________

|s| **ce**

1 ______________________
2 ______________________
3 ______________________
4 ______________________
5 ______________________

|j| **ge**

8 ______________________
9 ______________________
10 ______________________

Name ..............................................

# Spelling Spree

| Spelling Words | |
|---|---|
| 1. place | 6. dance |
| 2. edge | 7. village |
| 3. peace | 8. change |
| 4. once | 9. choice |
| 5. large | 10. judge |

**Hink Pinks** Write the Spelling Word that answers each question and rhymes with the word in dark type.

1. What are you doing if you step to music while holding a spear? **lance** ______________
2. What do you call the rim of a narrow stone shelf? **ledge** ______________
3. What thick, oily lotion is used in a ceremony to end a war? ______________ **grease**
4. Where is a dugout paddling contest held? **race** ______________
5. What is a huge raft used to carry goods? ______________ **barge**

**Proofreading** Find and circle five misspelled Spelling Words in this poster. Then write each word correctly.

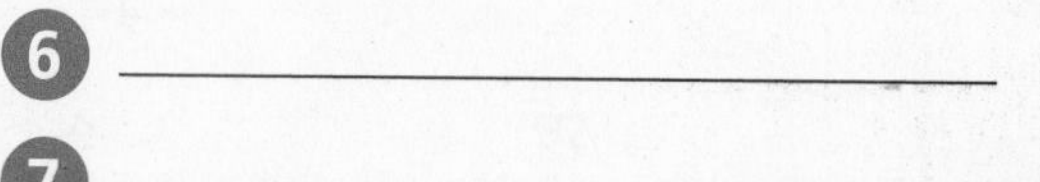

6. ______________________
7. ______________________
8. ______________________
9. ______________________
10. ______________________

**ALLIGATOR WRESTLING CONTEST**

**Do you want to chandge your dull, boring life? Are you ready to take your place in history? Well then, sign up now for Sunday's Alligator Wrestling Contest to be held in the villaje from 1–3 P.M. One-Hand Sam, who lost to a 'gator only onse, will be the judg. Those who sign up early will even get their choyce of alligators!**

**Long Overdue Treaty** The Florida Seminoles never signed a formal peace treaty with the United States. On a separate sheet of paper, write a draft of what the treaty might have said. Use Spelling Words from the list.

Name

# Past and Present

**The Verb *be*** Complete the sentences by writing a form of the verb *be*. In the first four sentences, use the past form. In the last four sentences, use the present form.

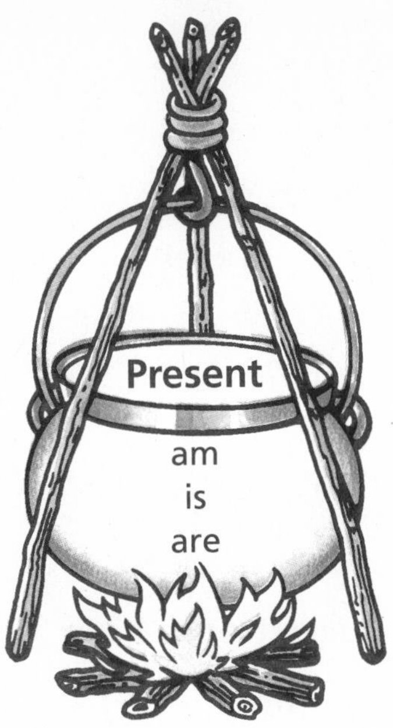


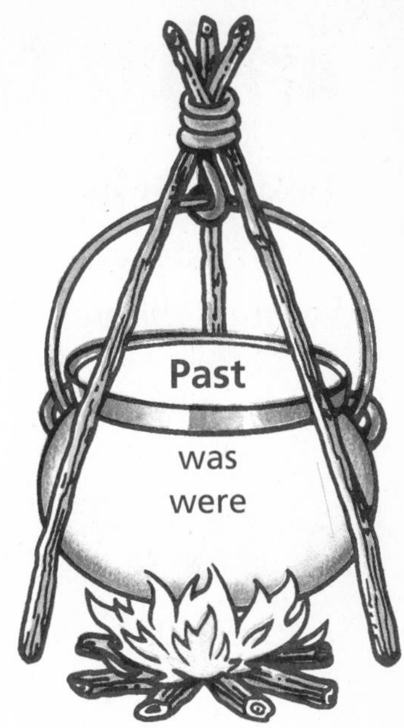


1. I ____________ anxious to read about Osceola.
2. Northern Florida ____________ the home of the Seminoles.
3. The Seminoles ____________ fearless explorers.
4. Animals ____________ important to their survival.

5. The Green Corn Dance __________ a Seminole ceremony.
6. I __________ proud of my Seminole ancestors.
7. More and more today, Seminoles __________ doctors, nurses, lawyers, engineers, and teachers.
8. They __________ still close to the land.

Name

# Arts and Crafts

**The Verb *be*** **Complete each sentence by writing the correct past or present form of the verb *be*.**

1. Traditional Seminole clothing ______________ very decorative. (past)
2. Seminole women ______________ able to create beautiful patterns from scraps of cloth they pieced together. (past)
3. Men's shirts ______________ quite colorful and had complex cloth designs. (past)
4. Women's skirts ______________ vivid with bands of patchwork and ribbon trim. (past)
5. This art form ______________ still alive today. (present)
6. Patchwork designs ______________ different at different locations. (present)
7. Some patterns ______________ variations on traditional designs. (present)
8. The creator of a new design ______________ likely to be greatly admired. (present)

**Now make up four sentences of your own, telling some things you have learned about the Seminoles. Use a different form of the verb *be* in each sentence.**

______________________________________________

______________________________________________

______________________________________________

______________________________________________

______________________________________________

Name

# What Would You Like to Know?

Do any of the topic ideas interest you?

## Topic Ideas

the United States flag
how coins are made
the origin of chess
manatees
pueblos
totem poles
the pony express
Chief Joseph
Frederick Douglass
Robert L. Ripley
Louisa May Alcott

## My Ideas

List five topics that you would like to research:

1. ____________________
2. ____________________
3. ____________________
4. ____________________
5. ____________________

Discuss your topic ideas with a classmate or your teacher. Then ask yourself these questions about each topic.

- Can I find enough information about this topic?
- Am I really interested in this?
- Is this topic too big? How can I narrow it?

We Want
YOU
to think about the questions in the box!

Circle the topic you want to research.

Name

# Get the Facts

Write the topic of your report as the title. Write five questions that you would like to answer about the topic. List sources such as books, magazines, videos, CD/ROMs, encyclopedia entries, atlases, and other materials that you can check to answer your questions.

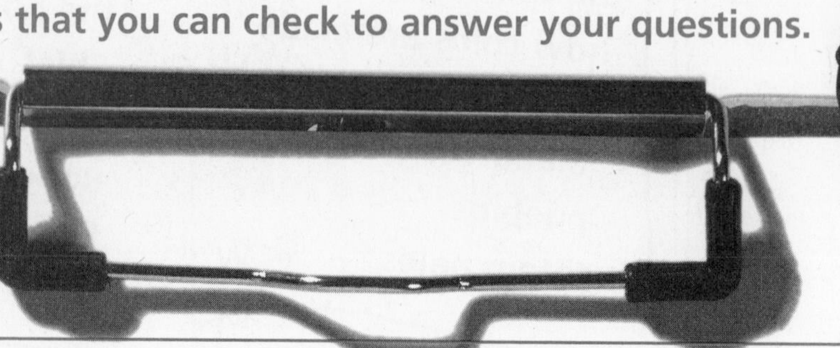

| Title |
|---|
| Question 1 |
| Question 2 |
| Question 3 |
| Question 4 |
| Question 5 |
| Sources |

Name

# Review the Facts

Read your report to yourself. Then make changes that will make it better.

## Revising Checklist

Use these questions to help you revise your report.

- ❑ Does the introduction present the topic?
- ❑ Did I write a topic sentence for each main idea?
- ❑ Do the details in each paragraph support the main idea?
- ❑ Have I included enough facts to explain each main idea?
- ❑ Does the conclusion sum up and close the report?

## Questions for a Writing Conference

Use these questions to discuss your report with a classmate.

- What do you like about this report?
- Does the introduction lead into the report?
- Do the topic sentences state the main ideas? Do the supporting details tell about the main ideas?
- Are any parts unclear? Why?
- What other information is needed?
- Does the conclusion make the report seem finished?

Write notes to help you remember the ideas discussed in your conference.

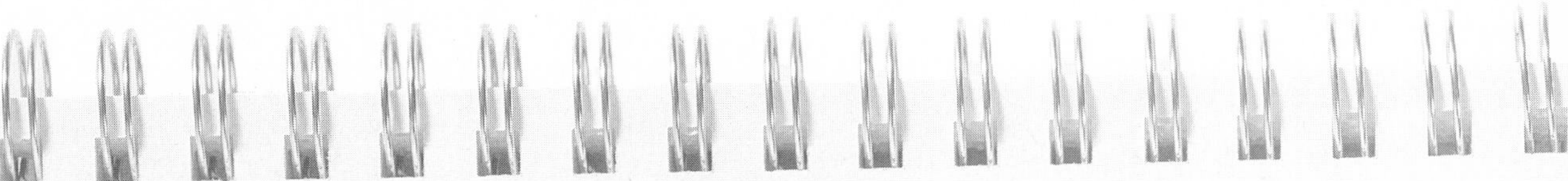

My Notes

_______________________________________________

_______________________________________________

_______________________________________________

_______________________________________________

_______________________________________________

Name

# Picturing the Old and the New

You, your relatives, or your ancestors once lived in a place that was very different from the place you or they moved to. Make a poster that shows and tells about the differences.

You can tell about yourself, a family member, or someone else. Think about the experiences of the grandfather in *Grandfather's Journey* or Evelina in *All for the Better.*

I will tell about (who) ______________________________

The old home was (where and when) ______________________

The new home is (where and when) _______________________

Use this chart to plan your poster. Think about how each place looks and what the people do there.

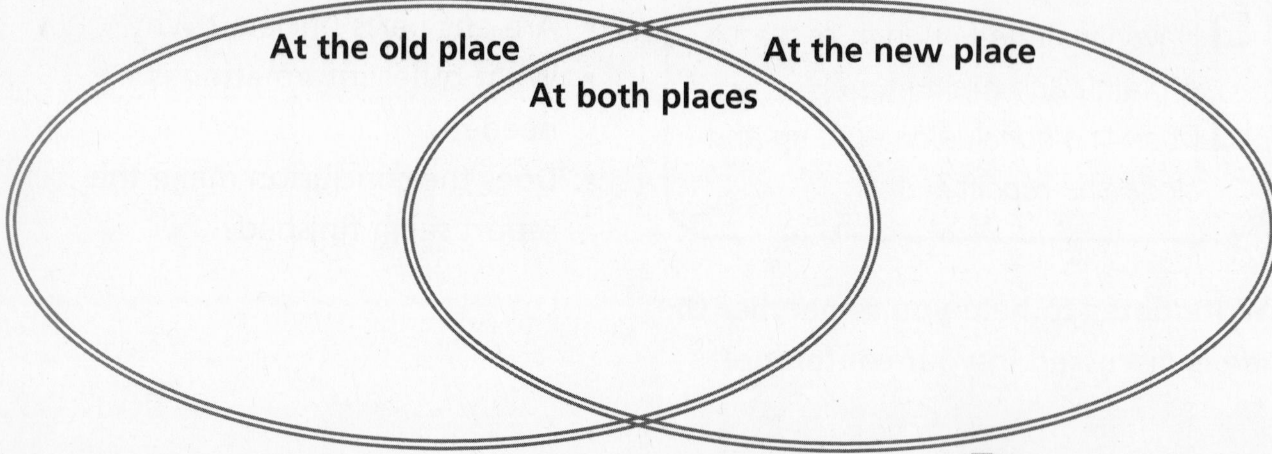


Before you make your poster, think about what you want to show. What would people who live there like about each place? In the new place, what would they miss about the old place?

Use pictures and words to make a poster that your classmates can enjoy. Be ready to tell them about your poster.

**✔ LIST**

- ❑ My poster shows two very different places where someone lived.
- ❑ It shows some interesting facts about both places.
- ❑ It shows at least two important ways in which the places are different.

Name

# Meet the Challenge

Have you ever had to meet a challenge? People meet challenges every day. Add three more examples of challenges to the list.

**Examples:** running a race ______

finishing a project ______

admitting a mistake ______

People use slogans like "Keep at it" or "Never fear" to help themselves and others meet difficult challenges. Write two new slogans on the buttons.

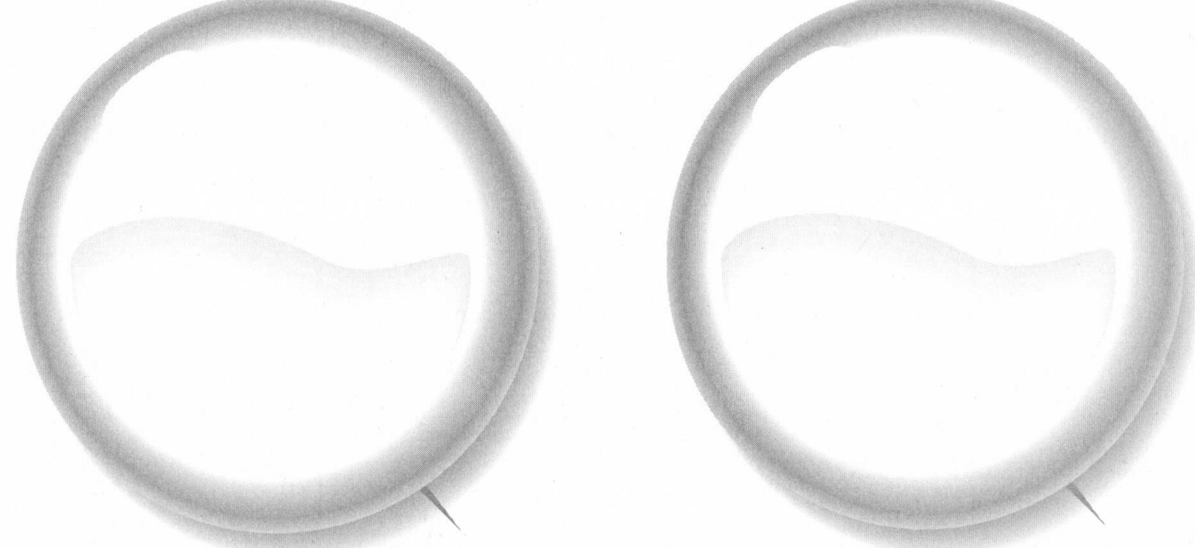

Write a short paragraph about a time when you had to meet a challenge.

Name

# Meet the Challenge

As you meet the challenge of reading the selections in this theme, keep track of the different types of challenges faced in the selections by filling in the appropriate part of this chart.

| | What was the challenge? | How was the challenge met? | When have you tried to meet a similar challenge? |
|---|---|---|---|
| The Marble Champ | | | |
| Thurgood Marshall and Equal Rights | | | |
| Sadako | | | |
| No One Is Going to Nashville | | | |





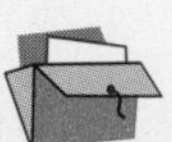

Name

# Deadline Vocabulary

**The editor of the sports page wants you to rewrite your article. Replace each word or words with a word from the box that means the same thing. Then write a headline for the story using the remaining word.**

**accurate awardee exhaustion honors opponent strengthen**

Rewrite this before the 5:00 deadline!

**Editor's Marks**

= delete word

∧ = insert word

______________________________
______________________________ ← Write a headline

Angela Maurici's ∧ ~~on-target~~ shooting helped her beat every ∧ ~~rival~~ in the basketball slam-dunk contest. After the contest, she was the ∧ ~~receiver~~ of the first prize. Angela had been exercising for weeks to ∧ ~~build up~~ her muscles. She suffered from ∧ ~~weakness~~ after the contest was over.

∧ ______________
∧ ______________
∧ ______________
∧ ______________
∧ ______________

Name

# Hollywood Hoopla

You want to convince an executive at a movie studio to produce a movie version of *The Marble Champ.* Fill in the missing information.

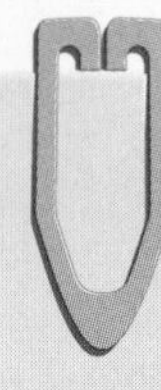

To: Larry Longlimo
Vice-president
SuperGigantic Studios
Movieville, California 55500

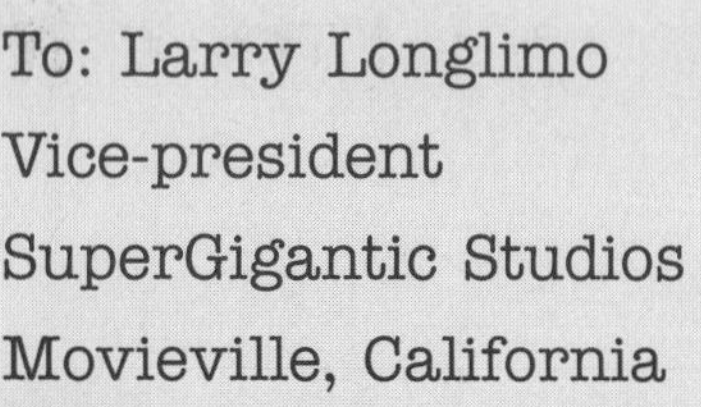

Dear Larry,

Read the idea I've enclosed. It's hot! You can tell me that you love it at lunch next week.

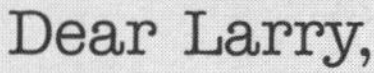

**Main Character's Name:**

**Description of Main Character:**

**Motivation: Lupe wants to become marble champ because**

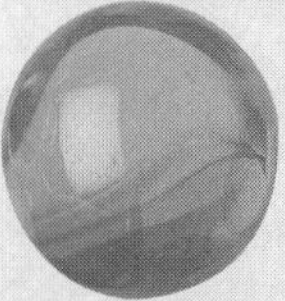

**Summary of Story:**

Name

# See the Sequence?

**Cut out and number the pieces in the order they occur in *The Marble Champ.* Then rewrite each sentence using one of the words in the box. Tape the pieces together in order, from top to bottom to make a trophy.**

| first | later | finally | after | then | before | last | next |
|---|---|---|---|---|---|---|---|

Lupe shakes hands with the girl in the baseball cap.

Lupe wins a match with a boy by eleven to four.

Lupe asks a girl named Rachel to join her.

The referee stops the game.

Lupe beats a fifth grader named Yolanda.



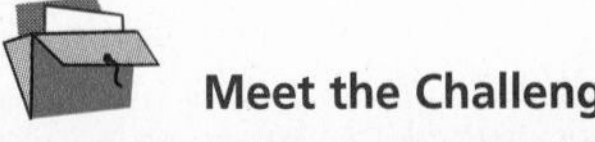

Name

# Q and A

**Read the paragraphs telling about the game of marbles. Then write answers to the questions. Be sure to write complete sentences.**

Marbles is a game played with small balls, usually made of glass. Marbles have also been made of wood, stone, plastic, and steel. People have found marbles made of baked clay in prehistoric caves.

Most marble games are played outside on a flat surface. Players balance a big marble between the thumb and index finger. They use their thumbs to flick a big marble toward one or more smaller marbles. The rules of most games say that players must keep at least one knuckle on the ground while they shoot.

Different kinds of marbles have their own nicknames. For example, the big marble is called a *shooter.* The smaller marbles are called *object marbles*. A glass marble with colored swirls is called a *glassy.*

1. What have marbles been made of?

________________________________________

________________________________________

2. Which fingers are used in playing marbles, and how are they used?

________________________________________

________________________________________

3. What is one way a player might break the rules?

________________________________________

________________________________________

4. What two sizes of marbles are used, and what are their nicknames?

________________________________________

________________________________________

5. Why is a game of marbles played on a flat surface?

________________________________________

________________________________________

Name

# Lupe's Thumb

**Write a sentence to explain the relationship between the words in the analogy.**

1. Lupe's thumb is to powerful as bodybuilder is to muscular.

______________________________

______________________________

**Now think about the relationship between the first two items in each analogy below. Write the word that best completes the analogy.**

2. Marble is to roll as baseball is to ______________.
   round mitt hit
3. Win is to lose as victory is to ______________.
   defeat award champion
4. Lazy is to hardworking as careless is to ______________.
   tired accurate messy
5. Succeed is to accomplish as goal is to ______________.
   target hockey sports
6. Car is to engine as body is to ______________.
   gasoline muscles people
7. Hand is to finger as foot is to ______________.
   knee thumbnail toe
8. Clap is to applaud as compliment is to ______________.
   noise congratulate despise
9. Umpire is to referee as player is to ______________.
   basketball athlete sport
10. Soccer is to kick as marbles is to ______________.
    shoot playground round
11. Honor is to respect as award is to ______________.
    shame speech trophy

Name

# Awarding Words

Cut out the medals and ribbons. Paste each ribbon to the back of the medal with the word that matches its definition. On a separate sheet of paper, write a sentence for each defined word.

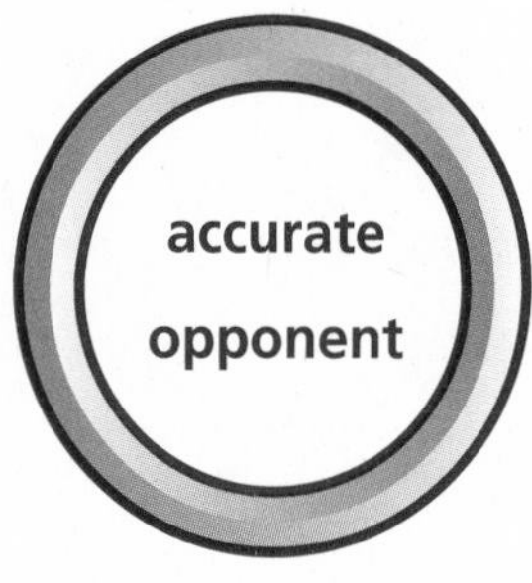

make more powerful

special recognition given to someone

person against you in a contest

someone who received a trophy or an honor

a competition

good at sports

feeling of extreme tiredness

free of mistakes; on target

Name

# Get Low and Aim!

**Words That End with schwa + *r*** Each Spelling Word has two syllables and ends with the schwa sound + ***r*** that you hear in ***finger***. The **schwa** sound is a weak vowel sound that is written as |ə|. The final |ər| sound can be spelled with the pattern ***er***, ***or***, or ***ar***.

|ər| finger honor dollar

**Spelling Words**

1. finger
2. gather
3. honor
4. number
5. favor
6. either
7. neighbor
8. mayor
9. dollar
10. cellar

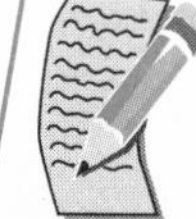

**My Study List**
What other words do you need to study for spelling? Add them to My Study List for *The Marble Champ* in the back of this book.

**Complete each word. Draw lines from each word to its spelling pattern. Then write each Spelling Word below the correct pattern.**

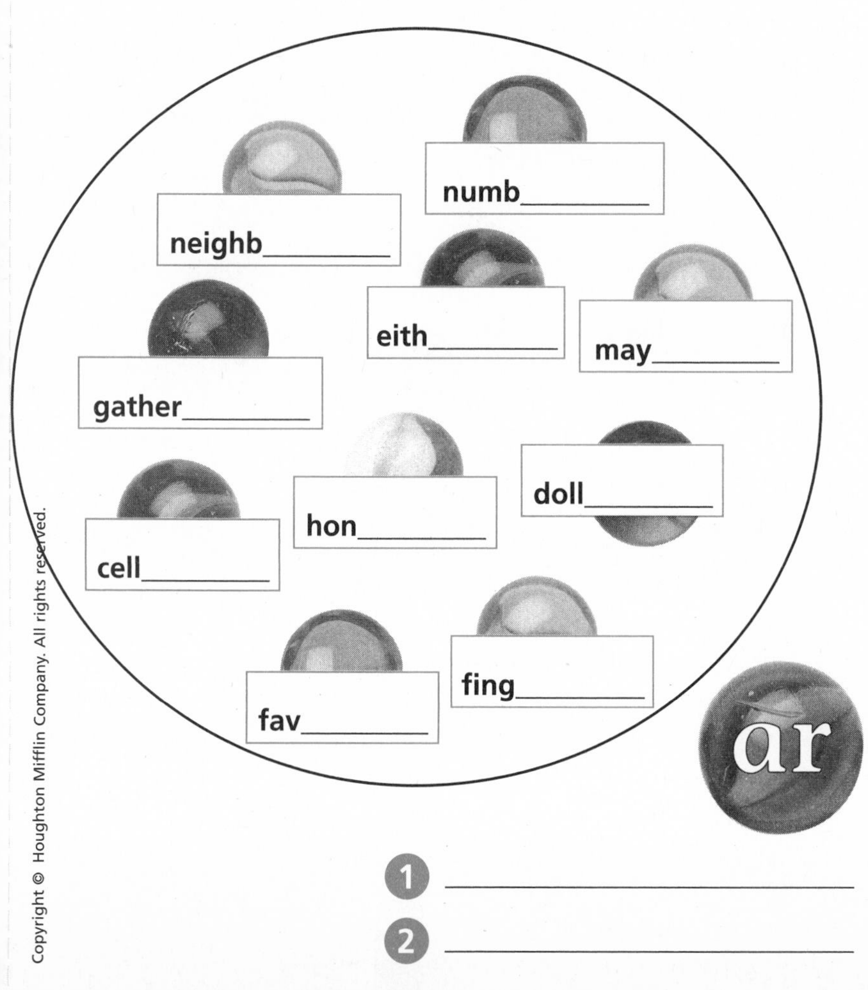


1. ____________________
2. ____________________

or

3. ____________________
4. ____________________
5. ____________________
6. ____________________

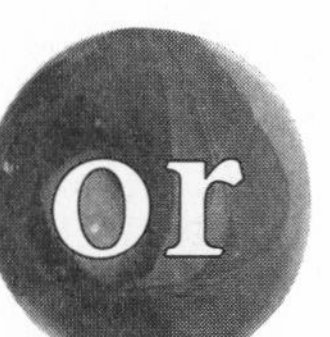

7. ____________________
8. ____________________
9. ____________________
10. ____________________

Name

# Spelling Spree

| Spelling Words | |
|---|---|
| 1. finger | 6. either |
| 2. gather | 7. neighbor |
| 3. honor | 8. mayor |
| 4. number | 9. dollar |
| 5. favor | 10. cellar |

**What's the Question?** Write a Spelling Word to complete each question.

1 The answer is "in City Hall."
The question is "Where is the office of the ____________?"

2 The answer is "one hundred."
The question is "How many cents are in a ____________?"

3 The answer is "my thumb."
The question is "What's your shortest, fattest ____________?"

4 The answer is *"or."*
The question is "What word is often paired with ____________?"

5 The answer is "basement."
The question is "What is another word for ____________?"

**Proofreading** Find and circle five misspelled Spelling Words in this announcement. Then write each word correctly.

6 ____________
7 ____________
8 ____________
9 ____________
10 ____________

Welcome, everyone, to the Marbles Championship! It's nice to see such a big crowd gathar for this event. Why, I see my next-door naybor, and wait, there's the mayor! What an honer! Baseball diamond nubmer three is really the place to be today. Say, who's in favvor of having a parade later?

**Congratulations, Lupe!** On a separate sheet of paper, make a congratulation card for Lupe. Write your message in sentences or as a poem. Use Spelling Words from the list.

Name

# Extra! Write All About It!

**Punctuating Dialogue** Scoop Sneed was a reporter at the marble championship. He took his notes in a hurry, and now he needs help. Write and punctuate each quotation. Use the sample to help you.

"Boy, that was a hard story to cover!" Scoop Sneed said.
"I hope you have all your notes," said Janice, the editor in chief.
"When do I have to turn in my article?" Sneed asked.
Janice replied, "Friday."

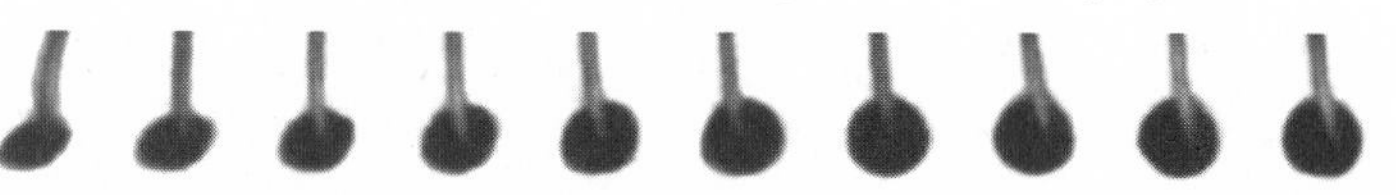

1. Mrs. Medrano said, I never knew Lupe could be so good at a sport.
2. Keep practicing, or your muscles will get weak again, said Alfonso.
3. Rachel said, You tried to make me feel better after I lost.
4. She's the best shooter I've ever played against! Yolanda exclaimed.
5. Mr. Medrano explained, I'm very proud of my daughter's hard work.
6. Lupe bragged, I worked out by squeezing an eraser.
7. Have you ever seen a better player? asked the referee.
8. This girl seems dead serious, said Lupe.
9. I think Lupe had a lot of luck, said the girl in the baseball cap.
10. Thanks for making me champion, Lupe said to her thumb.

Name

# Champions' Club

Each winner belongs to the Champions' Club. Write quotations in which they introduce themselves. Include each speaker's name and special ability. Use quotation marks and other punctuation correctly. Include each of the four types of sentences.

| | |
|---|---|
| Statement | "I have a beautiful agate marble," Lupe stated. |
| Question | "May I borrow it?" I asked. |
| Command | "Please give them room," said the referee. |
| Exclamation | The judge cried, "Lupe is the marble champion!" |

On a separate sheet of paper, write a short dialogue about something you are proud of. Vary your sentence types and check the punctuation of your quotations.

Name

# Brainstorming

## Story Ideas

Do these ideas for characters and settings give you any story ideas?

| Who??? | Where??? |
|---|---|
| astronauts | a kingdom in the Middle Ages |
| explorers | a playground |
| swamp animals | a city after an earthquake |
| two people your age | an airplane |
| statues that come to life | an ancient civilization |

## My Story Ideas

List your five best ideas for a story.

1. ______________________________

2. ______________________________

3. ______________________________

4. ______________________________

5. ______________________________

Think about your ideas. Ask yourself these questions about each one.

*Would this story interest my audience?*

*Do I have clear ideas about the plot, characters, and setting?*

*Would I enjoy writing this story?*

Circle the topic you would most like to write about.

Name

# The Big Plot

Make a story map to help you plan your story. Write notes or draw pictures of your ideas.

| Characters | Setting |
| --- | --- |
| | |

**Plot**

**Problem**

**What happens**

| Beginning | Middle | End |
| --- | --- | --- |
| | | |

**Solution**

Name

# Look It Over

Reread your story, and make changes to improve it.

## Revising Checklist

Ask yourself these questions.

- ❑ Does the story focus on one problem or one situation?
- ❑ Does the ending show how the problem works out?
- ❑ Is each character important to the story?
- ❑ Where can I add more details or dialogue?
- ❑ What other changes would improve my story?

## Questions for a Writing Conference

Use these questions to discuss your story.

- What do you like about this story?
- Do all the events relate to one main problem or situation?
- Does the ending make the story seem finished?
- Is anything confusing?
- Where would more details make the characters, the setting, or the action clearer?
- Should some dialogue be dropped? Where would more dialogue be useful?

## My Notes

Take notes to help you remember ideas from your writing conference.

___

___

___

___

___

___

___

___

Name

# Speaking of History . . .

**Using the vocabulary words below, complete the partially written speech about the history of equal rights.**

**Amendment** **Constitution** **integrated** **opportunity** **prejudice**

Ladies and Gentlemen,

In 1787, the people of the United States needed a new plan for governing the nation. Representatives met in Philadelphia and wrote the ____________________, which has been the basis for our government ever since.

One of the important changes made to the Constitution is the Fourteenth ____________________, which guarantees the full rights of citizenship to all Americans of all races. Unfortunately, African Americans have often been denied equal ____________________ and equal rights. This happened because of ____________________ against African Americans.

Until a few decades ago, many African American children were not allowed to go to the same schools as white children. In 1954, the Supreme Court decided that, according to the principles of the Constitution, all public schools must be ____________________. Now all children in the same neighborhood can attend school together.

Name

# On the Air Tonight

Complete each episode of a four-part documentary series about the life of Thurgood Marshall for the television guide in your local newspaper.

**Monday, 8:00 P.M., Episode 1:**

**Growing Up With the Constitution**

Thurgood Marshall sometimes misbehaved in school. He first learned about the Constitution when he had to ________________________________

before being permitted to return to class. Marshall felt angry when he learned that African Americans did not ________________________________

even though the Constitution promised equal rights for everyone.

**Tuesday, 8:00 P.M., Episode 2:**

**Getting an Education**

Thurgood Marshall got a law degree despite the obstacle of prejudice. After the University of Maryland would not accept him, ________________________________.

Marshall's favorite teacher, Charles Hamilton Houston, taught students that African Americans could use ________________________________ to win equal rights.

**Wednesday, 8:00 P.M., Episode 3:**

**A Very Unusual Lawyer**

Marshall's most famous case, *Brown* v. *Board of Education of Topeka, Kansas*, resulted in ________________________________.

The Supreme Court declared that separate educational facilities were inherently ________________.

**Thursday, 8:00 P.M., Episode 4:**

**Justice Marshall**

In 1967, Thurgood Marshall was ________________________________.

He was the first ________________________________.

Name

# The Letter of the Law

**What if a new law were passed to keep people from riding their skateboards downtown? Two people have written letters about the law to the editor of the local newspaper. Read the letters and fill in the chart.**

**Author A**

To Whom It May Concern:

I worry that one of these skateboards will run into me. Even worse, what if one accidentally goes into the street? The traffic downtown is too heavy to risk having someone hurt for the sake of fun. There are other, less crowded parts of town that are fine for skateboarding.

**Author B**

To Whom It May Concern:

I ride my skateboard home from school every day. These are public streets, and I have as much right to be on them as anyone else. I am very responsible with my skateboard. I wear a helmet and pads. I always watch where I'm going, and I never cross a street against the light.

| | Author A | Author B |
|---|---|---|
| Viewpoint on Skateboarding Downtown | | |
| Supporting Details | | |
| Message About the New Law | | |

Name

# Express Your Opinions!

Use this page to help you plan a personal essay. Write your topic. Then write two thoughts about your topic in the thought balloons. Write notes about examples that you could use to make each thought clear.

**My focus idea:** ______________________________

______________________________

**Thought**

**Thought**

**Example**

**Example**

On a separate sheet of paper, express your opinions in a short essay about your topic.

Name

# Uncover These Words

*Thurgood Marshall and Equal Rights* is about an unusual lawyer. *Unusual* means "not usual." The prefixes *un-*, *in-*, and *il-* often mean "not." In the puzzle, find and circle the words in the box. Then write each word by its meaning.

| | |
|---|---|
| incomplete | unconstitutional |
| illegible | illegal |
| injustice | inactive |
| uneven | inattentive |
| unprepared | unimportant |

| | | | | | | | | | | | | | |
|---|---|---|---|---|---|---|---|---|---|---|---|---|---|
| u | n | p | r | e | p | a | r | e | d | x | n | p | d |
| n | d | e | k | l | a | q | e | t | w | u | e | x | t |
| c | c | v | l | i | u | n | e | v | e | n | n | e | i |
| o | p | o | i | k | s | w | i | x | s | i | v | e | k |
| n | b | i | n | a | c | t | i | v | e | m | l | i | j |
| s | q | e | t | e | p | r | s | j | s | p | u | e | i |
| t | c | i | l | l | e | g | a | l | r | o | n | m | n |
| i | r | l | d | u | k | v | w | z | e | r | h | l | j |
| t | e | l | c | k | a | e | r | o | n | t | p | l | u |
| u | x | e | s | t | y | o | a | n | q | a | a | e | s |
| t | w | g | o | p | p | o | k | v | c | n | e | r | t |
| i | r | i | n | c | o | m | p | l | e | t | e | o | i |
| o | e | b | g | e | h | e | k | p | f | l | o | x | c |
| n | x | l | i | n | a | t | t | e | n | t | i | v | e |
| a | o | e | e | x | g | k | p | r | w | t | z | k | l |
| l | a | h | e | t | k | l | s | r | t | p | x | a | o |

1. not even
   ______________________
2. not in keeping with the Constitution
   ______________________
3. unfairness
   ______________________
4. not keeping one's mind on something
   ______________________
5. unreadable
   ______________________
6. not of importance
   ______________________
7. unlawful
   ______________________
8. not finished
   ______________________
9. not ready
   ______________________
10. not getting any exercise
    ______________________

Name

# Picture This

**You are the editor of a history book called *Thurgood Marshall and the Struggle for Equal Rights.* Use the vocabulary words to complete captions for the pictures. Then draw a picture for the last space.**

| | |
|---|---|
| **Amendment** | **Constitution** |
| **integrated** | **opportunity** |
| **justice** | **segregated** |
| **prejudice** | |

As a child, Thurgood Marshall learned that the Fourteenth ______________ to the ______________ promised equal rights for all Americans.

Because of ______________, African Americans were often kept ______________ from white people in public places.

As an adult, Marshall worked for ______________ schools.

In 1967 Marshall, who worked for equal ______________ for all, was made a ______________ of the Supreme Court.

Name

# Join the March!

**Words That End with schwa + *l*** Each Spelling Word has more than one syllable and ends with the schwa sound + *l* that you hear in ***equal.*** This sound, written as |əl|, can be spelled with the pattern ***al, il, le,*** or ***el.***

|əl| equal civil trouble travel

**Help to organize the march. Complete the Spelling Word on each sign by writing the correct |əl| spelling pattern. Then write each word by the matching spelling pattern.**

**Spelling Words**

1. equal
2. civil
3. legal
4. trouble
5. final
6. local
7. travel
8. puzzle
9. pupil
10. nickel

**My Study List**
What other words do you need to study for spelling? Add them to My Study List for *Thurgood Marshall and Equal Rights* in the back of this book.

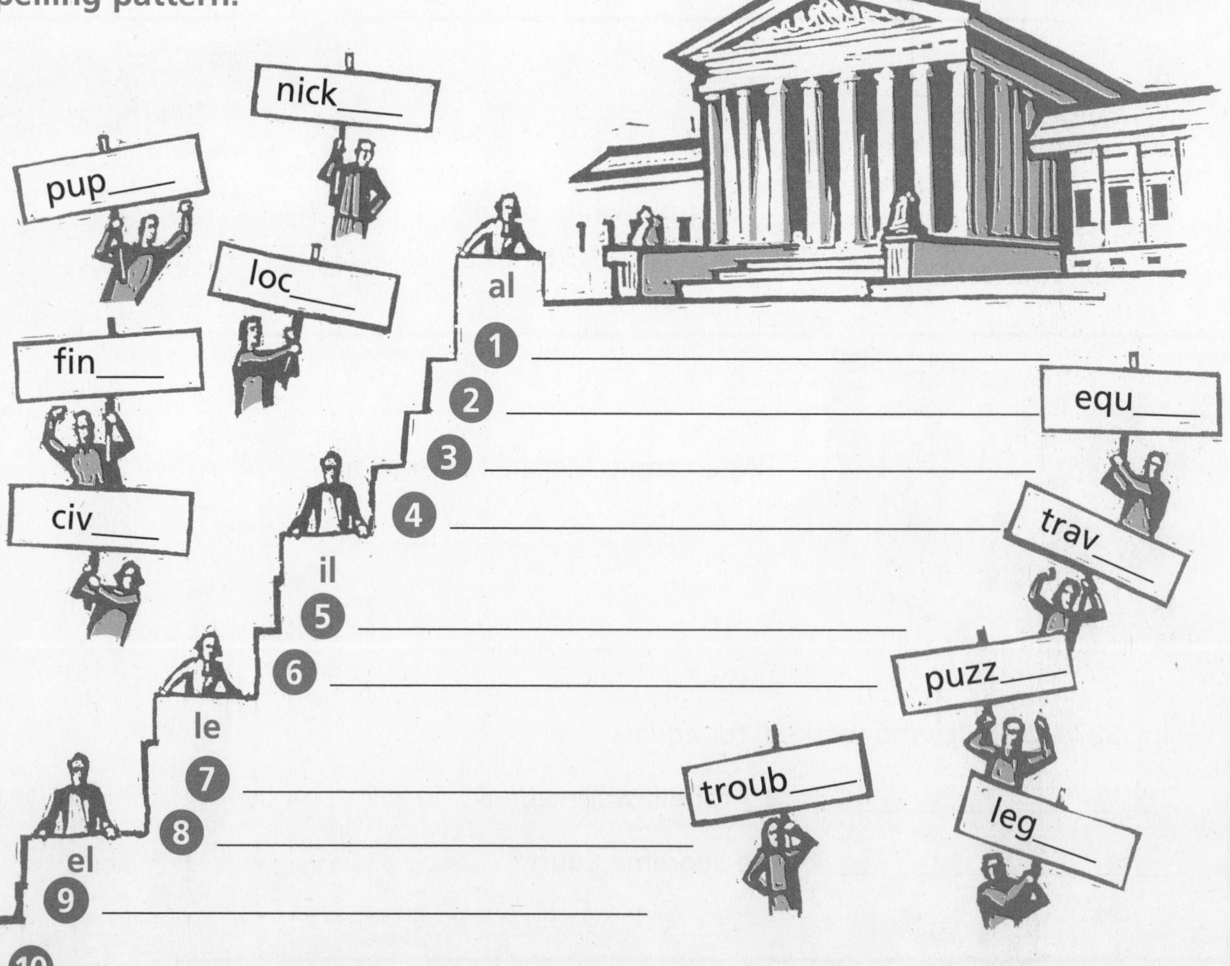


1. ______________________
2. ______________________
3. ______________________
4. ______________________
5. ______________________
6. ______________________
7. ______________________
8. ______________________
9. ______________________
10. ______________________

Name

# Spelling Spree

**Spelling Words**

1. equal
2. civil
3. legal
4. trouble
5. final
6. local
7. travel
8. puzzle
9. pupil
10. nickel

**Proofreading** Circle the four misspelled Spelling Words. Write each word correctly.

For three years, this civel action has been in the locale courts. In January, I will travil to Washington to argue this legal issue before the Supreme Court. With the law on our side, the justices will not have to puzle long over the matter.

1 ______
2 ______
3 ______
4 ______

**Word Search** Write the Spelling Word that fits each clue. Then circle the word in the puzzle.

5. student
6. having the same rights and privileges
7. a five-cent coin
8. authorized by law
9. last
10. a cause of difficulty or distress

| | | | | | | | | | |
|---|---|---|---|---|---|---|---|---|---|
| c | o | f | i | n | a | l | u | r | e |
| l | a | g | e | m | a | y | b | e | q |
| e | n | e | p | u | p | i | l | e | u |
| g | d | e | d | t | o | b | r | i | a |
| a | t | r | o | u | b | l | e | n | l |
| l | g | a | b | o | u | t | j | u | s |
| t | i | n | i | c | k | e | l | c | e |

5 ______ 8 ______
6 ______ 9 ______
7 ______ 10 ______

Write the remaining puzzle letters in order on another sheet of paper to find the secret message.

**Rest in Peace** An obituary, or death notice, may include a short biography. Marshall died at age 84 on January 24, 1993. Write a short obituary for him. Use Spelling Words.

Name

# Keys to Success

**Irregular Verbs** Complete each statement by writing the correct form of the verb in parentheses.

**The school principal had given Marshall a copy of the Constitution.**

**When Marshall grew up, he gave his best to the world.**

1. When young Thurgood misbehaved, his teacher ______________________ (take) him down to the school basement.
2. As Thurgood read the Constitution in the basement, he ______________________ (begin) to take an interest in law.
3. When Will Marshall went to court to watch trials, he ______________________ (bring) his son with him.
4. Thurgood decided to change things when he ______________________ (grow) up.
5. His college classmates have ______________________ (know) him to be a hard worker and a top student.
6. Thurgood Marshall never ______________________ (break) his promise to the "little folks."
7. Thurgood always has ______________________ (give) his best in the fight for equal rights for everyone.
8. From 1967 until 1991, he ______________________ (wear) the robes of a Supreme Court justice with great pride and commitment.

Name

# A Notable Career

**Irregular Verbs** Write at least five sentences to thank Justice Marshall for all he has done for the country. Use verbs in the box. Vary the verb tenses. A sample has been done for you.

| give | wear | know | take |
|---|---|---|---|
| begin | come | break | throw |
| bring | grow | | |

Your Honor,

I remember the first day you <u>wore</u> the robes of a Supreme Court Justice. I have <u>grown</u> up with you as my role model. Thank you for your courage and hard work.

Name

# Words for Thought

**Help finish a plaque dedicated to those who died at Hiroshima. Replace the underlined words with vocabulary words.**

**atom bomb** **comfort** **leukemia** **memorial** **monument**

This plaque is dedicated as a lasting reminder to those who died at Hiroshima. The first nuclear weapon ever dropped on human beings fell in 1945. More than 75,000 people lost their lives, either to the huge explosion, or to cancer of the blood and other forms of radiation sickness. It is hoped that by celebrating this remembrance day, we will ease the pain of the survivors, and create a warning to the future. May it never happen again.

1 ______________________

2 ______________________

3 ______________________

4 ______________________

5 ______________________

Name

# Kimono

**Complete the story map to summarize the main themes and events in *Sadako*. One answer has been filled in for you.**

**Who is the main character?**

**What is she like?**

**Beginning (pages 455-460)**

Sadako attends the Peace Day celebrations with her friend Chizuko. Peace Day is a memorial day for those killed by the atom bomb.

**Middle (pages 463-466)**

**Ending (pages 467-477)**

**Afterword (pages 478-480)**

**What personal quality does Sadako show throughout the story?**

**What are some examples?**

Name ..................................................

# Jumping to Judgments

**Read these letters from a newspaper advice column. Then fill in the chart with details supporting each plan.**

**Dear Gabby,**

**I sprained my ankle playing basketball a few weeks ago. It seemed to get better, but when I tried playing again, it hurt. My best friend says that I shouldn't tell my parents because then they won't let me play in the championship. She says that without me, our team will lose. It only hurts when I play basketball. What should I do?**

**Footloose in Fort Smith**

Dear Footloose,

You must have a screw loose if you have not told your parents, and your doctor. Sports injuries can take a while to heal. If you play basketball again too soon, you might even make your ankle worse. Besides, if you are still in pain, it may affect your playing. Your team may be better off with an uninjured player.

Gabby

| Footloose should keep the injury a secret. | Footloose should speak up about the injury. |
|---|---|
| | |
| | |

**Which plan do you think is right? Explain your judgment.**

______________________________________________

______________________________________________

______________________________________________

Name

# Use Your Senses

Use the chart to plan your poem. First, choose your subject and write it in the center of the chart. Then brainstorm ideas for as many of the six categories as you can. You'll help readers enjoy your poem by adding details telling what it's like to see, touch, feel with your heart, smell, taste, or hear the subject.

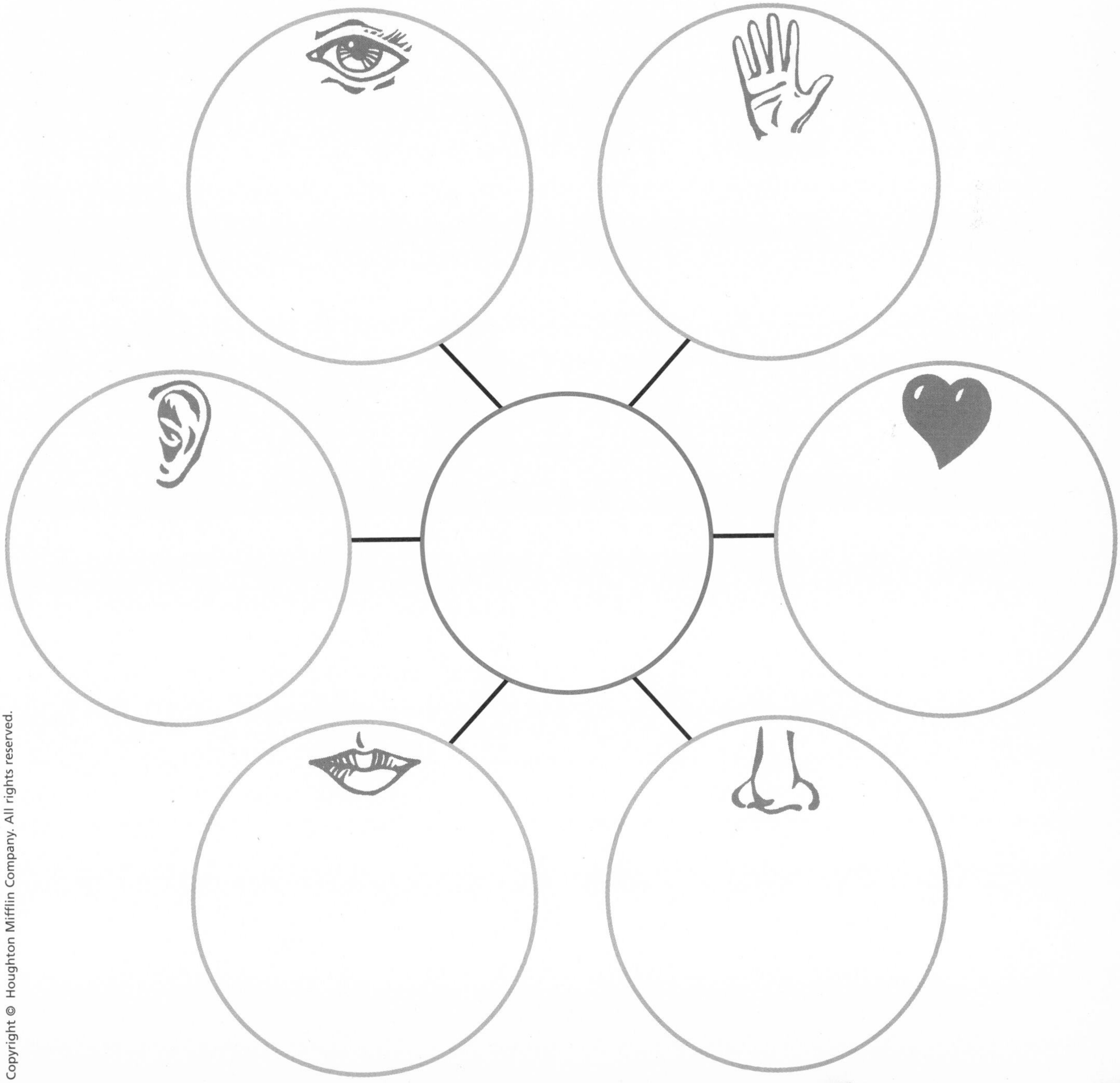

Name ............................................................

# Root It Out

**The word root *sign* means "mark or sign."**
**The word root *spect* means "watch or look at."**

The Japanese people **designed** a monument to the children who died from the atom bomb. A monument is a way of showing **respect**.

**Use the words in the box to complete the story. Write only one letter on a line.**

| spectacular | inspect | assign | signature |
|---|---|---|---|
| signifies | signaled | aspect | expectations |

Kyoko ___ ___ ___ ___ ___ ___ ___ (___) that he was turning left. Soon we were in Centennial Park, where there was an art fair. The exhibits we saw were ___ ___ ___ ___ ___ ___ ___ ___ ___ ___ (___)! We learned that the organizers of the art fair always ___ ___ (___) ___ ___ ___ a space to each artist for his or her exhibit. This year, every exhibitor had great ___ ___ ___ ___ ___ ___ ___ ___ ___ ___ (___) ___ of winning a ribbon. The judges took time to (___) ___ ___ ___ ___ ___ ___ each artist's exhibit carefully. They looked at design, color, and every other ___ ___ ___ (___) ___ ___ of each artist's work. A blue ribbon hung on one painting. Kyoko saw his art teacher's ___ ___ (___) ___ ___ ___ ___ ___ ___ in the corner of one painting. We were thrilled! A blue ribbon always ___ ___ ___ ___ ___ ___ ___ ___ (___) ___ "best in the show"!

**Unscramble the circled letters to find the answer to the question.**

What did the road worker do when he installed the wrong signs?

He ___ ___ ___ ___ ___ ___ ___ ___.

Name

# Words of Memory

**Help Nurse Yasunaga write a letter to her family. Finish the incomplete sentences.**

| | | | |
|---|---|---|---|
| **miracle** | **leukemia** | **respect** | **memorial** |
| **atom bomb** | **comfort** | **symbols** | **monument** |

Dear Mother and Father,

A brave little girl named Sadako was recently staying at the hospital where I work. She was very weak because she had ____________________. Despite her weakness, Sadako folded more than six hundred paper cranes in an effort to get well. Cranes are ____________________ of good health.

After a while, we were amazed. Sadako seemed to get better, as if a ____________________. She was allowed to go home for O Bon. O Bon is a ____________________ celebration held in honor of the damage and suffering caused ____________________. It gives a feeling of ____________________ to the survivors and their families.

After Sadako died, other young people helped to build a ____________________. This is just a symbol of the affection and ____________________ she earned through her courage. I wish that this had been enough to save her.

Love,

Your daughter

Name

# Clouds Get in Your Eyes

**Adding *-ed* or *-ing*** Each Spelling Word has a base word and the ending ***-ed*** or ***-ing***. Some Spelling Words have a base word that ends with **e**. Drop the **e** before adding ***-ed*** or ***-ing***.

care + ed = cared      race + ing = racing

Other Spelling Words have a base word that ends with a consonant. If the consonant follows one vowel, double the consonant before adding ***-ed*** or ***-ing***. If the consonant follows another consonant, do not change the spelling of the base word.

run + ing = running      fold + ed = folded

**Spelling Words**

1. racing
2. cared
3. folded
4. running
5. rushed
6. letting
7. shining
8. smiling
9. tapped
10. sniffed

**My Study List**
What other words do you need to study for spelling? Add them to My Study List for *Sadako* in the back of this book.

**Join the base words and the endings to make Spelling Words. Then write the Spelling Words under their correct headings.**

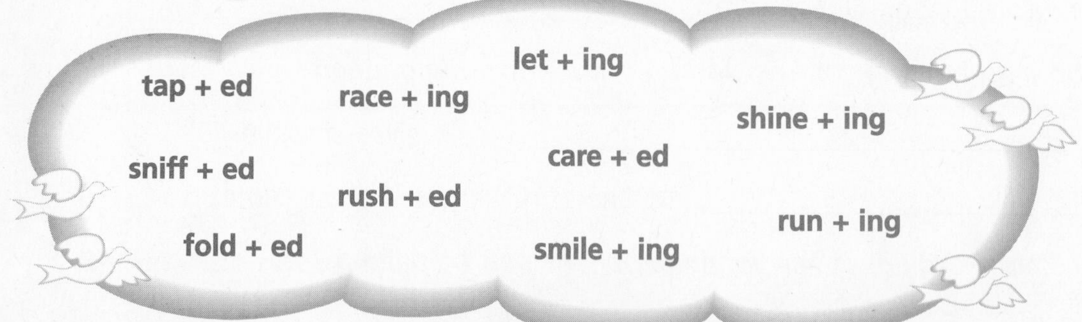


| Spelling Change<br>Drop *e* | Spelling Change<br>Double Final Consonant | No Spelling Change |
|---|---|---|
| 1 ______ | 5 ______ | 8 ______ |
| 2 ______ | 6 ______ | 9 ______ |
| 3 ______ | 7 ______ | 10 ______ |
| 4 ______ | | |

Name

# Spelling Spree

**Spelling Words**

1. racing
2. cared
3. folded
4. running
5. rushed
6. letting
7. shining
8. smiling
9. tapped
10. sniffed

**Original Origami** Write the Spelling Word that fits each clue.

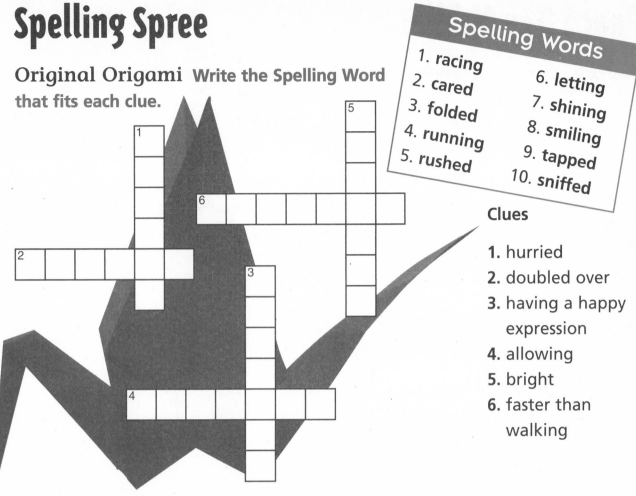

1 2 3 4 5 6

**Clues**

1. hurried
2. doubled over
3. having a happy expression
4. allowing
5. bright
6. faster than walking

**Proofreading** Find and circle four misspelled Spelling Words in these notes. Then write each word correctly.

*Folded Crane Club Notes: Hiroko tapt on the table to call the meeting to order. We discussed letting new members join the club. Next Hiroko asked if we carred to do something special on the anniversary of Sadako's death. A few members wanted to have a raceing event. Others snifed at the idea.*

7 __________
8 __________
9 __________
10 __________

**Poetic Images** A **haiku** is a short Japanese poem, usually having 17 syllables. It gives an image of something in nature, and it creates a mood. On a separate sheet of paper, write a few haiku about the story's nature subjects. Use Spelling Words from the list.

Name

# Peace Day Riddles

| Adverbs that tell ***how*** | Adverbs that tell ***when*** | Adverbs that tell ***where*** |
|---|---|---|
| happily | once | downtown |
| softly | finally | there |
| sadly | sometimes | somewhere |

**Adverbs** **Read these riddles about things that are part of Peace Day in Japan. Underline the adverb in each riddle. Next to each picture clue, write the word that answers the riddle.**

1. People silently walk through the memorial building to see these reminders of the bomb's damage.

______________

2. These fly gracefully when they are released.

______________

3. These explode brightly in the night sky.

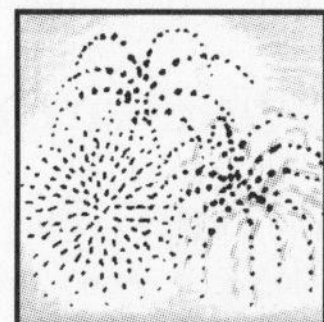

______________

4. People carefully launch these on the river.

______________

5. People arrive early and place these at the foot of Sadako's statue.

______________

**On a separate sheet of paper, write two riddles about other things in the story. Use an adverb in each and underline it. Draw a clue for each riddle.**

Name

# Party Time!

**Adverbs** Some fourth graders are planning a party for children in a local hospital. Help them complete their schedule by writing adverbs that tell *how*, *when*, or *where*.

| | | |
|---|---|---|
| early | suddenly | quickly |
| cheerfully | then | silently |
| downstairs | loudly | next |
| finally | softly | happily |
| quietly | upstairs | |

**Example:** Andy and Luis arrive **early** (when) with the decorations.

## Schedule

- ✔ We meet ____________. (where)
- ✔ Joe and Terri ____________ (how) dress as clowns.
- ✔ Together we go ____________. (where)
- ✔ ____________ (when) we open the door to the children's wing and ____________ (how) shout, "Surprise!"
- ✔ We greet the patients ____________ (how).
- ✔ The clowns ____________ (how) give the children favors while Tina climbs into the box for our first song, "Pop Goes the Weasel."
- ✔ We sing the song's beginning ____________ (how).
- ✔ ____________ (when) we sing "Pop Goes the Weasel" really ____________ (how), and Tina jumps from the box.
- ✔ ____________ (when), everyone sings "Little Bunny Foo Foo" while the clowns ____________ (how) do the motions.
- ✔ ____________ (when), we sing "If You're Happy and You Know It" and wave good-bye.

On a separate sheet of paper, write two sentences telling the fourth graders what else to do at the party. Use at least one adverb in each sentence.

Name

# Be a Pet Detective

Complete the sentences in this ad for a lost-pet detective agency. Use each vocabulary word once.

relieved abandoned responsibility disposition companion

## AWOL Animal Detective Agency

Has your beloved pet run off and heartlessly ______________________?

Don't worry yourself sick. Leave all of the ______________________.

When we find your roving rover, you will be so ______________________!

We have experience with all types of pets. Whether your pet is good-natured or has a ______________, we will find it.

Just call us today, and your missing ______________________.

 Dial PET-FIND 

Write your own sentence for the ad using two vocabulary words.

______________________________________________

______________________________________________

Name

# Sonia's Play

**Help Sonia finish the first scene of a play about Max. In this scene, Max is talking to Fangs, the lizard.**

(Max is walking by Fangs's tank. Fangs speaks.)

**Fangs:** Hi, I'm Fangs. We haven't been introduced.

**Max:** Oh, sorry, I didn't notice you. I'm Max.

**Fangs:** That's okay. How did you get your name?

**Max:** I was named after ______________________________

______________________________________________.

**Fangs:** Did Annette find you?

**Max:** No, ______________________________________.

I was eating ____________________________________.

**Fangs:** How disgusting! Wouldn't you prefer a juicy termite?

**Max:** Uh, no thanks! So are these people as nice as they seem?

**Fangs:** Yes, especially Sonia. She wants to be ______________

______________________________________________.

When she's not around, the big ones take care of us. I took a bite out of Richard once.

**Max:** Where does Sonia go?

**Fangs:** Sonia lives with ______________________________

and only stays here ______________________________.

Are you going to stay here?

**Max:** I think so. Richard wanted ______________________

but, at the last minute, Annette ____________________

______________________________________________.

Name

# The Story Structure Special

***No One Is Going to Nashville* has a story within a story. Read the summary of the story about Annette's dog Maxine. Then fill in the chart.**

When Annette was a girl, she had a dog named Maxine. Her father was a railroad engineer, and they lived near the railroad tracks. One day Maxine disappeared. One night, some time later, Annette's father came home and told her what may have happened to Maxine. He said that Maxine may have hopped a freight train and gone to Nashville, Tennessee, to be a country and western music star.

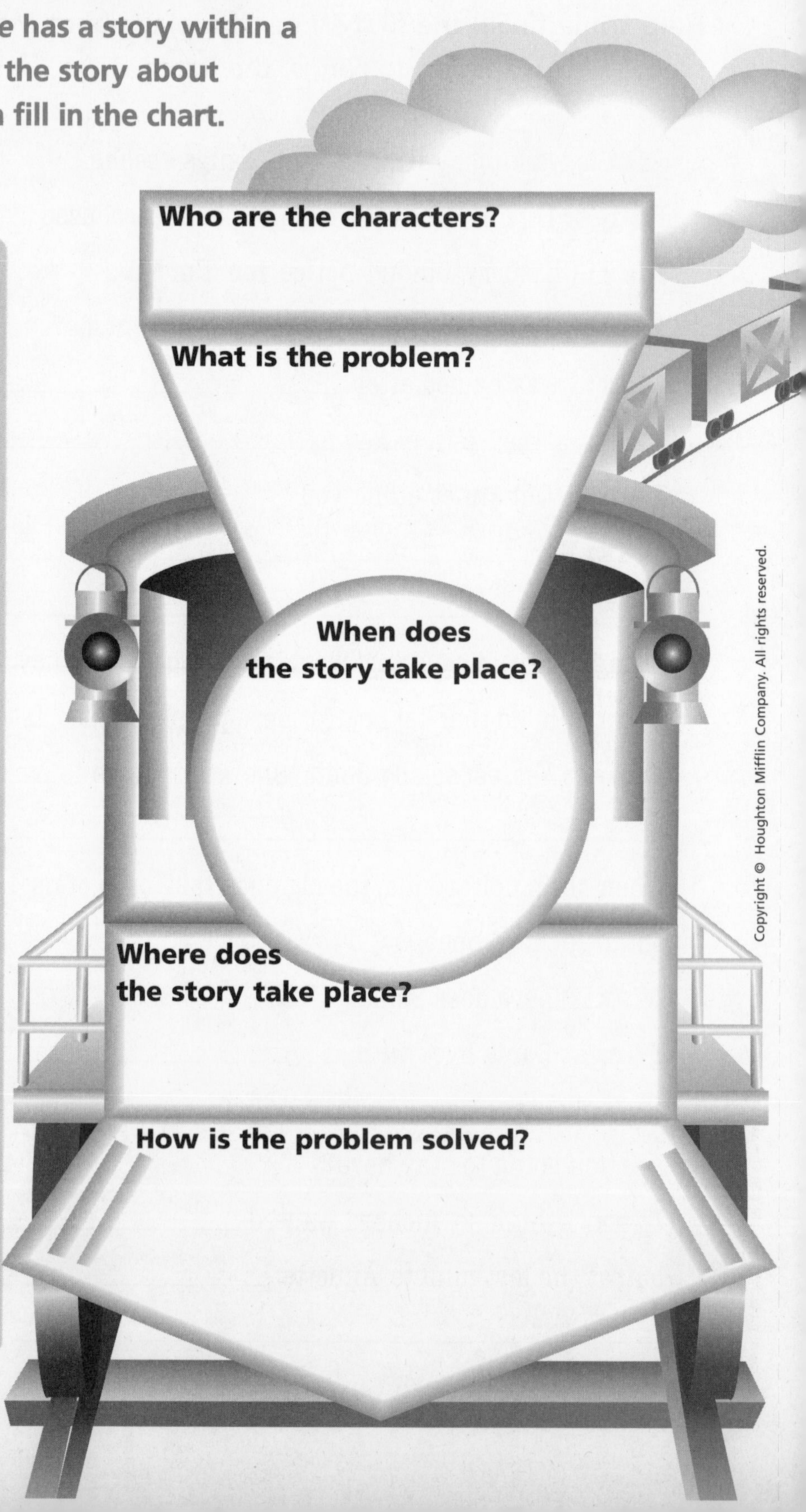

**Who are the characters?**

**What is the problem?**

**When does the story take place?**

**Where does the story take place?**

**How is the problem solved?**

Name

# Leopard on the Loose

**Dr. Ann E. Mahl, a zoo veterinarian, wrote this story for *Zoo Monthly* magazine. Add adverbs to make it more interesting. Choose adverbs from the Adverb Bank, or use adverbs of your own. Begin each sentence with a capital letter.**

| Adverb Bank | | |
|---|---|---|
| here | there | nearby |
| outside | first | then |
| suddenly | soon | lazily |
| loudly | excitedly | firmly |
| softly | quickly | slowly |
| happily | sadly | today |
| peacefully | lazily | often |

Larry the leopard yawned ___(1)___. Things were slow ___(2)___ in his part of the zoo. "Not much happening," he thought. "I wonder what goes on in the rest of the zoo." ___(3)___ Larry looked at the gate. It was open! He looked both ways—and then he ___(4)___ walked ___(5)___.

___(6)___ Larry wandered to the pool to look at the seals. He had ___(7)___ heard them barking and wondered what they were. They barked ___(8)___ at him. He head another noise. It was people yelling ___(9)___. They were running in the other direction. "What's all the fuss?" Larry wondered.

Larry didn't like fuss. He saw a soft grassy spot and ___(10)___ lay down. He yawned. ___(11)___ he snoozed ___(12)___.

___(13)___ he heard a familiar voice saying, "Larry, it's time to go home." The voice spoke ___(14)___. It was Zach the zookeeper.

"Sure thing," Larry said—or growled. He got up and ___(15)___ walked back to his part of the zoo with Zach.

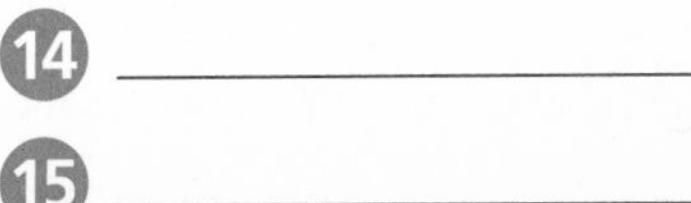

1. ______________
2. ______________
3. ______________
4. ______________
5. ______________
6. ______________
7. ______________
8. ______________
9. ______________
10. ______________
11. ______________
12. ______________
13. ______________
14. ______________
15. ______________

Name

# Wanted: Prefixes

**Circle the words below with prefixes. Then answer the questions.**

**WANTED**

***Ex***perienced students who do not ***mis***read words beginning with ***ex-***, ***re-***, and ***mis-***. Students must ***re***call how these prefixes are used.

1. Why do teachers expect respect? ______________________

2. Why might a book with a misprint need to be reprinted? ______________________

3. Why should you try to respell a word that you have misspelled? ______________________

4. Mr. Fogget misplaced his eyeglasses. Should he replace them? Why or why not? ______________________

5. If soldiers wish to repel the enemy, is it wise for them to expel spies? Why or why not? ______________________

**Draw a picture to go with each caption.**

| | |
|---|---|
| I must redo my mishandled experiment. | Fearsome, a misnamed dog, always has an extreme reaction to the doorbell. |

Name

# Vamoosed Varmint Vocabulary Blues

**Max has written a country-and-western song in honor of Maxine. Replace the underlined sections of the song with vocabulary words.**

| abandoned | relieved | expressive | disposition |
|---|---|---|---|
| companion | responsibility | restless | decision |

## Ode to Maxine
by Max

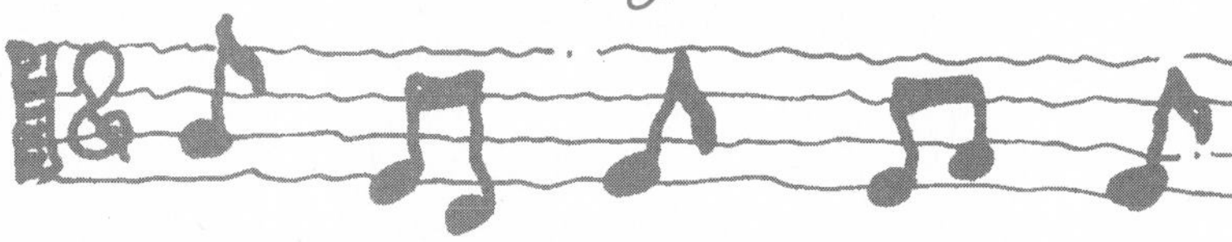

She was a dog of sweet personality, ____________
but she had a fidgety heart. ____________
She never told her young friend ____________
of her determination to depart. ____________

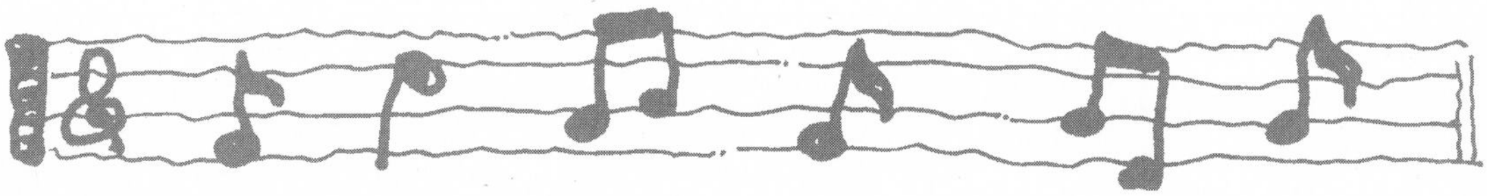

Oh, my full of meaning Maxine! ____________
You left behind tranquility. ____________
I'm free from worry that I have a home now, ____________
Staying's my duty. ____________

Name

# Waltzing with Max

**Changing Final *y* to *i*** Each Spelling Word has the ending ***-ed***, ***-es***, ***-er***, or ***-est*** added to a base word that ends with a consonant and ***y***. When the ending is added, change the ***y*** to ***i***.

carry + ed = carried
story + es = stories
sorry + er = sorrier
funny + est = funniest

**TIP**: Does a vowel or a consonant come before the final *y*?

**Spelling Words**

1. easiest
2. carried
3. stories
4. sorrier
5. cities
6. funniest
7. families
8. angrier
9. copied
10. studied

**My Study List**
What other words do you need to study for spelling? Add them to My Study List for *No One Is Going to Nashville* in the back of this book.

**Help Sonia teach Max to do the box step. Join the words and endings to write Spelling Words.**

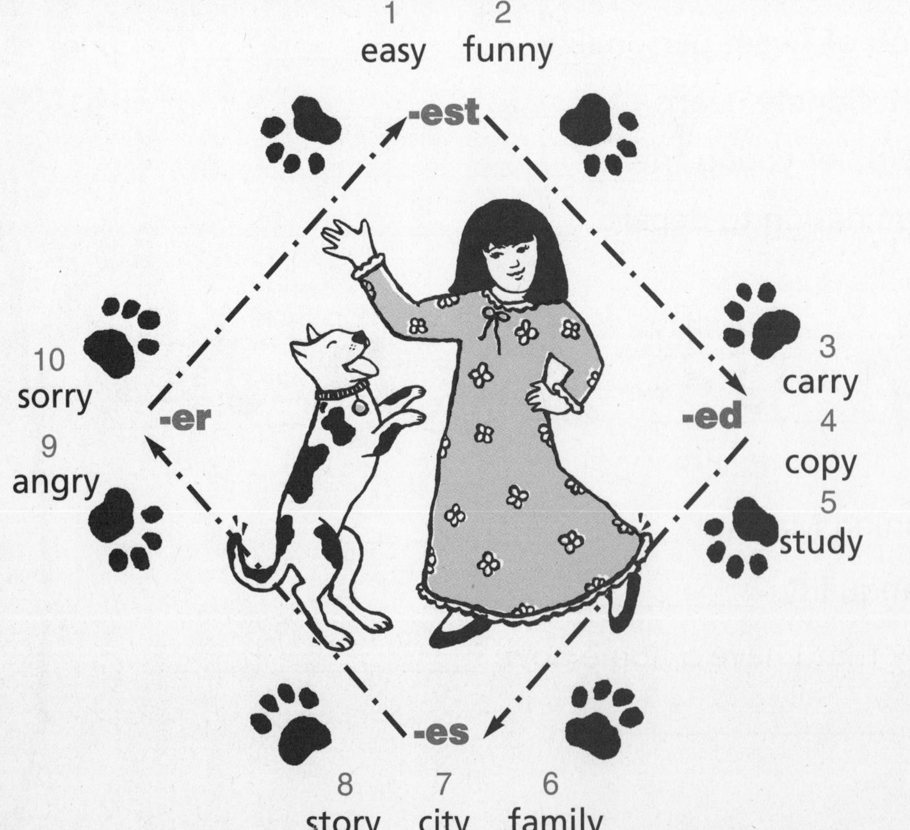


1. ______
2. ______
3. ______
4. ______
5. ______
6. ______
7. ______
8. ______
9. ______
10. ______

Name

# Spelling Spree

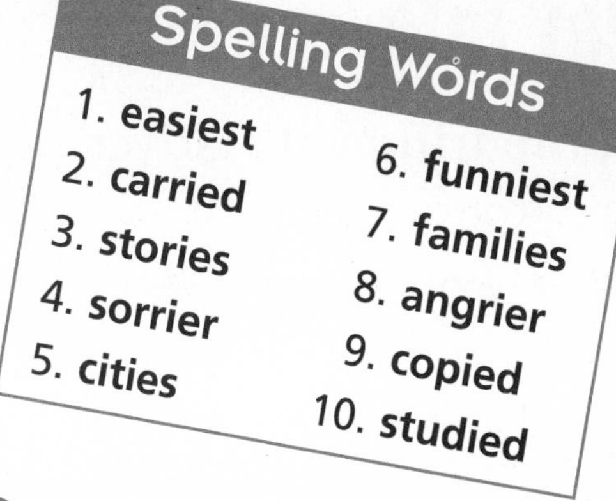


**Proofreading** Circle five misspelled Spelling Words. Write each word correctly.

Each year, stray pets are found all over our citties. Sometimes, whole famalies of puppies and kittens are abandoned. If these animals could talk, many would have shocking storys to tell. Is neglecting an animal really the eaziest way to get rid of it? This makes me angryer than I have ever been.

1. ______
2. ______
3. ______
4. ______
5. ______

**Rhyme Time** Write the Spelling Word that best completes each rhyme.

6. There's no ______ sound than a dog's wail in the pound.

7. I've ______ white mice, and I've decided they're nice.

8. The ______ song was about a cat named Kong.

9. I ______ you. When you smiled, I did too.

10. We ______ Wag home in a small bag.

**Dogs and You** An opinion tells how you feel about something. Richard has a strong opinion about dogs. On a separate sheet of paper, write your opinion of dogs. Use Spelling Words from the list.

Name

# Pet Talk

**Comparing with Adverbs** Each of these animals wants to convince you that it would be a perfect pet. Write the correct form of the adverb to complete each statement.

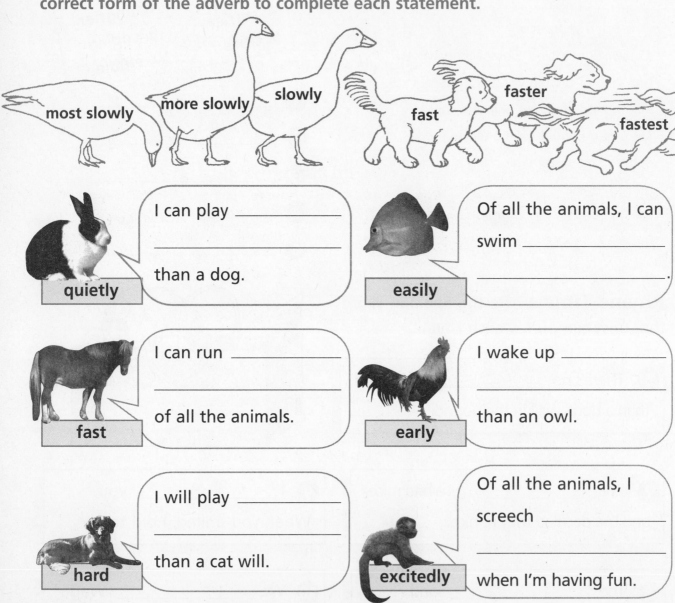

most slowly | more slowly | slowly | fast | faster | fastest

**quietly** — I can play ____________ ____________ than a dog.

**easily** — Of all the animals, I can swim ____________ ____________.

**fast** — I can run ____________ ____________ of all the animals.

**early** — I wake up ____________ ____________ than an owl.

**hard** — I will play ____________ ____________ than a cat will.

**excitedly** — Of all the animals, I screech ____________ ____________ when I'm having fun.

**late** — I can stay awake ____________ than a rabbit.

**gracefully** — I can fly ____________ ____________ than a rooster.

Name

# Promises to Keep

**Comparing with Adverbs** Complete the list of promises Sonia gave to her father by filling in the correct form of each adverb. Then add one more promise that makes a comparison using an adverb.

**If you let me keep Max, I, Sonia, do hereby promise that**

- I will wake up ____________ (early) of anyone to walk the dog.
- Max will behave ____________ (calmly) than Ms. Mackey.
- Max will obey ____________ (eagerly) of all my pets.
- I will try ____________ (hard) in school than I did last semester.
- I will score ____________ (high) of all on math.
- I will be quiet on Saturday mornings so that you can sleep ____________ (long) than I do.
- When you call me, I will run ____________ (fast) than a racer.
- I will watch my pets ____________ (carefully) than I have in in the past.
- ______________________________________________
______________________________________________

Name

# And the Nominee Is . . .

Write a letter to nominate one of the main characters in this theme for an award for being courageous, persistent, or resourceful. Answer the questions to help you plan your letter.

Character you think deserves award:

_______________

Challenge or challenges the character faced:

1. _______________
2. _______________
3. _______________

What did the character do that showed courage, persistence, or resourcefulness?

1. _______________
2. _______________
3. _______________

Make sure your letter explains your viewpoint about the character. Describe whether you think the character did a good job in meeting the challenge. Summarize the main points of the story to explain how your character met a challenge.

**Checklist**

Before you share your letter, use this box to check your work.

- ❑ My letter explains why my character deserves to win an award for meeting a challenge.
- ❑ My letter explains what challenge my character faced.
- ❑ My letter describes my viewpoint about my character.

Name

# Could It Really Happen?

Have you ever heard about a remarkable event that really happened? Add three amazing real-life events to the list.

people walking on the moon ______________________

winning an Olympic medal ______________________

seeing a rainbow ______________________

Add to the list three amazing events from books that could never happen in real life.

a mouse riding a motorcycle ______________________

animals talking ______________________

dinosaurs living today ______________________

Draw pictures of two amazing events, one that could really happen and one that could not.

It Could Really Happen. It Couldn't Really Happen.

On a separate sheet of paper, write a short paragraph about an amazing event that happened to you.

Name

# Could It Really Happen?

**As you read the stories in this theme, keep track of the different strange events. Fill out the appropriate part of this chart as you finish each story.**

| | What amazing thing happened? | How did the characters react? | How would you react if it happened to you? | Could it really happen? Why or why not? |
|---|---|---|---|---|
| Jumanji | | | | |
| Elliot's House | | | | |
| June 29, 1999 | | | | |
| Charlotte's Web | | | | |

Name

# Eat Your Words

**Begin on the space marked Start and follow the instructions as you move counterclockwise. Inside the lion's mouth, write the vocabulary word that has the same meaning as the underlined word or phrase.**

**casually   bored   disappointed   sighed   restless   slouched**

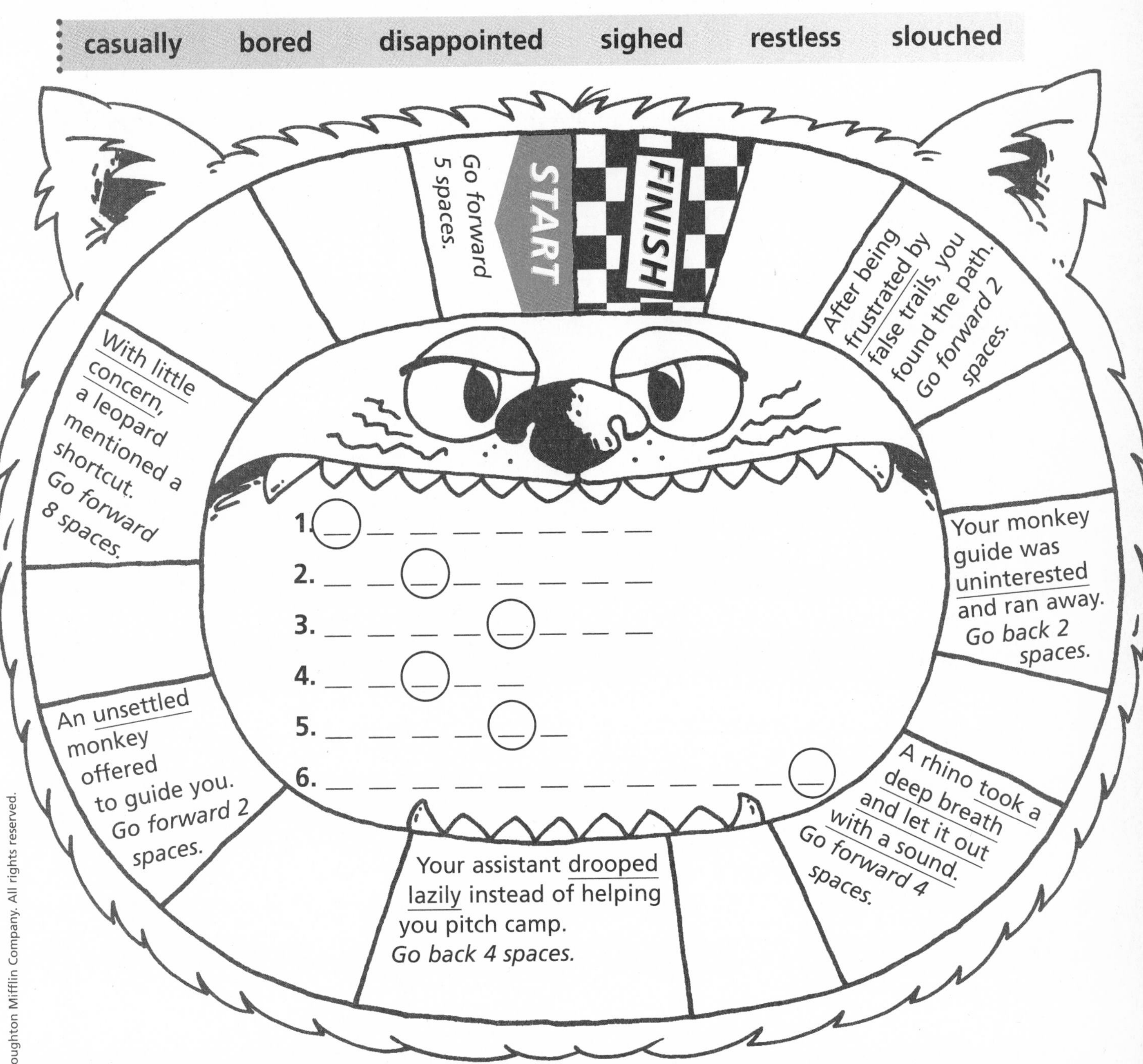

START
Go forward 5 spaces.
FINISH
With little concern, a leopard mentioned a shortcut. Go forward 8 spaces.
After being frustrated by false trails, you found the path. Go forward 2 spaces.
Your monkey guide was uninterested and ran away. Go back 2 spaces.
An unsettled monkey offered to guide you. Go forward 2 spaces.
A rhino took a deep breath and let it out with a sound. Go forward 4 spaces.
Your assistant drooped lazily instead of helping you pitch camp. Go back 4 spaces.
1. _ _ _ _ _ _ _ _
2. _ _ _ _ _ _ _ _
3. _ _ _ _ _ _ _ _
4. _ _ _ _ _
5. _ _ _ _ _ _
6. _ _ _ _ _ _ _ _ _ _ _ _

**Write the letters from the circles to solve the riddle.**

What did the lion do when it got bored? It __ __ __ __ __ __!

Name

# Published

**You are trying to get *Jumanji* published in another country. Your assistant was supposed to write a summary, but he got the story mixed up. Read the summary and draw a line through the mistakes. Then write what really happened, using a separate sheet of paper if necessary.**

Judy and Peter's parents go out. The children get tired of watching TV and go to the mall, where they find a game under a tree. The game is called Jumanji.

When Judy and Peter play the game at home, strange things start to happen. A real lion appears in the house. Later, turtles, a monsoon, a kangaroo, stampeding hedgehogs, a snake, and a volcano appear. Judy and Peter are afraid to stop, because the lion says that a game of Jumanji does not end until both players reach the ivory-tower. Judy returns the house to normal by landing on the last space and shouting, "Cowabunga!" Judy and Peter throw the game out the window, where two other children find it.





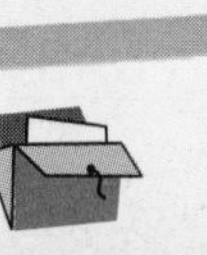

Name

# Directions to Paradise

Follow the steps to make a pencil puppet bird of paradise. You will need safety scissors, paste, tape, an unsharpened pencil, and colored markers. Check each box as you complete the directions.

1. Read each step carefully.
2. Follow the steps in order.
3. Picture the steps in your mind.

- ❑ Step 1. Read all the steps and collect the materials you will need.
- ❑ Step 2. Cut out the three large shapes.
- ❑ Step 3. Lay the body down and put a thin coating of paste inside area A.
- ❑ Step 4. Lay flap A on the head over area A on the body.
- ❑ Step 5. Put a thin coating of paste inside area B on the body.
- ❑ Step 6. Lay flap B on the tail over area B on the body.
- ❑ Step 7. When the paste has dried, decorate the other side of the puppet with colored markers.
- ❑ Step 8. Finally, tape the pencil on the undecorated side of the body so that one end covers area C.

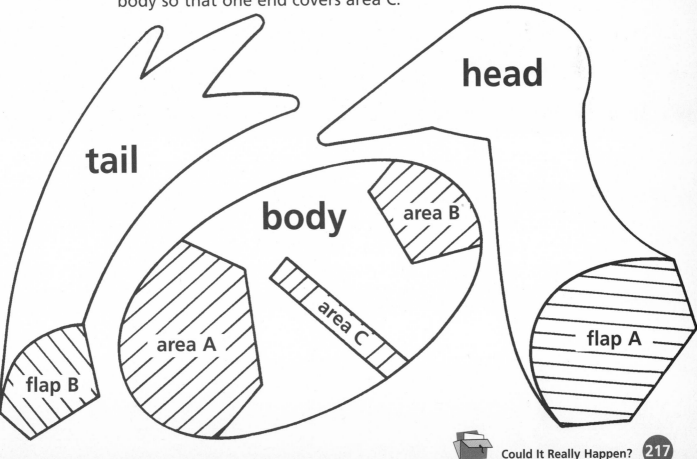

Name

# Who? What?

Decide whether the meaning of each underlined pronoun is clear or unclear. Put a check mark in the proper column.

| | Clear | Unclear |
|---|---|---|
| 1. Peter and Judy went to the park after playing in the house. They left it a terrible mess. | | |
| 2. Peter and Judy were bored. They went to the park. | | |
| 3. Peter found a box. In it was a game. | | |
| 4. A lion chased Peter under the bed. He got his head stuck. | | |
| 5. The children found monkeys in the kitchen. They tore the room apart. | | |
| 6. The thunder scared the monkeys. They ran out of the kitchen. | | |
| 7. Judy reached the golden city. She yelled, "Jumanji!" | | |
| 8. Mother and Father woke up Peter and Judy. They put on their pajamas. | | |

Rewrite each unclear sentence so that the meaning of the pronouns is clear.

Name ______________________________

# Root Out the Roots

Write the missing root to complete each word. Then write the word to complete each sentence.

| interrupt | rupture | disruptive | attractive |
|---|---|---|---|
| eruption | tractor | extract | distraction |

Root Reminder
*tract* means "to draw or pull"
*rupt* means "to break"

1. a sudden breakup or explosion: e ________________ion

   The ________________ of a volcano behind our house surprised my family.

2. to stop an activity by breaking into it: inter ________________

   The noise was so loud we had to ________________ our dinner.

3. to break apart: ________________ ure

   The force of the volcano caused the basement floor to ________________.

4. pleasing, drawing attention: at ________________ ive

   Volcanoes can be beautiful, but they are not ________________ in your yard.

5. breaking things up and causing confusion: dis ________________ ive

   In fact, the volcano's sudden appearance was ________________ to our lives.

6. to pull out: ex ________________

   We had to ________________ the broken chunks of concrete.

7. farm machine used for pulling: ________________ or

   We tied the chunks to a ________________ and dragged them out.

8. something that draws attention away: dis________________ion

   Having a volcano in your yard can be a terrible ________________.

**Now write your own sentence using two words with the root *tract* or *rupt*.**

______________________________________________________________

______________________________________________________________

Name

# Woefully Weary Words

Complete the crossword puzzle. Use the words in the box.

| bored | unexcited | disappointed | restless |
|---|---|---|---|
| slouched | ignored | sighed | casually |

**Across**

1. took a deep breath and let it out with a sound
5. frustrated or let down
7. not interested

**Down**

1. sat, stood, or walked with a bent posture
2. in a relaxed, informal manner
3. not excited
4. unable to relax
6. paid no attention to

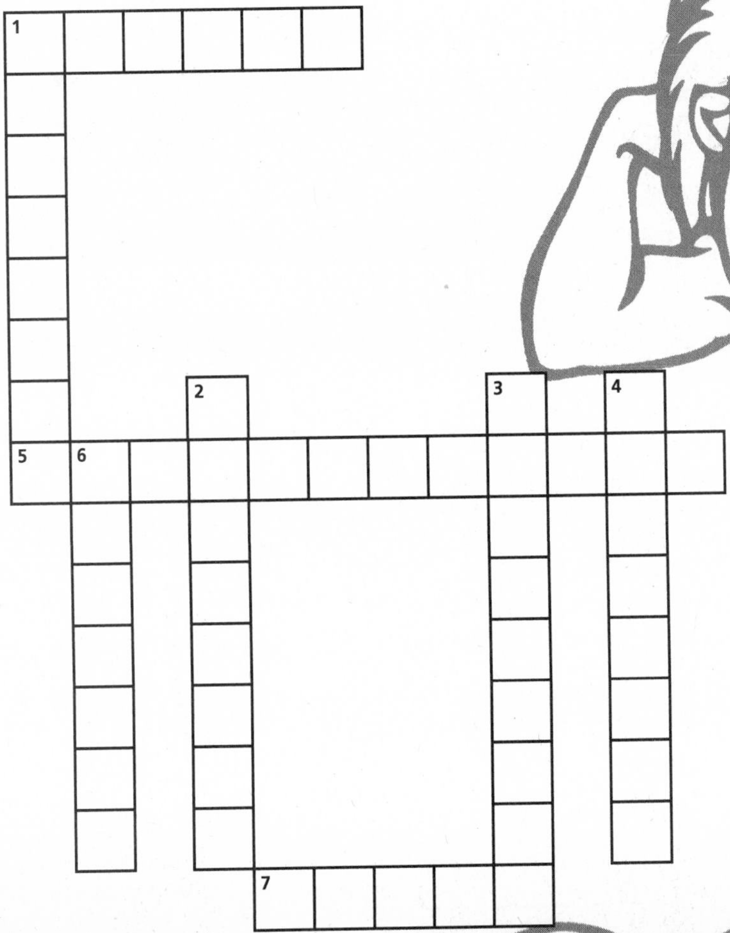

1 2 3 4 5 6 7

Name

# Into the Jungle

**Words with Prefixes** Each Spelling Word begins with the prefix ***re-***, ***un-***, or ***dis-***. A ***prefix*** is a word part that comes at the beginning of a base word. A prefix adds meaning to the word.

The prefix ***re-*** means "again." The prefix ***un-*** means "not" or "the opposite of." The prefix ***dis-*** means "not."

reread = to read again
unfold = the opposite of fold
dislike = to not like

## Spelling Words

1. **reread**
2. **unfold**
3. **unclear**
4. **dislike**
5. **reuse**
6. **unsure**
7. **displease**
8. **unwrap**
9. **discolor**
10. **rejoin**

**My Study List**
What other words do you need to study for spelling? Add them to My Study List for *Jumanji* in the back of this book.

**Play a jungle board game. Begin at START and use the game piece codes to decide which prefix goes with each word. Then write the Spelling Word you form.**

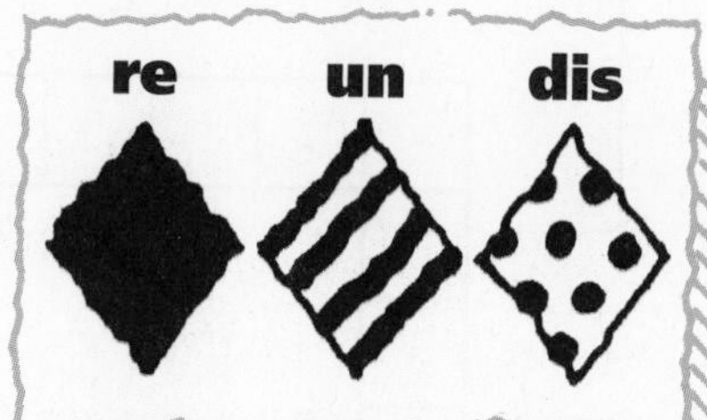


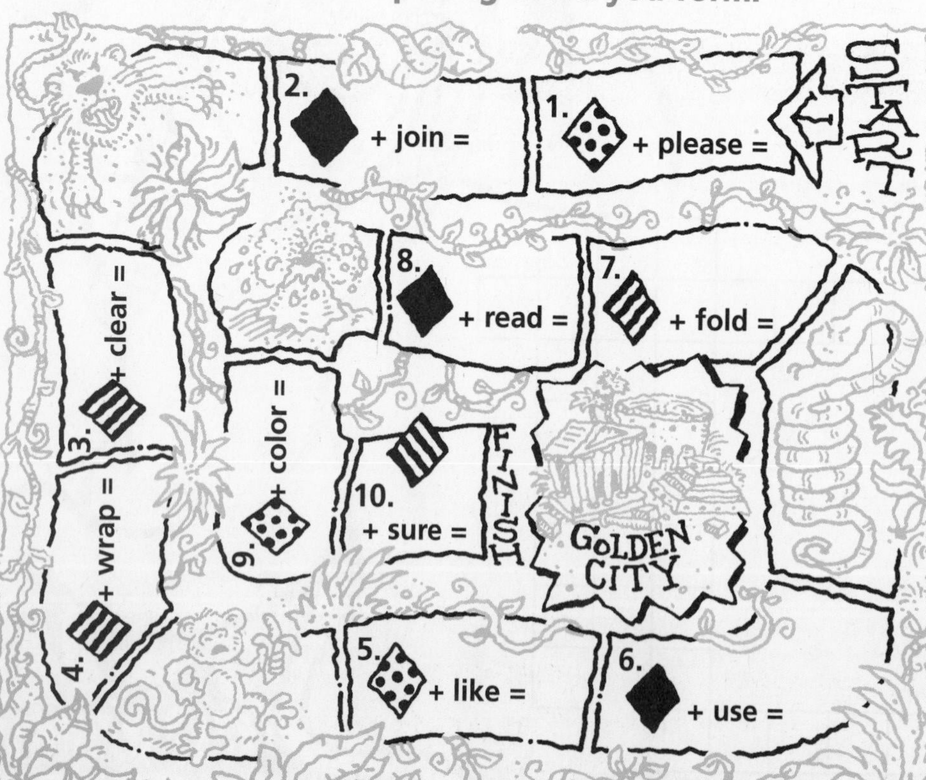


1 ______________
2 ______________
3 ______________
4 ______________
5 ______________
6 ______________
7 ______________
8 ______________
9 ______________
10 ______________

Name

# Spelling Spree

**Spelling Words**

1. reread
2. unfold
3. unclear
4. dislike
5. reuse
6. unsure
7. displease
8. unwrap
9. discolor
10. rejoin

**Proofreading** Find and circle four misspelled Spelling Words in these game instructions. Then write each word correctly.

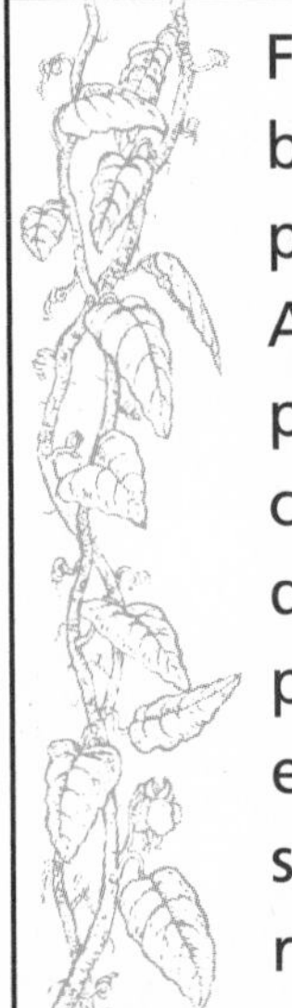

First, unfoled the game board. Then unrap the package of game pieces. Ask all players to choose a piece in their favorite color. In order not to displease anyone, we have provided several pieces in each color. Players who disslike some colors can feel free to reyuse their game pieces.

1. ______
2. ______
3. ______
4. ______

**Animal Answers** Write the Spelling Word that fits each clue. Write your words next to the jungle animals.

5. not certain
6. not satisfy
7. join again
8. spoil the color of
9. not clear
10. read again

5 ______

8 ______

9 ______

6 ______

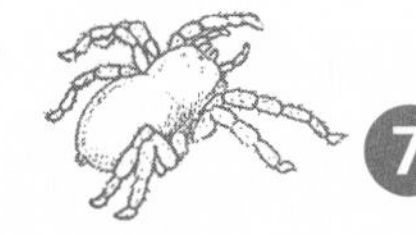

7 ______

10 ______

**Safari Speech** Imagine that you are a safari guide lost in the jungle. The tourists in your party are nervous. On a separate sheet of paper, write a short speech that you can give to make the tourists more at ease. Use Spelling Words from the list.

Name

# The Key to the Golden City

mine, yours, hers, his, its, ours, theirs — **Pronouns That Stand Alone**

**Pronouns That Appear Before Nouns**

**Possessive Pronouns** **Finish Queen Ajuji's greeting by completing the sentences with possessive pronouns. Then find each piece hidden in the picture and write a sentence describing its location. In each sentence, use a possessive pronoun and underline it.**

"The golden city belongs to me, and everything in it is ____________. But I am happy to share its riches. The people who live here know that whatever they need will be ____________ if they only ask. We will share what is ____________, but first you must find the five pieces missing from the key to the city. If you do, the city's treasures will be ____________ too."

**Example: Piece #1.** The queen has it on <u>her</u> headdress.

**Piece #2.** ________________________

**Piece #3.** ________________________

**Piece #4.** ________________________

**Piece #5.** ________________________

Name

# It's a Jungle Out There!

**Possessive Pronouns** Here's a jungle game you can play. First, fill in the missing possessive pronouns in the players' conversation and on the game path. Then use coins for markers and roll one die to move around the board. Good luck.

ours my your theirs our their mine yours

Start

The lions want ______________ dinner. Lose a turn.

Queen Ajuji gives you one of ______________ elephants. Take another turn.

The river overflows ______________ banks. Move back 2 spaces.

King Abasi chooses you for ______________ advisor. Move ahead 5 spaces.

Friendly inhabitants share ______________ food with you. Take another turn.

Chimpanzees raid ______________ tent. Lose a turn.

A mother rhino charges when you photograph ______________ baby! Move back 5 spaces.

A monsoon ruins ______________ equipment. Lose a turn.

Queen Ajuji has lots of film and gives you some of ______________. Move ahead 2 spaces.

The guide takes your compass because he has lost ______________. Lose a turn.

Finish

Sammy: Is it ______________ turn?

Erica: I just took ______________ turn so it's ______________.

Sammy: OK. I rolled a three so I'll move ______________ marker three spaces.

Erica: OK. You know I'll always remind you when it's ______________ turn and when it's ______________.

Sammy: Right, and I'll record the score. Is that ______________ scorecard?

Erica: No. Tracy and Cedric played last night. That's ______________. I have ______________ in ______________ hand.

Name ........................................

## Instructions Ideas

Can you do any of these things? Do they make you think of other things you can do?

- inflate a bike tire
- wash dishes so Mom is impressed
- make a chart on the computer
- set the table for guests
- take care of pets
- play a new game
- set the alarm on a clock
- make an ornament
- build a campfire
- make a splint
- make a linoleum print

**My Ideas** **Write down five things that you could tell someone how to do.**

1. ______________________________
2. ______________________________
3. ______________________________
4. ______________________________
5. ______________________________

**Think about each idea you wrote. Ask yourself these questions.**

*Would I enjoy explaining how to do this?*

*Is this too hard to explain in a few steps or paragraphs?*

*Is this something I have done recently or can do again as I plan my writing?*

**Circle the topic you would most like to write about.**

Name

# Step by Step

List materials that would be needed for following your instructions. Then write each step of your instructions, and list details that your audience would need to know to do each one.

| MATERIALS | |
|---|---|
| | |
| **STEPS** | **DETAILS** |
| Step 1 | |
| Step 2 | |
| Step 3 | |
| Step 4 | |
| Step 5 | |

Name

# Look It Over

Read your instructions and make changes to make them clearer.

## Revising Checklist

Use these questions to help you revise your instructions.

- ❑ Does my topic sentence introduce the topic in an interesting way?
- ❑ Did I include all the steps?
- ❑ Did I give enough details so that my reader knows exactly what to do?
- ❑ Are the steps in order? Did I use order words?
- ❑ Did I include all the materials?

## Questions for a Writing Conference

Use these questions to discuss your instructions with a classmate.

- What do you like about these instructions?
- Does the first sentence make the topic clear and interesting?
- Are the steps in order? Are they easy to follow?
- Which steps need more explanation?
- Which steps are confusing?
- How could the instructions be made even clearer?

Write notes to help you remember ideas from your writing conference.

**My Notes**

Name

# Where Does It Go?

Make a storyboard showing what happens to the garbage you throw away. Draw a picture in each box and write a sentence about it using the vocabulary words. Use each word at least once.

mounds landfill garbage collected depositing

**Stage 1: Picking It Up**

**Stage 2: Taking It Away**

**Stage 3: Covering It Up**

Name

# Digging for a Story

**You are an archaeologist of the future. Write a paragraph telling the story of Elliot based on these objects you dug up. Mention the clues in your paragraph.**

a child's drawing

SPECIAL REPORT

**August 2, 2345**

Name

# Cat Conclusions

**A pet cat has disappeared. Examine the picture and draw a conclusion about what happened to the cat.**

| Clues from the cartoon | What I know about cats |
| --- | --- |
| | |

| Conclusion: Where is the cat? |
| --- |
| |

Name

# Bigger Bins

Students at Clutterton Elementary School ordered 50-gallon recycling bins but received 5-gallon bins, which fill up too fast. On a separate sheet of paper, write a letter to Customer Service for the container company to request new bins. Use this page to plan your letter.

The container company's address is:

Clutterton Containers, Inc.
555 Littery Lane
Clutterton, OH 44444

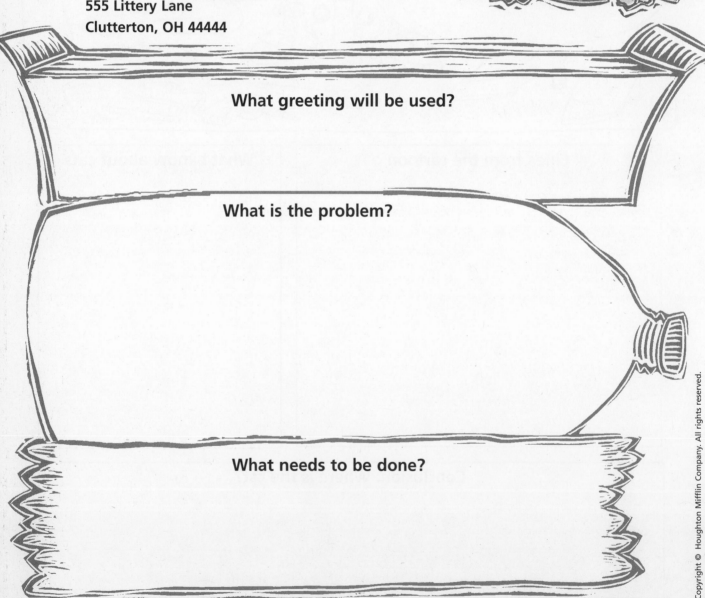

What greeting will be used?

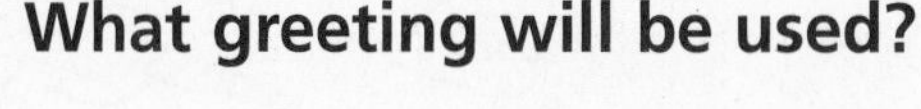

What is the problem?

What needs to be done?

Name

# Name That Category!

You are on a TV game show. To win, write the category that fits all the words in each list. Then add one more word to each category.

1 **Category:** ______________________

rats giraffes cats penguins

2 **Category:** ______________________

trees flowers weeds grass

3 **Category:** ______________________

dress shirt shoes socks

GRAND PRIZE

Circle another word that belongs in each category. Write a sentence that explains why it belongs there.

**Example:**

yellow green white red — dark (brown)

The category is colors. Brown is a color.

4 poodle spaniel German shepherd greyhound — collie Fido

______________________________________________

5 tulip marigold rose daisy — zinnia garden

______________________________________________

6 rectangle oval square circle — inch triangle

______________________________________________

Name ______________________________

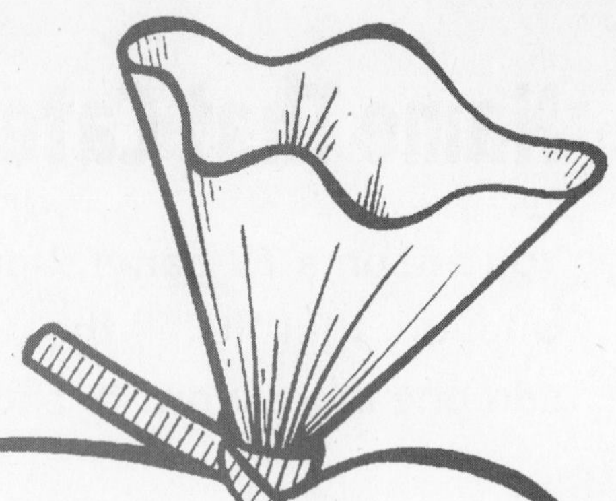

# Wasted Words

**Dispose of the used-up words waiting to be thrown away. Connect each word to the correct definition with a line. (Two words share the same definition.)**

**putting or laying down**

**gathered or brought together**

**reusing waste products**

**unwanted or useless material**

**piles or hills**

**an area in which trash is buried beneath layers of dirt**

**Write three sentences that use two vocabulary words each. Use each word only once.**

______________________________________________________________

______________________________________________________________

______________________________________________________________

______________________________________________________________

Name

# Landfill Maneuvers

**Words with Suffixes** Each Spelling Word ends with the suffix *-ful*, *-less*, *-ness*, or *-ment*. A **suffix** is a word part that comes at the end of a word. It adds meaning to the word.

| Suffix | Meaning | | |
|---|---|---|---|
| -ful | full of | careful | = full of care |
| -less | without | homeless | = without a home |
| -ness | quality of | goodness | = quality of being good |
| -ment | act of | movement | = act of moving |

## Spelling Words

1. homeless
2. careful
3. goodness
4. colorless
5. darkness
6. wishful
7. smoothness
8. restless
9. movement
10. treatment

**My Study List**
What other words do you need to study for spelling? Add them to My Study List for *Elliot's House* in the back of this book.

**Draw a line from each base word to the suffix that completes each Spelling Word. Then write each Spelling Word under the correct suffix meaning.**

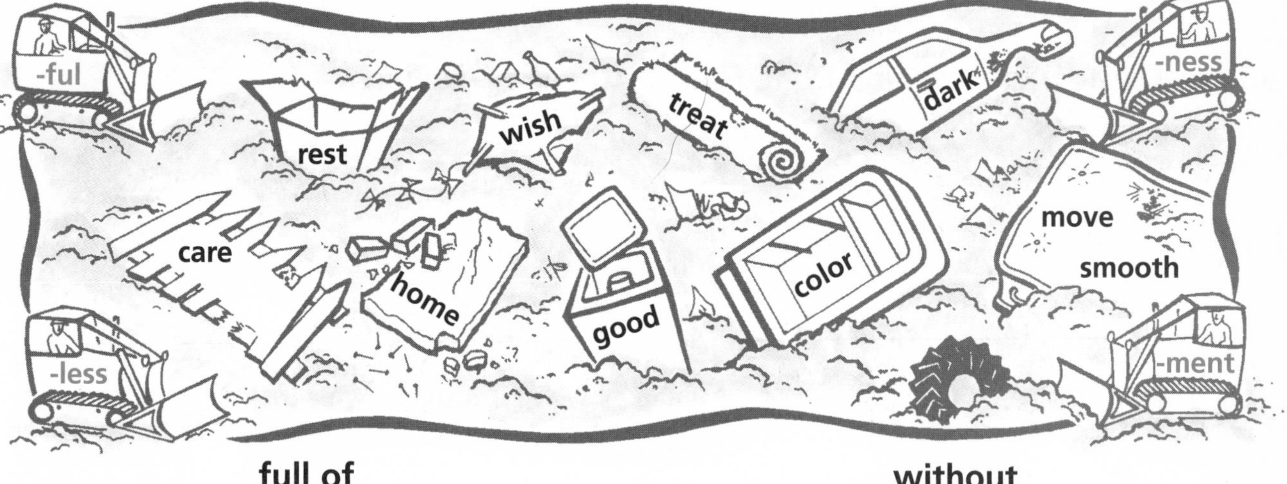


**full of**

1 ____________________

2 ____________________

**quality of**

3 ____________________

4 ____________________

5 ____________________

**without**

6 ____________________

7 ____________________

8 ____________________

**act of**

9 ____________________

10 ____________________

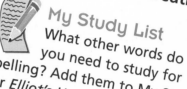

Name

# Spelling Spree

| Spelling Words | |
|---|---|
| 1. homeless | 6. wishful |
| 2. careful | 7. smoothness |
| 3. goodness | 8. restless |
| 4. colorless | 9. movement |
| 5. darkness | 10. treatment |

**Recycled Opposites** For each sentence write the Spelling Word that means the opposite of the underlined word.

1. Thank evilness that more people are recycling now!
2. A trucking firm handles the stillness of our town's trash to recycling centers.
3. We are always careless to sort our aluminum, glass, plastic, and paper trash.
4. I spent a calm night dreaming that I was buried in mounds of trash.
5. My friend has invented a new use for colorful glass.
6. Dad was amazed by the roughness of the car's ride on the recycled rubber tires.

1 ____________
2 ____________
3 ____________
4 ____________
5 ____________
6 ____________

**Proofreading** Find and circle four misspelled Spelling Words in this essay. Then write each word correctly.

To sum up, we must all give careful thought to what we throw away. Granted, landfills are not eyesores when covered by darckness. But in the light of day, swarming with homless cats and dogs, they are awful. Our treetment of trash simply MUST change. When it does, the idea of a trash-free world will no longer be mere wishfull thinking.

   9 ____________

7 ____________

8 ____________ 10 ____________

**Save-Our-Planet Survey** The Save-Our-Planet group has asked you to survey your neighbors' opinions on recycling. On a separate sheet of paper, write a list of questions to ask your neighbors. Use Spelling Words from the list.

Name ______________________________

# Rita Recycler

**Prevent Pileups! Use Commas.**

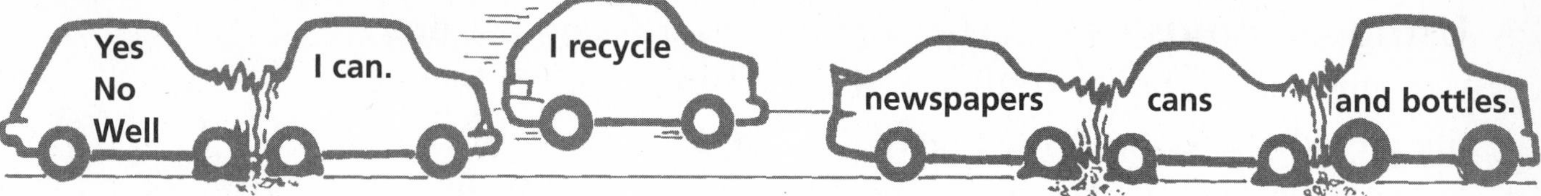


**Using Commas Correctly** Look at the picture of Rita Rat's house and write the names of three items to complete each statement. Use commas and the words *and* and *or* to separate the items.

stamp
pencil
comb
sponge
earrings

matchbox
spool
block
toothpaste cap
buttons

cup
necklace
paper clips
birthday candles
bottle caps
locket
bolts
watch

## Elliot's Trash is Rita's Treasure

Rita Rat uses ______________________________ for dishes. She uses ______________________________ as bedroom furniture. Rita Rat has made the place look nice by hanging ______________________________ on her wall. Rita has a sofa made of ______________________________. To hang up her clothes, Rita Rat uses ______________________________ ______________________________. Rita made a chandelier from ______________________________. Folks call her Rita Recycler!

Name

# Elliot, Can You Hear Me?

**Using Commas Correctly** A trained search dog has dug its way into Elliot's house to deliver a walkie-talkie to his family. You are a reporter recording the rescuers' conversation with Elliot. Add commas where needed to the questions. Then write one-sentence answers. Begin each answer with *yes, no,* or *well.*

**Rescuer:** Elliot is everyone OK?

**Elliot:** ______________________________

**Rescuer:** How many people are in the house right now Elliot?

**Elliot:** ______________________________

**Rescuer:** Elliot are you the smallest person there?

**Elliot:** ______________________________

**Rescuer:** Do you think you could tunnel out through an upstairs window Elliot?

**Elliot:** ______________________________

**Rescuer:** Elliot is there enough food in the house to last for two days while a bulldozer moves the trash away from the house?

**Elliot:** ______________________________

**Rescuer:** Is anyone feeling faint Elliot from lack of oxygen?

**Elliot:** ______________________________

**Rescuer:** There's one thing I just don't understand. Why is there garbage piled up to the top of your house Elliot?

**Elliot:** ______________________________

Name ______________________

# Vast Vegetable Vocabulary

Dr. Bean wants to grow giant vegetables. He wrote a draft of a report but is too busy to write a final copy. Rewrite his report using each vocabulary word at least once.

| concludes | experiment | conditions |
|---|---|---|
| effects | development | specimens |

**UltraVeg Food Corp. Research Laboratory**

**Office of Dr. James Bean**

**Purpose:** My group has been trying to conduct a test on radishes. I wanted to find out what changes the SuperSprout X formula causes in them.

**Description:** I grew radishes in a sealed room so I could control the amount of light, water, and other things that might be important. The examples that we were studying were sprayed with SuperSprout X. The way they grew was remarkable.

**Recommendations:** My partner, Dr. Jean Green, believes, after much thought, that we should cancel the project. These radishes are growing out of control!

**UltraVeg Food Corp. Research Laboratory**

**Office of Dr. James Bean**

**Purpose:** ______________________

______________________

______________________

**Description:** ______________________

______________________

______________________

**Recommendations:** ______________________

______________________

______________________

Name

# Ionospheric Investigator

You are an Arcturian investigator. You must explain the *Alula Borealis* incident to Chief Inspector T'Sphftys. Answer the questions to complete the accident report.

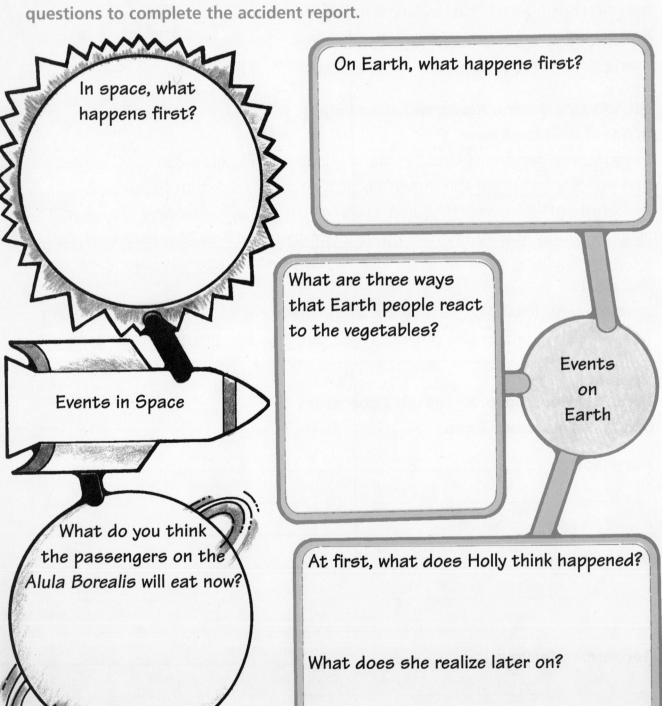

In space, what happens first?

Events in Space

What do you think the passengers on the *Alula Borealis* will eat now?

On Earth, what happens first?

What are three ways that Earth people react to the vegetables?

Events on Earth

At first, what does Holly think happened?

What does she realize later on?

Name

# Reality or Fantasy? You Decide

Which picture shows a fantastic scene, and which one shows a realistic scene? Circle the fantastic scene and explain what makes it fantastic.

Draw a picture of a fantastic scene and a realistic scene. Explain what is fantastic or realistic about each picture.

**This picture is fantastic because**

**This picture is realistic because**

Name

# Extra! Extra!

**Read the interviews and the police report about a strange incident at the beach. Then write a newspaper story and a headline about it.**

**Eyewitness #1,** *surfer Wayne Wipeout:* It was amazing. The big thing fell out of the sky into the ocean! It must have been one hundred feet wide! The splash was huge. I rode some cool waves.

**Eyewitness #2,** *dog owner Damp Tanner:* I was having a picnic with my dog on the beach when a giant wave soaked me. Everyone in the water ran away and trampled my lunch. Now my dog faints at the sight of cabbage! I'm going to find out who is responsible for this.

**Police report:** About 2 P.M. yesterday, a giant cabbage fell into the ocean near Santa Kapusta. No one was hurt. The cabbage was towed away by a police boat. When found, the owner of the vegetable may be fined for littering and charged for storage.

## THE BERGSBURY BUGLE

Name

# Could It Really Be a Noun?

Did you find any **silliness** in *June 29, 1999*? What was your **reaction?** Perhaps you felt **amazement.**

The boldfaced words are nouns. Each ends with the suffix ***-ment***, ***-ion***, or ***-ness***.

| | | |
|---|---|---|
| **illustration** | **announcement** | **stubbornness** |
| **government** | **dizziness** | **expression** |
| **confusion** | **wickedness** | **refreshment** |

**Draw a line to connect each root word to the suffix that will make it a noun. Then write the complete noun next to the suffix. Remember that some suffixes change the spelling of the root word.**

| ROOT | SUFFIX | |
|---|---|---|
| illustrate | ment | 1 __________ |
| govern | | 2 __________ |
| dizzy | | 3 __________ |
| announce | ness | 4 __________ |
| stubborn | | 5 __________ |
| express | | 6 __________ |
| refresh | ion | 7 __________ |
| wicked | | 8 __________ |
| confuse | | 9 __________ |

**On a separate sheet of paper, write three sentences. Use one of the words above in each sentence. Each word should have a different suffix.**

Name ______________________

# Whirling Words

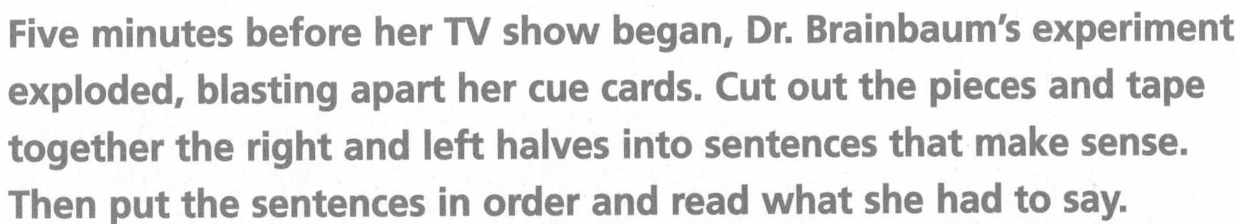

Five minutes before her TV show began, Dr. Brainbaum's experiment exploded, blasting apart her cue cards. Cut out the pieces and tape together the right and left halves into sentences that make sense. Then put the sentences in order and read what she had to say.

| | | | |
|---|---|---|---|
| concludes | experiment | results | conditions |
| effects | development | research | specimens |

| | |
|---|---|
| 3. We will expose the rutabaga to | growing part of the science world. |
| 7. See the results next time on | fascinating vegetable, the rutabaga. |
| 6. Let's see how the development | about rutabagas in space on next week's show. |
| 4. First, we will place the specimens | of a rutabaga is changed by space. |
| 2. Today, we'll experiment with that | *Bea Brainbaum, Woman of Science.* |
| 5. This test will show the effects | conditions like those in outer space. |
| 1. Research about vegetables is a | into the outer-space tank. |
| 8. Find out what special guest Dr. James Bean concludes | of outer space on rutabaga growth. |

Name

# Syllable Vegetables

**The VCCV Pattern** Each Spelling Word has two syllables and the vowel-consonant-consonant-vowel (VCCV) pattern. To find the syllables of many words with the VCCV pattern, divide between the consonants.

| VC\|CV | VC\|CV |
|---|---|
| hap\|pen | tur\|nip |

**Spelling Words**

1. happen
2. pepper
3. turnip
4. twenty
5. supper
6. carpet
7. entire
8. ribbon
9. member
10. captain

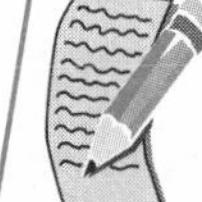

**My Study List**
What other words do you need to study for spelling? Add them to My Study List for *June 29, 1999* in the back of this book.

**Help the Arcturians find their food supply. Draw lines to match the syllables of the Spelling Words. Then write each word correctly on the giant green bean. Draw a line between the syllables.**

| | |
|---|---|
| sup | tain |
| mem | per |
| tur | pen |
| cap | bon |
| car | nip |
| twen | tire |
| pep | ty |
| rib | ber |
| hap | pet |
| en | per |

1. ______
2. ______
3. ______
4. ______
5. ______
6. ______
7. ______
8. ______
9. ______
10. ______

Name ____________________

# Spelling Spree

| Spelling Words | |
|---|---|
| 1. happen | 6. carpet |
| 2. pepper | 7. entire |
| 3. turnip | 8. ribbon |
| 4. twenty | 9. member |
| 5. supper | 10. captain |

**Proofreading** Find and circle five misspelled Spelling Words in this TV news script. Then write each word correctly.

Here's some late-breaking news from a membre of our staff. Just twennty minutes ago, thousands of huge vegetables fell from the sky. One-ton peas carpit the entire city of Springfield. A giant ternip landed atop Seattle's Space Needle. A blimp-sized green peper sits on the White House lawn. No one will go hungry tonight!

1. ____________________
2. ____________________
3. ____________________
4. ____________________
5. ____________________

**Tongue Twisters** Write the Spelling Word that completes each tongue twister.

6. The river is a ________________ of rhubarb, radishes, and rutabaga.
7. An enormous eggplant engulfed the ________________expressway.
8. Should Sue steam some super-sized spinach and squash for ______________?
9. Can the cruiser's ________________ capture all the cabbages and carrots?
10. Does Hal ________________ to be hungry for a huge helping of horseradish?

**Star Cruiser S.O.S.** You are the radio operator aboard the *Alula Borealis*. On a separate sheet of paper, write a message requesting that food be rushed to the spacecraft. Use Spelling Words from the list.

Name

# Who's Who at the Arcturian Party?

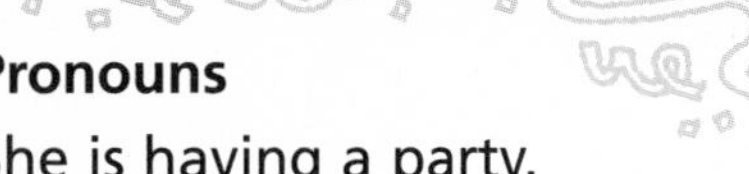

| Nouns | Pronouns |
|---|---|
| Glitzy is having a party. | She is having a party. |
| Iza and Itab are guests. | They are guests. |

**Arcturian Glitzy Planetska is having a party. Complete this conversation between Glitzy and her guest Bleep. Write a subject pronoun to replace the word or words in parentheses.**

**Bleep:** Thanks for inviting us. (Zid and I) ______________ enjoy your parties so much.

**Glitzy:** You're welcome. (Glitzy) ______________ try to have interesting people at my parties.

**Bleep:** I'll say! (Glitzy) ______________ really do! Who is that in the red cape?

**Glitzy:** Oh, that's Lilo. (Lilo) ______________ plays the piano beautifully.

**Bleep:** I can hardly wait to hear her, but those two aren't waiting.

**Glitzy:** Do you mean Aza and Itab? No, (Aza and Itab) ______________ dance whether there's music or not.

**Bleep:** The tall fellow in the corner seems to have a lot to say.

**Glitzy:** Yes, that's Atre. (Atre) ______________ talks nonstop. He's lucky to be with Rina, the woman in green. (Rina) ______________ listens nonstop.

**Bleep:** Is that Zort by the refreshment table?

**Glitzy:** Oh my, yes! (Zort) ______________ eats everything if you don't watch him.

**Bleep:** With this food, who can blame him? (The food) ______________ tastes great.

**Glitzy:** Oh good, Ipp is here. (Ipp) ______________ keeps her eye on Zort so that he doesn't eat the flowers.

**Bleep:** What???

Name ______________________

# At the 1999 County Fair

**Subject Pronouns** These gardeners had out-of-this-world results with their crops! Use subject pronouns and present tense verbs to write two captions for each vegetable and grower or team of growers.

Example

1

2

3

4

**Examples:**

She grows strawberries as big as pumpkins.
They make huge fruit pies!

1 ______________________________________________

______________________________________________

2 ______________________________________________

______________________________________________

3 ______________________________________________

______________________________________________

4 ______________________________________________

______________________________________________

Now draw yourself and a friend with a prize-winning vegetable you have grown. Write two sentences as a caption.

5 ______________________________

______________________________

______________________________

______________________________

5

Name

# Web Weaving Wonders

**News of amazing events has reached the local papers. Write headlines for the stories, using each word at least once.**

**wonders    wondrous    miracle    miraculous    bewilderment**

## The County Commentator

| Weather today: sunny, warm | *"All the news that fits, we print."* | Farm Report Inside |
|---|---|---|

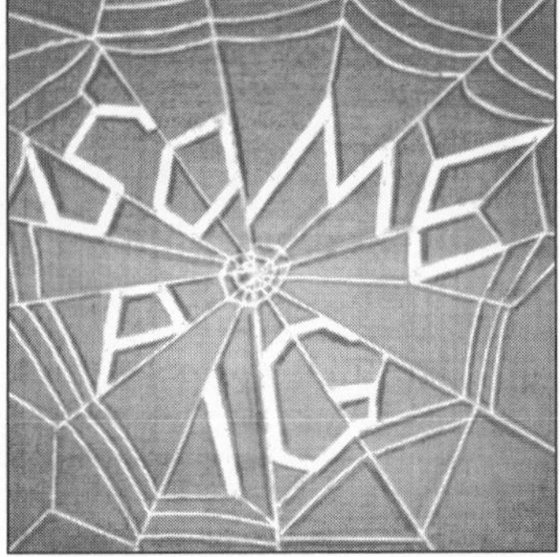

A farm hand discovered a spider web with an incredible message in it yesterday. The words "Some Pig" were spelled out across the web, sources say.

The message was discovered on the Zuckerman farm early in the morning by a hired hand known only as Lurvy.

(continued on A3)

"I don't see why everyone is talking about the pig," commented Mrs. Edith Zuckerman. "The spider wrote the message," she explained. "The pig sure didn't."

(continued on A3)

**"It's a sign," said Mr. Homer Zuckerman, owner of the farm where the message was discovered. "It's a mysterious sign that my pig Wilbur is no ordinary animal," he said.**

(continued on A3)

"I don't know what to make of it," said Dr. Webb Spinner, a local spider buff. "I've never heard of anything like this happening before," he added. "Spiders are amazing creatures."

(continued on B7)

Governor Bulrush sent animal experts to examine the pig, Wilbur. "I hope they will be able to establish if this is truly some pig," the Governor declared.

(continued on B2)

Name

# Spider Events

**Cut out the event spiders. Paste them on the web in the order that the events happened. Then fill in the other circles in order with the rest of the main events from *Charlotte's Web*.**

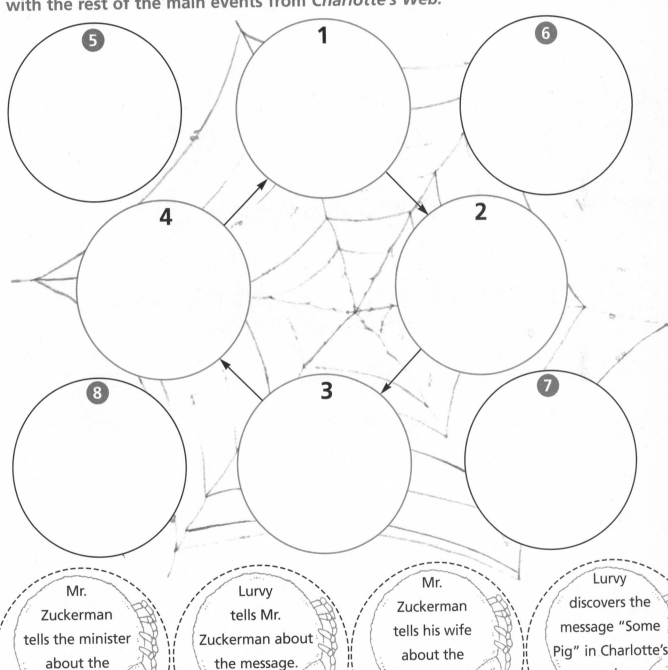

5

1

6

4

2

8

3

7

Mr. Zuckerman tells the minister about the web.

Lurvy tells Mr. Zuckerman about the message.

Mr. Zuckerman tells his wife about the messsage.

Lurvy discovers the message "Some Pig" in Charlotte's web.

Name

# Cause-and-Effect Chaos

Causes and effects can form a chain of events. Each effect becomes the cause of another effect. Examine the picture. Then finish the cause-and-effect chain.

BARK

The spider drops from its web. This causes the farm hand to be startled.

This causes

This causes

This causes

This causes

What do you think will happen next?



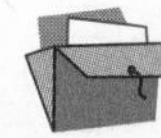

Name

# Some Sentences!

**Read each sentence. Decide if the underlined word or words can be moved to another place in the sentence without changing the meaning of the sentence. If yes, write the new sentence. If no, explain how the meaning of the sentence would change.**

**Example:** The farmer saw the pigs napping in the mud. Moving the words would make it seem as if the farmer were in the mud.

1. A spider spun its web in the far corner.

2. The spider web fluttered gently in the breeze.

3. A tall tree shaded a pond near the barn.

4. The hired hand mixed the pig's breakfast in the bucket.

5. The goat hungrily ate the old shoes.

6. The tractor ran out of gas in the middle of the field.

7. The mice scampered across the barn floor quietly.

8. The girl saw the sparkling dew on the spider web.

Name

# Complete Prefix Control

**Write two words from the box that together match each description. Use each word only once.**

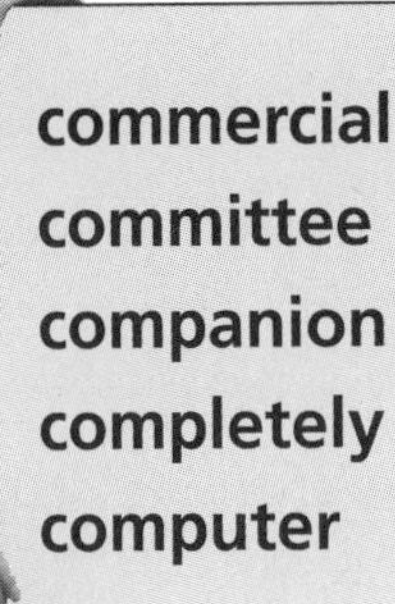

**Example:** A spider's message is not "exactly expected."
In other words, it is not **precisely predicted.**

| | | | |
|---|---|---|---|
| commercial | concert | congratulations | preowned |
| committee | concise | constant | prerecorded |
| companion | concrete | construction | preserved |
| completely | condition | consumer | preteen |
| computer | confused | prehistoric | preventable |

1. steady friend: ______
2. mixed-up group: ______
3. advertisement taped earlier: ______
4. buyer between the ages of 9 and 12: ______
5. totally saved from an earlier time: ______
6. used machine that runs programs: ______
7. very old musical performance: ______
8. brief words to express joy for someone's good luck: ______
9. avoidable situation: ______
10. building or structure made of hard material: ______

Name

# Lurvy's Speech

**Lurvy wrote a speech to give to visitors to the farm. Help make the speech more exciting by rewriting it, using words from the box to replace the underlined words.**

**wonders**
**important**
**miracle**
**miraculous**
**bewilderment**
**mysterious**
**wondrous**

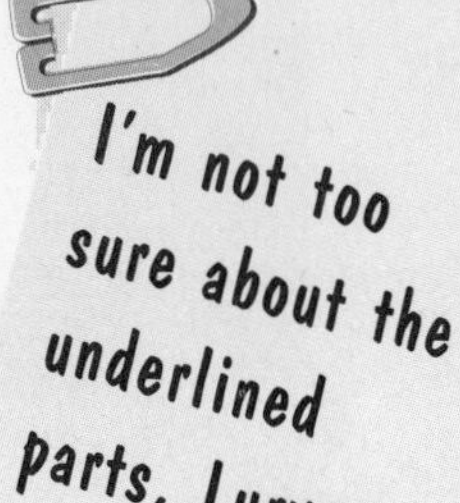

I'm not too sure about the underlined parts, Lurvy.

Lurvy's speech:

Gather around, ladies and gentlemen. Take a look at this pig. He is not just a good pig, he is a very good pig.

Not too long ago, unusual things occurred right here in this pig pen. A strange message appeared in this spider's web. You can see it if you look close enough. It says "Some Pig."

No one knows how this odd message got here. Imagine my confusion when I first saw it. I knew that it was a great thing. I told Mr. Zuckerman that a very unusual event had taken place.

Lurvy's rewritten speech:

Name

# Wordy Webs

**The VCV Pattern** Each Spelling Word has two syllables and the vowel-consonant-vowel (VCV) pattern. Some words begin with the short vowel pattern. They are divided into syllables after the consonant.

In the other words, the first syllable ends with a vowel sound. These words are divided before the consonant.

| V C \| V | V\| C V |
|---|---|
| b u s\| y | s p i\| d e r |

**Spelling Words**

1. spider
2. busy
3. tiny
4. finish
5. alone
6. visit
7. silent
8. human
9. magic
10. wagon

**My Study List**
What other words do you need to study for spelling? Add them to My Study List for *Charlotte's Web* in the back of this book.

**In the webs, write the missing syllables to form Spelling Words. Then write each Spelling Word under the correct pattern and draw a line between the syllables.**

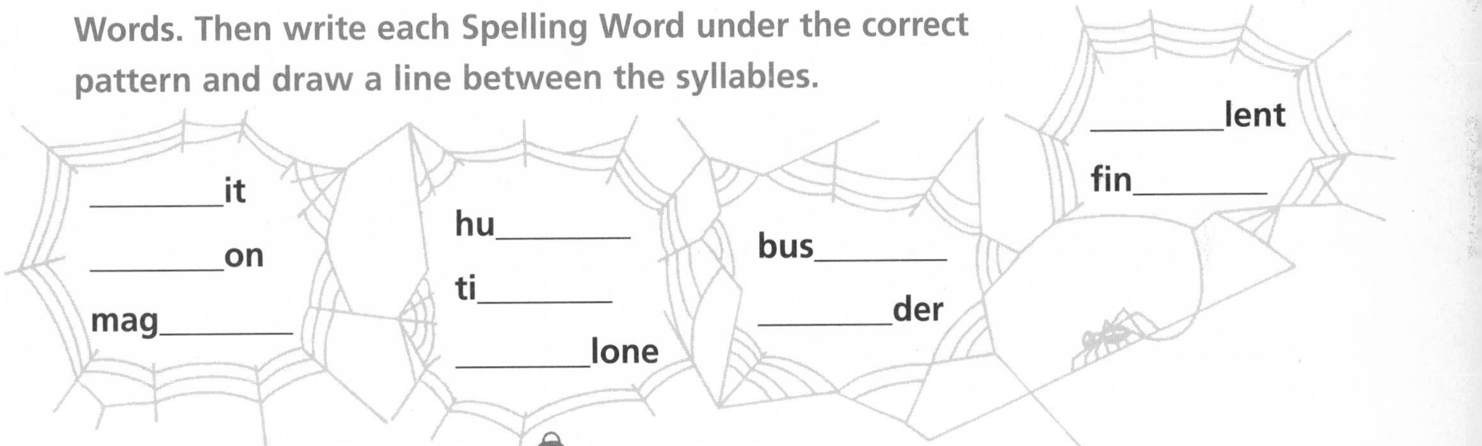

_______it
_______on
mag_______

hu_______
ti_______
_______lone

bus_______
_______der

_______lent
fin_______

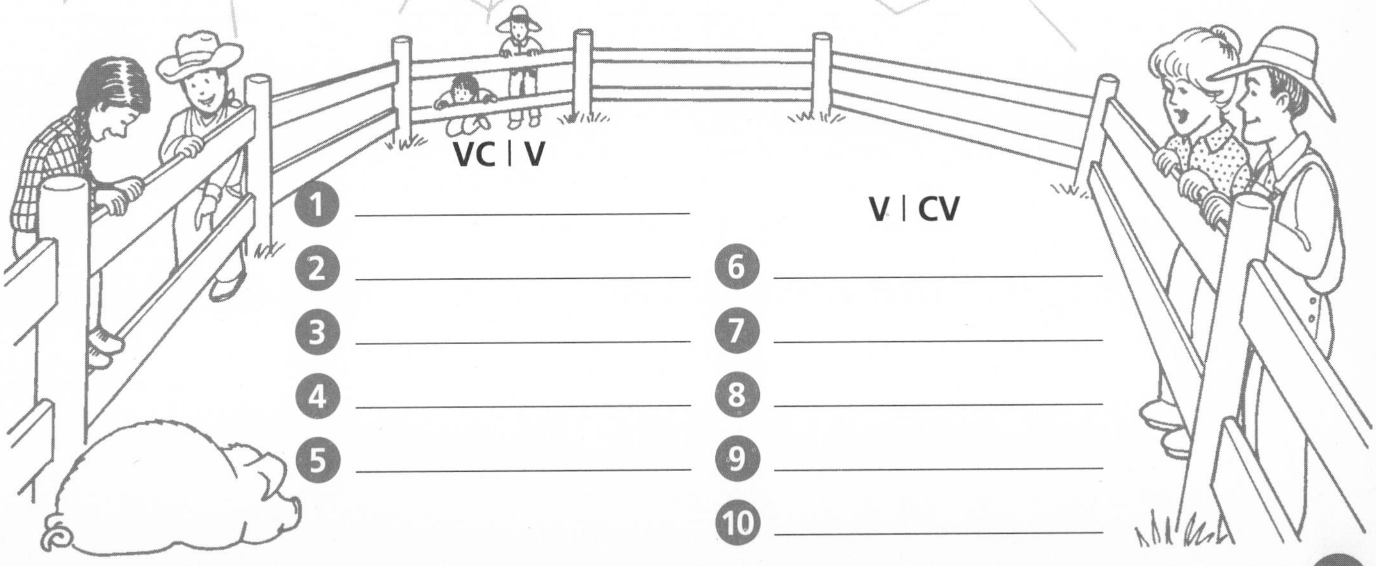

**VC | V**

1. ____________________
2. ____________________
3. ____________________
4. ____________________
5. ____________________

**V | CV**

6. ____________________
7. ____________________
8. ____________________
9. ____________________
10. ____________________

Name

# Spelling Spree

**Spelling Words**

1. spider
2. busy
3. tiny
4. finish
5. alone
6. visit
7. silent
8. human
9. magic
10. wagon

**Word Pen** Write the Spelling Word that fits each clue. The letters in the pen will spell a synonym for pigpen.

1. an eight-legged animal ___ ___ ___ ___ ___ ___
2. bring to an end ___ ___ ___ ___ ___ ___
3. a four-wheeled vehicle ___ ___ ___ ___ ___
4. making no sound ___ ___ ___ ___ ___ ___
5. to go see ___ ___ ___ ___ ___
6. engaged in activity ___ ___ ___ ___

**Proofreading** Find and circle four misspelled Spelling Words in this speech. Then write each Spelling Word correctly.

My good people, this past week a magick event took place here in our community. A tiney spider gave the Zuckermans a sign that they had a wondrous pig. It is not often that heuman beings get to see such miracles. I urge you to stop by the Zuckermans, aloan or with your families, to see the marvelous pig for yourselves.

7. ______________________
8. ______________________
9. ______________________
10. ______________________

**See Wilbur the Wonder Pig!** Homer Zuckerman wants some billboards to be posted along roads leading to his farm. On a separate sheet of paper, make signs inviting tourists to the farm. Use Spelling Words from the list.

Name

# A Warm, Fuzzy Web

**Object Pronouns** A class that visited the Zuckermans' farm made a friendship web. Everyone stood in a circle. Then the first player said something nice about another player and, holding the end of a ball of yarn, threw the ball to the player. The second player caught the ball, said something nice about the third player, and threw the ball to him or her. Read this story to find out what happened. You will have to fill in the object pronouns—so read carefully.

Jana said she loved Mike's sense of humor and threw the yarn to ______________. Mike said Sherry and I were nice to help him clean the garage. Then he threw the ball to ______________. We said Marco wrote great stories and threw the yarn to ______________. Marco told Kioshi that the pictures she drew were awesome. He tossed the ball to ______________. Kioshi thanked Jeff and Quincy for teaching her to pitch a curve ball. Then she threw ______________ a curve! They dropped the yarn, but Jeff picked ______________ up and kept the game going. He and Quincy said they thought Jonathan was a great athlete. Then Quincy threw the yarn to ______________. Jonathan complimented Jana on her solo in the chorus program. He tossed the ball to ______________.

Jana started a second round of compliments and picked Kioshi. Jana told ______________ she liked the way Kioshi was always friendly to new kids.

When we had used all the yarn, we were all tangled up. If you ask ______________, that's the kind of tangle I don't mind being in!

Name

# Working for Wilbur

**Lurvy hired five workers to help him take care of the famous pig. YOU are one of them! Fill in the schedule by writing your name next to every *. Then use the schedule and the pronoun *I* or *me* to answer each question with a complete sentence.**

| | Monday | Tuesday | Wednesday | Thursday | Friday |
|---|---|---|---|---|---|
| Clean stall;<br>bathe Wilbur | *<br>Enrique | Hannah<br>* | *<br>Teisha | Enrique<br>* | Lin<br>Teisha |
| 6:00 A.M.<br>feeding | Lin<br>Enrique | Enrique<br>Hannah | *<br>Lin | Hannah<br>Teisha | Hannah<br>Teisha |
| 10:00 A.M.<br>feeding | *<br>Enrique | Hannah<br>Teisha | Enrique<br>Teisha | *<br>Lin | Lin |
| 1:00 P.M.<br>feeding | Hannah<br>Teisha | *<br>Hannah | Lin<br>Teisha | Enrique<br>* | *<br>Enrique |
| 6:00 P.M.<br>feeding | *<br>Lin | Enrique<br>Hannah | Hannah<br>Teisha | *<br>Teisha | Lin<br>Teisha |

1. If no one arrives Monday at 6:00 P.M., whom should Lurvy call?

   ______________________________

2. Who is supposed to bathe Wilbur on Tuesday?

   ______________________________

3. Lurvy gives the key to the workers who do the earliest feeding. To whom should he give the key Tuesday afternoon?

   ______________________________

4. Who will do the 1:00 P.M. feeding on Thursday?

   ______________________________

5. The mail carrier always gives the mail to the workers who are doing the 10:00 A.M. feeding. To whom will she give the mail on Friday?

   ______________________________

Name

# Writing a News Story

**Write a news story for the 6 o'clock news. Imagine you're reporting an event from either *June 29, 1999* or *Charlotte's Web*. Fill out the chart to help you plan your project.**

Story you're going to write about:

_______________________________________________

The amazing event you'll report:

_______________________________________________

| What happened during the event | | What caused each happening |
|---|---|---|
| **1.** | → | **1.** |
| **2.** | → | **2.** |
| **3.** | → | **3.** |
| **4.** | → | **4.** |
| **5.** | → | **5.** |



**Use the information to write your news story. Then present your story to your class or group. Explain which parts of your story are real and which are fantasy. Before you share your project, use the checklist to check your work.**

✔ **LIST**

- ❑ My news story tells about an amazing event from *June 29, 1999* or *Charlotte's Web*.
- ❑ I can explain how the events in my news story happened.
- ❑ I can explain which events in my news story are real and which are fantasy.

# STUDENT HANDBOOK

# Contents

# INDEPENDENT READING LOG

**Use this log to record the books or other materials you read on your own.**

Date ______________________

Author ______________________

Title ______________________

Notes and Comments ______________________

______________________

______________________

______________________

______________________

Date ______________________

Author ______________________

Title ______________________

Notes and Comments ______________________

______________________

______________________

______________________

______________________

Date

Author

Title

Notes and Comments

Date

Author

Title

Notes and Comments

Date

Author

Title

Notes and Comments

Date

Author

Title

Notes and Comments

Date

Author

Title

Notes and Comments

Date

Author

Title

Notes and Comments

Date

Author

Title

Notes and Comments

Date

Author

Title

Notes and Comments

Date

Author

Title

Notes and Comments

# How to Study a Word

**1 LOOK at the word.**
- What does the word mean?
- What letters are in the word?
- Name and touch each letter.

**2 SAY the word.**
- Listen for the consonant sounds.
- Listen for the vowel sounds.

**3 THINK about the word.**
- How is each sound spelled?
- Close your eyes and picture the word.
- What familiar spelling patterns do you see?
- Do you see any prefixes, suffixes, or other word parts?

**4 WRITE the word.**
- Think about the sounds and the letters.
- Form the letters correctly.

**5 CHECK the spelling.**
- Did you spell the word the same way it is spelled in your word list?
- If you did not spell the word correctly, write the word again.

# WORDS OFTEN MISSPELLED

| | | | | |
|---|---|---|---|---|
| accept | busy | fourth | nickel | to |
| ache | buy | Friday | ninety | too |
| again | by | friend | ninety-nine | tried |
| all right | calendar | goes | ninth | tries |
| almost | cannot | going | often | truly |
| already | can't | grammar | once | two |
| although | careful | guard | other | tying |
| always | catch | guess | people | unknown |
| angel | caught | guide | principal | until |
| angle | chief | half | quiet | unusual |
| | | | | |
| answer | children | haven't | quit | wasn't |
| argue | choose | hear | quite | wear |
| asked | chose | heard | really | weather |
| aunt | color | heavy | receive | Wednesday |
| author | cough | height | rhythm | weird |
| awful | cousin | here | right | we'll |
| babies | decide | hers | Saturday | we're |
| been | divide | hole | stretch | weren't |
| believe | does | hoping | surely | we've |
| bother | don't | hour | their | where |
| | | | | |
| bought | early | its | theirs | which |
| break | enough | it's | there | whole |
| breakfast | every | January | they're | witch |
| breathe | exact | let's | they've | won't |
| broken | except | listen | those | wouldn't |
| brother | excite | loose | though | write |
| brought | expect | lose | thought | writing |
| bruise | February | minute | through | written |
| build | finally | muscle | tied | you're |
| business | forty | neighbor | tired | yours |

## Take-Home Word Lists

### *Koya DeLaney and the Good Girl Blues*

**Spelling long *i* and Long *o***

|ī| → **side, high**

|ō| → **rope, coach, know**

### Spelling Words

1. rope
2. coach
3. know
4. side
5. spoke
6. high
7. blow
8. bright
9. wipe
10. goal

### Challenge Words

1. microphone
2. surprise
3. recognize
4. narrow
5. approach

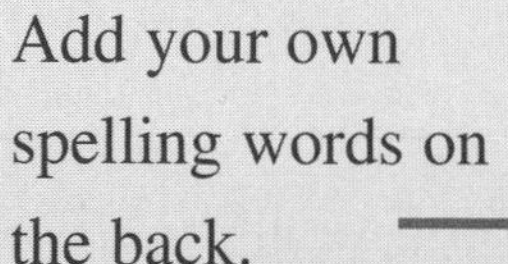

**My Study List**

Add your own spelling words on the back. →



## Take-Home Word Lists

### *I'm New Here*

**Spelling Long *a* and Long *e***

|ā| → grade, wait, away

|ē| → neat, meet

### Spelling Words

1. grade
2. meet
3. seem
4. neat
5. wait
6. away
7. safe
8. afraid
9. least
10. crayon

### Challenge Words

1. playground
2. repeat
3. United States
4. squeeze
5. Wednesday

**My Study List**

Add your own spelling words on the back. →

273

## Take-Home Word Lists

### *Tales of a Fourth Grade Nothing*

**Short Vowels**

|ă| → class

|ĕ| → desk

|ĭ| → still

|ŏ| → drop

|ŭ| → dull

### Spelling Words

1. class
2. plan
3. desk
4. still
5. check
6. dull
7. drop
8. trust
9. snip
10. knock

### Challenge Words

1. topic
2. traffic
3. sketch
4. whisper
5. script

**My Study List**

Add your own spelling words on the back. →

273

## Spelling and Writing Word Lists

Name ____________

### My Study List

1. ____________
2. ____________
3. ____________
4. ____________
5. ____________
6. ____________
7. ____________
8. ____________
9. ____________
10. ____________

### Selection Vocabulary

You may want to use these words in your own writing.

1. project
2. committees
3. arranged
4. solution
5. method
6. schedule

### How to Study a Word

LOOK at the word.
SAY the word.
THINK about the word.
WRITE the word.
CHECK the spelling.



## Spelling and Writing Word Lists

Name ____________

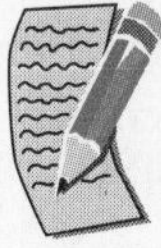

### My Study List

1. ____________
2. ____________
3. ____________
4. ____________
5. ____________
6. ____________
7. ____________
8. ____________
9. ____________
10. ____________

### Selection Vocabulary

You may want to use these words in your own writing.

1. register
2. papers
3. customs

### How to Study a Word

LOOK at the word.
SAY the word.
THINK about the word.
WRITE the word.
CHECK the spelling.



## Spelling and Writing Word Lists

Name ____________

### My Study List

1. ____________
2. ____________
3. ____________
4. ____________
5. ____________
6. ____________
7. ____________
8. ____________
9. ____________
10. ____________

### Selection Vocabulary

You may want to use these words in your own writing.

1. routine
2. competition
3. poised
4. rhythm
5. somersaulted
6. participants

### How to Study a Word

LOOK at the word.
SAY the word.
THINK about the word.
WRITE the word.
CHECK the spelling.

## *Just a Dream*

### The Vowel Sound in *walk*

/ô/ → **walk, aw**ful, bec**au**se, th**ough**t, c**augh**t

### Spelling Words

1. walk
2. awful
3. because
4. lawn
5. thought
6. always
7. caught
8. bought
9. fault
10. taught

### Challenge Words

1. quality
2. cough
3. laundry
4. naughty
5. automobile

### My Study List

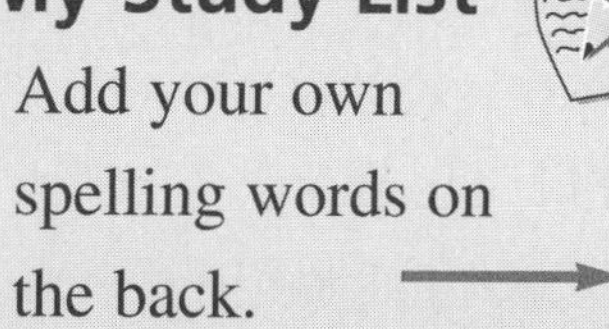

Add your own spelling words on the back. →

Take-Home Word Lists

## *The Great Kapok Tree: A Tale of the Amazon Rain Forest*

### The Vowel Sounds in *ground* and *point*

/ou/ → gr**ou**nd, fl**ow**er

/oi/ → p**oi**nt, enj**oy**

### Spelling Words

1. ground
2. flower
3. sound
4. soil
5. howl
6. voice
7. about
8. point
9. enjoy
10. loyal

### Challenge Words

1. destroy
2. doubt
3. surround
4. avoid
5. coward

### My Study List

Add your own spelling words on the back. →

Take-Home Word Lists

## *The Great Yellowstone Fire*

### Spelling Long *u*

/yo͞o/ or

/o͞o/ → r**u**l**e**, gr**ew**, tr**ue**, r**oo**ts, fr**ui**t

### Spelling Words

1. grew
2. roots
3. rule
4. few
5. June
6. tool
7. true
8. fruit
9. glue
10. suit

### Challenge Words

1. continue
2. parachute
3. subdue
4. refuse
5. schedule

### My Study List

Add your own spelling words on the back. →

## Spelling and Writing Word Lists

Name ____________

### My Study List

1. ____________
2. ____________
3. ____________
4. ____________
5. ____________
6. ____________
7. ____________
8. ____________
9. ____________
10. ____________

### Selection Vocabulary

You may want to use these words in your own writing.

1. ignited
2. scorching
3. singeing
4. kindled
5. smoldering
6. charred

### How to Study a Word

LOOK at the word.
SAY the word.
THINK about the word.
WRITE the word.
CHECK the spelling.



## Spelling and Writing Word Lists

Name ____________

### My Study List

1. ____________
2. ____________
3. ____________
4. ____________
5. ____________
6. ____________
7. ____________
8. ____________
9. ____________
10. ____________

### Selection Vocabulary

You may want to use these words in your own writing.

1. environment
2. generations
3. ancestors
4. pollinate
5. hesitated

### How to Study a Word

LOOK at the word.
SAY the word.
THINK about the word.
WRITE the word.
CHECK the spelling.



## Spelling and Writing Word Lists

Name ____________

### My Study List

1. ____________
2. ____________
3. ____________
4. ____________
5. ____________
6. ____________
7. ____________
8. ____________
9. ____________
10. ____________

### Selection Vocabulary

You may want to use these words in your own writing.

1. sort
2. foul
3. enormous
4. haze
5. suspected

### How to Study a Word

LOOK at the word.
SAY the word.
THINK about the word.
WRITE the word.
CHECK the spelling.

## Take-Home Word Lists

### *Encyclopedia Brown and the Case of the Disgusting Sneakers*

**More Vowel + *r* Sounds**

|ôr| → wore, torn

|ûr| → third, worse, turn

**Spelling Words**

1. third
2. wore
3. girl
4. worse
5. turn
6. urge
7. torn
8. score
9. storm
10. worm

**Challenge Words**

1. normal
2. surface
3. foreign
4. purchase
5. tornado

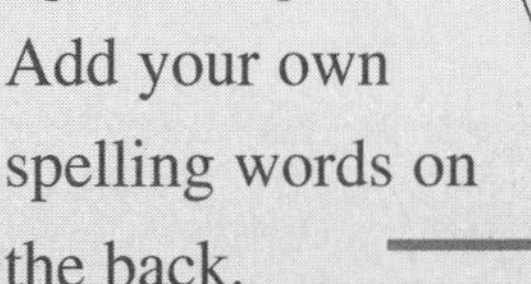

**My Study List**

Add your own spelling words on the back. →



## Take-Home Word Lists

### *Julian, Secret Agent*

**Vowel + *r* Sounds**

|är| → park

|âr| → care, air

|îr| → ear, peer

**Spelling Words**

1. park
2. care
3. cart
4. glare
5. ear
6. peer
7. air
8. chair
9. beard
10. cheer

**Challenge Words**

1. supermarket
2. article
3. barely
4. compare
5. dreary

**My Study List**

Add your own spelling words on the back. →



## Take-Home Word Lists

### *Meg Mackintosh and the Case of the Curious Whale Watch*

**Unusual Vowel Spellings**

|ā| → great

|ŭ| → touch, nothing

|ĕ| → meant

**Spelling Words**

1. great
2. touch
3. meant
4. break
5. nothing
6. young
7. weather
8. money
9. ton
10. breath

**Challenge Words**

1. treasure
2. rough
3. nervous
4. company
5. pleasant

**My Study List**

Add your own spelling words on the back. →

Name ____________

## My Study List

1. ____________
2. ____________
3. ____________
4. ____________
5. ____________
6. ____________
7. ____________
8. ____________
9. ____________
10. ____________

## Selection Vocabulary

You may want to use these words in your own writing.

1. deduce
2. suspects
3. motives
4. alibi
5. red herring
6. amateur
7. theory

## How to Study a Word

LOOK at the word.
SAY the word.
THINK about the word.
WRITE the word.
CHECK the spelling.



Spelling and Writing Word Lists

Name ____________

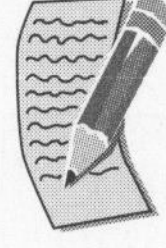

## My Study List

1. ____________
2. ____________
3. ____________
4. ____________
5. ____________
6. ____________
7. ____________
8. ____________
9. ____________
10. ____________

## Selection Vocabulary

You may want to use these words in your own writing.

1. investigate
2. mighty
3. glared
4. mischievous

## How to Study a Word

LOOK at the word.
SAY the word.
THINK about the word.
WRITE the word.
CHECK the spelling.

278

Spelling and Writing Word Lists

Name ____________

## My Study List

1. ____________
2. ____________
3. ____________
4. ____________
5. ____________
6. ____________
7. ____________
8. ____________
9. ____________
10. ____________

## Selection Vocabulary

You may want to use these words in your own writing.

1. champion
2. sponsors
3. judges
4. rival
5. defeat

## How to Study a Word

LOOK at the word.
SAY the word.
THINK about the word.
WRITE the word.
CHECK the spelling.

278

## *Sarah, Plain and Tall*

### Homophones

**Homophones** are words that sound alike but have different spellings and meanings.

### Spelling Words

1. plain
2. plane
3. would
4. wood
5. dear
6. deer
7. mail
8. male
9. fourth
10. forth

### Challenge Words

1. course
2. coarse
3. vain
4. vane
5. vein

### My Study List

Add your own spelling words on the back. →





## *All for the Better*

### Silent Consonants

Some words have silent consonants.

**knife**

**write**

### Spelling Words

1. island
2. palm
3. climb
4. knew
5. answer
6. wrong
7. often
8. half
9. honest
10. knee

### Challenge Words

1. whistle
2. bustle
3. glisten
4. debt
5. muscle

### My Study List

Add your own spelling words on the back. →





## *Grandfather's Journey*

### Compound Words

A **compound word** may be written as one word, as two words joined by a hyphen, or as two separate words.

### Spelling Words

1. grandparents
2. homesick
3. sweetheart
4. weekend
5. sunlight
6. post office
7. great-aunt
8. breakfast
9. pen pal
10. make-believe

### Challenge Words

1. North America
2. Pacific Ocean
3. Atlantic Ocean
4. old-fashioned
5. nevertheless

### My Study List

Add your own spelling words on the back. →

## Spelling and Writing Word Lists

Name ____________________

### My Study List

1. ____________________
2. ____________________
3. ____________________
4. ____________________
5. ____________________
6. ____________________
7. ____________________
8. ____________________
9. ____________________
10. ____________________

### Selection Vocabulary

You may want to use these words in your own writing.

1. astonished
2. amazed
3. bewildered
4. excited
5. marveled
6. longed
7. homesick

### How to Study a Word

LOOK at the word.
SAY the word.
THINK about the word.
WRITE the word.
CHECK the spelling.



## Spelling and Writing Word Lists

Name ____________________

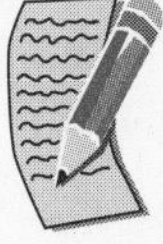

### My Study List

1. ____________________
2. ____________________
3. ____________________
4. ____________________
5. ____________________
6. ____________________
7. ____________________
8. ____________________
9. ____________________
10. ____________________

### Selection Vocabulary

You may want to use these words in your own writing.

1. loomed
2. forbidding
3. dreary
4. bustled
5. uptown
6. community
7. scurried

### How to Study a Word

LOOK at the word.
SAY the word.
THINK about the word.
WRITE the word.
CHECK the spelling.



## Spelling and Writing Word Lists

Name ____________________

### My Study List

1. ____________________
2. ____________________
3. ____________________
4. ____________________
5. ____________________
6. ____________________
7. ____________________
8. ____________________
9. ____________________
10. ____________________

### Selection Vocabulary

You may want to use these words in your own writing.

1. prefer
2. pesky
3. greetings
4. alarmed
5. perfect

### How to Study a Word

LOOK at the word.
SAY the word.
THINK about the word.
WRITE the word.
CHECK the spelling.

## *Thurgood Marshall and Equal Rights*

**Words That End with Schwa + *l***

/əl/ → equa**l**, civi**l**, troub**le**, trave**l**

### Spelling Words

1. equal
2. civil
3. legal
4. trouble
5. final
6. local
7. travel
8. puzzle
9. pupil
10. nickel

### Challenge Words

1. social
2. example
3. several
4. general
5. potential

**My Study List**
Add your own spelling words on the back. →





## *The Marble Champ*

**Words That End with Schwa + *r***

/ər/ → fing**er**, hon**or**, doll**ar**

### Spelling Words

1. finger
2. gather
3. honor
4. number
5. favor
6. either
7. neighbor
8. mayor
9. dollar
10. cellar

### Challenge Words

1. shoulder
2. quiver
3. soccer
4. eraser
5. razor

**My Study List**
Add your own spelling words on the back. →





## *The Seminoles*

**The Final Sounds in *place* and *edge***

/s/ → pla**ce**

/j/ → e**dge**, lar**ge**

### Spelling Words

1. place
2. edge
3. peace
4. once
5. large
6. dance
7. village
8. change
9. choice
10. judge

### Challenge Words

1. necklace
2. voyage
3. porridge
4. influence
5. college

**My Study List**
Add your own spelling words on the back. →

## Spelling and Writing Word Lists

Name ____________

### My Study List

1. ____________
2. ____________
3. ____________
4. ____________
5. ____________
6. ____________
7. ____________
8. ____________
9. ____________
10. ____________

### Selection Vocabulary

You may want to use these words in your own writing.

1. territory
2. treaty
3. reservation
4. adapted
5. sacredness

### How to Study a Word

LOOK at the word.
SAY the word.
THINK about the word.
WRITE the word.
CHECK the spelling.



## Spelling and Writing Word Lists

Name ____________

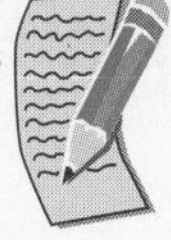

### My Study List

1. ____________
2. ____________
3. ____________
4. ____________
5. ____________
6. ____________
7. ____________
8. ____________
9. ____________
10. ____________

### Selection Vocabulary

You may want to use these words in your own writing.

1. awardee
2. honor
3. accurate
4. strengthen
5. exhaustion
6. opponent

### How to Study a Word

LOOK at the word.
SAY the word.
THINK about the word.
WRITE the word.
CHECK the spelling.



## Spelling and Writing Word Lists

Name ____________

### My Study List

1. ____________
2. ____________
3. ____________
4. ____________
5. ____________
6. ____________
7. ____________
8. ____________
9. ____________
10. ____________

### Selection Vocabulary

You may want to use these words in your own writing.

1. Constitution
2. amendment
3. prejudice
4. opportunity
5. integrated

### How to Study a Word

LOOK at the word.
SAY the word.
THINK about the word.
WRITE the word.
CHECK the spelling.

## Take-Home Word Lists

### *Jumanji*

**Words with Prefixes**

| | | | | |
|---|---|---|---|---|
| **re** | + | read | = | **re**read |
| **un** | + | fold | = | **un**fold |
| **dis** | + | like | = | **dis**like |

**Spelling Words**

1. reread
2. unfold
3. unclear
4. dislike
5. reuse
6. unsure
7. displease
8. unwrap
9. discolor
10. rejoin

**Challenge Words**

1. unexcited
2. discover
3. disagree
4. unimportant
5. unscramble

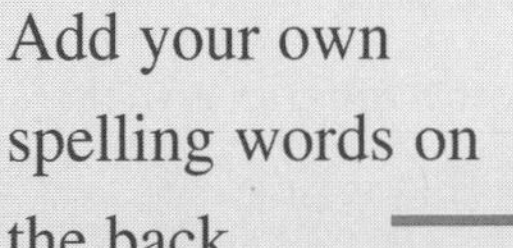

**My Study List**
Add your own spelling words on the back. →



## Take-Home Word Lists

### *No One Is Going to Nashville*

**Changing Final *y* to *i***

carry - y + i + **ed** = carried
story - y + i + **es** = stories
sorry - y + i + **er** = sorrier
easy - y + i + **est** = easiest

**Spelling Words**

1. easiest
2. carried
3. stories
4. sorrier
5. cities
6. funniest
7. families
8. angrier
9. copied
10. studied

**Challenge Words**

1. memories
2. beauties
3. countries
4. blotchier
5. responsibilities

**My Study List**
Add your own spelling words on the back. →



## Take-Home Word Lists

### *Sadako*

**Adding *-ed* or *-ing***

care - **e** + ed = cared
race - **e** + ing = racing
tap + **p** + ed = tapped

**Spelling Words**

1. racing
2. cared
3. folded
4. running
5. rushed
6. letting
7. shining
8. smiling
9. tapped
10. sniffed

**Challenge Words**

1. tired
2. wheeled
3. scrubbed
4. stroking
5. launched

**My Study List**
Add your own spelling words on the back. →

## Spelling and Writing Word Lists

Name ____________

### My Study List

1. ____________
2. ____________
3. ____________
4. ____________
5. ____________
6. ____________
7. ____________
8. ____________
9. ____________
10. ____________

### Selection Vocabulary

You may want to use these words in your own writing.

1. memorial
2. atom bomb
3. leukemia
4. comfort
5. monument

### How to Study a Word

LOOK at the word.
SAY the word.
THINK about the word.
WRITE the word.
CHECK the spelling.



## Spelling and Writing Word Lists

Name ____________

### My Study List

1. ____________
2. ____________
3. ____________
4. ____________
5. ____________
6. ____________
7. ____________
8. ____________
9. ____________
10. ____________

### Selection Vocabulary

You may want to use these words in your own writing.

1. abandoned
2. responsibility
3. relieved
4. companion
5. disposition

### How to Study a Word

LOOK at the word.
SAY the word.
THINK about the word.
WRITE the word.
CHECK the spelling.



## Spelling and Writing Word Lists

Name ____________

### My Study List

1. ____________
2. ____________
3. ____________
4. ____________
5. ____________
6. ____________
7. ____________
8. ____________
9. ____________
10. ____________

### Selection Vocabulary

You may want to use these words in your own writing.

1. slouched
2. bored
3. sighed
4. restless
5. disappointed
6. casually

### How to Study a Word

LOOK at the word.
SAY the word.
THINK about the word.
WRITE the word.
CHECK the spelling.

Take-Home Word Lists

*Charlotte's Web*

**The VCV Pattern**

VC|V → bus|y

V|CV → spi|der

## Spelling Words

1. spider
2. busy
3. tiny
4. finish
5. alone
6. visit
7. silent
8. human
9. magic
10. wagon

## Challenge Words

1. special
2. notice
3. solid
4. dozen
5. jealous

**My Study List**

Add your own spelling words on the back. →



Take-Home Word Lists

*June 29, 1999*

**The VCCV Pattern**

VC|CV → hap|pen, tur|nip

## Spelling Words

1. happen
2. pepper
3. turnip
4. twenty
5. supper
6. carpet
7. entire
8. ribbon
9. member
10. captain

## Challenge Words

1. intend
2. expect
3. channel
4. advance
5. galley

**My Study List**

Add your own spelling words on the back. →



Take-Home Word Lists

*Elliot's House*

**Words with Suffixes**

care + **ful** = care**ful**

home + **less** = home**less**

good + **ness** = good**ness**

move + **ment** = move**ment**

## Spelling Words

1. homeless
2. careful
3. goodness
4. colorless
5. darkness
6. wishful
7. smoothness
8. restless
9. movement
10. treatment

## Challenge Words

1. apartment
2. nervousness
3. togetherness
4. appointment
5. shovelful

**My Study List**

Add your own spelling words on the back. →

Spelling and Writing Word Lists

Name ____________

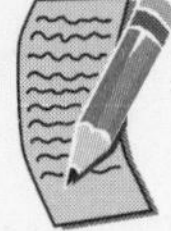

## My Study List

1. ____________
2. ____________
3. ____________
4. ____________
5. ____________
6. ____________
7. ____________
8. ____________
9. ____________
10. ____________

## Selection Vocabulary

You may want to use these words in your own writing.

1. mound
2. garbage
3. collected
4. depositing
5. landfill

## How to Study a Word

LOOK at the word.
SAY the word.
THINK about the word.
WRITE the word.
CHECK the spelling.



Spelling and Writing Word Lists

Name ____________

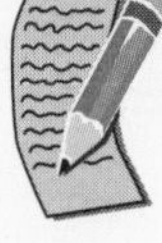

## My Study List

1. ____________
2. ____________
3. ____________
4. ____________
5. ____________
6. ____________
7. ____________
8. ____________
9. ____________
10. ____________

## Selection Vocabulary

You may want to use these words in your own writing.

1. experiment
2. effects
3. conditions
4. development
5. concludes
6. specimens

## How to Study a Word

LOOK at the word.
SAY the word.
THINK about the word.
WRITE the word.
CHECK the spelling.



Spelling and Writing Word Lists

Name ____________

## My Study List

1. ____________
2. ____________
3. ____________
4. ____________
5. ____________
6. ____________
7. ____________
8. ____________
9. ____________
10. ____________

## Selection Vocabulary

You may want to use these words in your own writing.

1. bewilderment
2. miracle
3. wondrous
4. miraculous
5. wonders

## How to Study a Word

LOOK at the word.
SAY the word.
THINK about the word.
WRITE the word.
CHECK the spelling.

# SPELLING GUIDELINES

## Short Vowel Patterns

| | | | |
|---|---|---|---|
| **1.** | A short vowel sound is usually spelled *a*, *e*, *i*, *o*, or *u* and is followed by a consonant sound. | class<br>desk<br>still | drop<br>dull |
| **2.** | The short *e* sound can be spelled with the pattern *ea*. | meant | |
| **3.** | The short *u* sound can be spelled with the pattern *ou* or *o*. | touch | nothing |

## Long Vowel Sounds

| | | | |
|---|---|---|---|
| **4.** | The long *a* sound can be spelled with the pattern *a*-consonant-*e*, *ai*, *ay*, or *ea*. | grade<br>wait | away<br>great |
| **5.** | The long *e* sound is often spelled with the pattern *e*-consonant-*e*, *ea*, or *ee*. | these<br>meet | neat |
| **6.** | The long *e* sound at the end of a word may be spelled *y*. | penny | funny |
| **7.** | The long *i* sound can be spelled with the pattern *i*-consonant-*e*, *igh*, or *ie*. | side<br>high | tie |
| **8.** | The long *i* sound at the end of a word may be spelled *y*. | cry | reply |
| **9.** | The long *o* sound can be spelled with the pattern *o*-consonant-*e*, *oa*, or *ow*. | rope<br>coach | know |
| **10.** | The long *u* sound \|yo͞o\| or \|o͞o\| may be spelled with the pattern *u*-consonant-*e*, *ew*, *ue*, *oo*, or *ui*. | rule<br>grew<br>true | roots<br>fruit |

## Other Vowel Sounds

| | | | |
|---|---|---|---|
| **11.** | The sound \|ou\| is often spelled with the pattern *ow* or *ou*. | flower | ground |
| **12.** | The sound \|oi\| is spelled with the pattern *oi* or *oy*. | point | enjoy |
| **13.** | The vowel sound in *walk* can be spelled with the pattern *a* before *l*, *aw*, *au*, *ough*, or *augh*. | always<br>awful<br>because | thought<br>caught |
| **14.** | The vowel sound in *cook* may be spelled with the pattern *oo* or *u*. | woods | pull |

# SPELLING GUIDELINES

## Vowel + *r* Sounds

| | | |
|---|---|---|
| **15.** The vowel + *r* sounds you hear in *park* can be spelled with the pattern *ar*. | c**ar**t | |
| **16.** The vowel + *r* sounds you hear in *care* can be spelled with the pattern *are* or *air*. | gl**are** | ch**air** |
| **17.** The vowel + *r* sounds you hear in *ear* can be spelled with the pattern *ear* or *eer*. | b**ear**d | ch**eer** |
| **18.** The vowel + *r* sounds you hear in *more* can be spelled with the patterns *or* and *ore*. | t**or**n | w**ore** |
| **19.** The vowel + *r* sounds you hear in *first* can be spelled with the pattern *er*, *ir*, *ur,* or *or*. | h**er**<br>th**ir**d | **ur**ge<br>w**or**m |

## Consonant Sounds

| | | |
|---|---|---|
| **20.** The /s/ sound you hear in *city* may be spelled *c* when the *c* is followed by *i* or *e*. The /s/ sound at the end of a word is often spelled with the pattern *ce*. | **c**ity<br>sli**ce** | pea**ce** |
| **21.** The /j/ sound you hear in *edge* can be spelled with the consonant *j*, the pattern *dge*, or the pattern *ge*. | **j**ust<br>e**dge** | lar**ge** |

## Syllable Patterns

| | | |
|---|---|---|
| **22.** The schwa + *r* sounds you hear in *finger* can be spelled with the pattern *er, or,* or *ar*. | numb**er**<br>hon**or** | doll**ar** |
| **23.** The schwa + *l* sounds you hear in *equal* can be spelled with the pattern *al, il, le,* or *el*. | leg**al**<br>civ**il** | troub**le**<br>trav**el** |
| **24.** Some two-syllable words have the vowel-consonant-consonant-vowel pattern (VCCV). Divide a word with this pattern between the two consonants to find the syllables. Look for spelling patterns you have learned. Spell the word by syllables. | hap \| pen | tur \| nip |
| **25.** Some two-syllable words have the vowel-consonant-vowel pattern (VCV) and begin with the short vowel pattern. Divide a word with this pattern after the consonant to find the syllables. Look for spelling patterns you have learned. Spell the word by syllables. | bus \| y | vis \| it |

## Syllable Patterns (continued)

**26.** Some two-syllable words have the vowel-consonant-vowel pattern (VCV), and the first syllable ends with a vowel sound. Divide a word with this pattern before the consonant to find the syllables. Look for spelling patterns you have learned. Spell the word by syllables.

spi | der    si | lent

## Word Endings

**27.** If a base word ends with *e*, drop the *e* before adding the ending *-ed* or *-ing*.

car**e** - car**ed**
rac**e** - rac**ing**

**28.** If a base word ends with a vowel and a single consonant, double the consonant before adding *-ed* or *-ing*.

**run** - run**ning**
**tap** - tap**ped**

**29.** If a base word ends with a double consonant, do not change the spelling of the base word when adding *-ed* or *-ing*.

fo**ld** - fold**ed**
ru**sh** - rush**ed**

**30.** When a base word ends with a consonant and *y*, change the *y* to *i* before adding *-ed, -es, -er, -ness,* or *-est*.

car**ry** - car**ried**
sto**ry** - sto**ries**
sor**ry** - sor**rier**
hap**py** - hap**piness**
fun**ny** - fun**niest**

**31.** Add *s* to most words to name more than one. Add *es* to words that end with *s, x, sh,* or *ch* to name more than one.

trip**s**    wish**es**
bus**es**    peach**es**
box**es**

## Prefixes and Suffixes

**32.** A **prefix** is a word part added to the beginning of a word. *Re-*, *un-*, and *dis-* are prefixes.

| prefix | meaning | word | meaning |
|---|---|---|---|
| **re-** | again | **re**read | read again |
| **un-** | not | **un**fair | not fair |
| **dis-** | not | **dis**like | have a feeling of not liking |

## Prefixes and Suffixes (continued)

**33.** A **suffix** is a word part that comes at the end of a word. These word parts are suffixes: *-ful*, *-ly*, *-er*, *-less*, *-ness*, *-ment*.

| suffix | meaning | word | meaning |
|---|---|---|---|
| **-ful** | full of | thought**ful** | full of thought |
| **-ly** | in a certain way | soft**ly** | in a soft way |
| **-er** | someone who | writ**er** | a person who writes |
| **-less** | without | home**less** | without a home |
| **-ness** | quality of | good**ness** | the quality of being good |
| **-ment** | act of | move**ment** | the act of moving |

## Special Spellings

**34.** A **compound word** is made up of two or more smaller words. It can be written as one word, as two words joined by a hyphen, or as two separate words.

homesick
make-believe
post office

**35.** **Homophones** are words that sound alike but have different meanings and spellings.

dear - deer
mail - male

**36.** In **contractions**, an apostrophe takes the place of the letters that are dropped.

doesn't
they're

**37.** **Silent consonants** are consonants that are not pronounced.

**w**rong, pal**m**, **h**onest, **k**nee, clim**b**, is**l**and, of**t**en, **k**new, ha**l**f

# GRAMMAR GUIDE

## SENTENCES

### Definition

A **sentence** is a group of words that expresses a complete thought. It has a subject (who or what) and a predicate (what the subject does or is). A sentence begins with a capital letter.

**L**ightning flashed in the sky. **T**he alert ranger spotted the fire.

- A group of words that does not express a complete thought is called a **sentence fragment**. A fragment is not a sentence. A fragment is missing a subject, a predicate, or both.

  Flashed in the sky. The alert ranger.
  During the storm. When the tree fell.

### Kinds of Sentences

There are four kinds of sentences.

- A **statement** tells something. It ends with a period.

  **D**eserts are dry**.**

- A **question** asks something. It ends with a question mark.

  **D**o you like deserts**?**

- A **command** tells someone to do something. It ends with a period.

  **A**lways carry water**.**

- An **exclamation** shows strong feeling. It ends with an exclamation point.

  **H**ow hot it was**!** **I**t was so hot**!**

### Subjects and Predicates

Every sentence has a **subject** and a **predicate.**

- The **subject** tells whom or what the sentence is about. The **complete subject** includes all the words in the subject. It may be either one word or more than one word.

  **The pilots of the plane** waved. **They** were preparing for take-off.

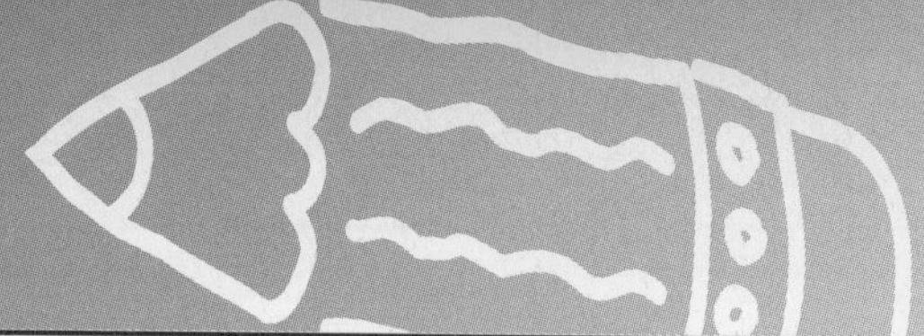

### Subjects and Predicates (continued)

- The **simple subject** is the main word or words in the complete subject.

  **The pilots of the plane** waved. **South America** is their destination.

- The **predicate** tells what the subject is or does. The **complete predicate** includes all the words in the predicate. It may be either one word or more than one word.

  Captain Ortega **is a good pilot.** The large jet **landed.**

- The **simple predicate** is the main word or words in the complete predicate.

  Several helicopters **landed in the field.** They **have landed there before.**

### Run-on Sentences

A **run-on sentence** has two or more complete thoughts that are run together.

- Correct a run-on sentence by writing each complete thought as a separate sentence.

  RUN-ON: Our class visited a museum we saw whaling ships.
  CORRECTED: Our class visited a museum. We saw whaling ships.

## NOUNS

### Definition

A **noun** names a person, a place, or a thing.

| Nouns | | |
|---|---|---|
| **Persons** | boy<br>student | writer<br>Jim Johnson |
| **Places** | lake<br>Hillside Park | Florida<br>mountain |
| **Things** | boat<br>calendar | sweater<br>*Little Women* |

## Common and Proper Nouns

A **common noun** names any person, place, or thing. A **proper noun** names a particular person, place, or thing. Capitalize proper nouns. Capitalize each important word in proper nouns of more than one word.

**Common and Proper Nouns**

| Common nouns | Proper nouns | Common nouns | Proper nouns |
|---|---|---|---|
| street | North Drive | river | Hudson River |
| city | Chicago | building | White House |
| state | Maryland | law | Bill of Rights |
| continent | North America | author | Beverly Cleary |
| ocean | Pacific Ocean | holiday | Fourth of July |
| mountain | Mt. McKinley | month | November |
| lake | Great Salt Lake | day | Monday |

## Singular and Plural Nouns

**Singular nouns** name one person, place, or thing.

The **farmer** drove to the **market** with the **box**.

**Plural nouns** name more than one person, place, or thing.

The **farmers** drove to the **markets** with the **boxes**.

- Form the plural of most nouns by adding *s* or *es* to the singular. Look at the ending of the singular noun to decide how to form the plural. Some nouns have special plural forms. (See the chart on the next page.)

## Singular and Plural Nouns (continued)

| Rules for Forming Plural Nouns | | |
|---|---|---|
| **Most singular nouns:**<br>Add *s* | street<br>house | street**s**<br>house**s** |
| **Nouns ending with *s*, *x*, *ch*, or *sh*:**<br>Add *es*. | dress<br>ax<br>bench<br>dish | dress**es**<br>ax**es**<br>bench**es**<br>dish**es** |
| **Nouns ending with a consonant and *y*:**<br>Change the *y* to *i* and add *es*. | city<br>strawberry | cit**ies**<br>strawberr**ies** |
| **Nouns that have special plural spellings** | woman<br>mouse<br>foot<br>ox | wom**en**<br>m**ice**<br>f**ee**t<br>ox**en** |
| **Nouns that remain the same in the singular and the plural** | sheep<br>moose<br>trout<br>deer | sheep<br>moose<br>trout<br>deer |

## Singular and Plural Possessive Nouns

A **singular possessive noun** shows that one person, place, or thing has or owns something.

- To form the possessive of a singular noun, add an apostrophe and *s*.

  the **car's** horn　　a **student's** papers　　**Rosa's** opinion

A **plural possessive noun** shows that more than one person, place, or thing has or owns something.

- If a plural noun ends with *s*, add only an apostrophe.

  the **cars'** horns　　two **students'** books　　two **girls'** ideas

- If a plural noun does not ends with *s*, add an apostrophe and *s*.

  the **children's** choice　　the **oxen's** tracks　　the **people's** cheers

**Singular and Plural Possessive Nouns** (continued)

| Singular | Singular possessive | Plural | Plural possessive |
|---|---|---|---|
| girl | girl's | girls | girls' |
| fox | fox's | foxes | foxes' |
| pony | pony's | ponies | ponies' |
| child | child's | children | children's |
| deer | deer's | deer | deer's |

## VERBS

### Definition

A **verb** shows action or a state of being. It is the main word in the predicate.

ACTION: The fire **burns** brightly. BEING: It **is** warm.

### Action Verbs

An **action verb** shows what the subject does or did, including action that you cannot see.

Roberta **swings** at the ball. The coach **thought** about the players.

### Main Verbs and Helping Verbs

When a verb has more than one word, the **main verb** shows the action. A **helping verb** works with the main verb. The helping verb comes before the main verb.

Kiran **has passed** everyone.

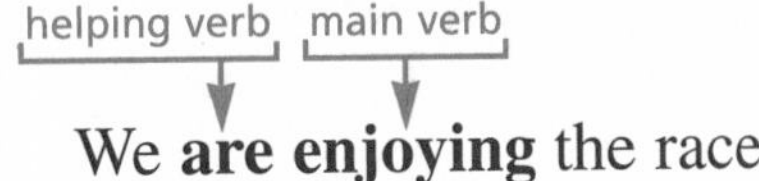

We **are enjoying** the race.

| Common Helping Verbs | | | | |
|---|---|---|---|---|
| am | are | were | shall | has |
| is | was | will | have | had |

# GRAMMAR GUIDE

## Verb Tense

The **tense** of the verb lets you know when something happens.

PRESENT: Bats hunt at night.
PAST: They hunted last night.
FUTURE: They will hunt tonight also.

## Present Tense

A **present tense verb** shows action that is happening now. Add *s* or *es* to most verbs to show the present tense if the subject is singular.

**Rules for Subject-Verb Agreement**

| | | |
|---|---|---|
| **Singular subject:** Add *s* or *es* to the verb. | The driver **trains** his dogs.<br>He **teaches** one dog to lead. | He **studies** his map. |
| **Plural subject or *I* or *you*:** Do not add *s* or *es* to the verb. | The dogs **pull** the sleds.<br>A driver and her dog **travel** far.<br>They **work** together. | I **like** your report on dogs.<br>You **write** well. |

- Change the spelling of some verbs when adding *s* or *es*.

**Rules for Forming the Present Tense**

| | | |
|---|---|---|
| **Most verbs:** Add *s*. | get - gets | play - plays |
| **Verbs ending with *s*, *ch*, *sh*, *x*, and *z*:** Add *es*. | pass - passes<br>punch - punches<br>push - pushes | mix - mixes<br>fizz - fizzes |
| **Verbs ending with a consonant and *y*:** Change the *y* to *i* and add *es*. | try - tries<br>empty - empties | |

## Verb Tense (continued)

### Past Tense

A **past tense verb** shows action that has already happened. Form the past tense of most verbs by adding *-ed*.

We **cooked** our dinner over a campfire last night.

- Change the spelling of some verbs when adding *-ed*.

A squirrel **hoped** for a few crumbs. It **begged** for a peanut.

Then it **hurried** back to its nest.

| Rules for Forming the Past Tense | |
|---|---|
| **Most verbs:** Add *-ed*. | play - play**ed**<br>reach - reach**ed** |
| **Verbs ending with *e*:** Add *-ed*. | believ**e** - believ**ed**<br>hop**e** - hop**ed** |
| **Verbs ending with a consonant and *y*:** Change the *y* to *i* and add *-ed*. | stud**y** - stud**ied**<br>hur**ry** - hur**ried** |
| **Verbs ending with a single vowel and a consonant:** Double the final consonant and add *-ed*. | st**op** - sto**pped**<br>pl**an** - pla**nned** |

### Future Tense

A **future tense verb** tells what is going to happen. Use the main verb with the helping verb *will* or *shall* to form the future tense.

Ken **will bring** his bird book tomorrow.

Ken and I **will look** for some nests.

**Shall** we **invite** Melissa?

## Verb Tenses with *be* and *have*

*Be* and *have* have special forms in the present and past tense. Change the forms of *be* and *have* to agree with their subjects.

**Present tense forms of *be***

I **am** a reporter.
You **are** a photographer.
She **is** an editor.

We **are** journalists.
You **are** proofreaders.
They **are** advertisers.

**Past tense forms of *be***

I **was** a reporter.
You **were** a photographer.
She **was** an editor.

We **were** journalists.
You **were** proofreaders.
They **were** advertisers.

**Present tense forms of *have***

I **have** a big story.
You **have** the photos.
It **has** a big headline.

We **have** a big edition.
You **have** a lot of work.
They **have** a midnight deadline.

**Past tense forms of *have***

I **had** a big story.
You **had** the photos.
It **had** a big headline.

We **had** a big edition.
You **had** a lot of work.
They **had** a midnight deadline.

| Subject | Form of *be* | | Form of *have* | |
|---|---|---|---|---|
| | **Present** | **Past** | **Present** | **Past** |
| **Singular subjects:** | | | | |
| I | am | was | have | had |
| You | are | were | have | had |
| He, She, It or singular noun | is | was | has | had |
| **Plural subjects:** | | | | |
| Plural noun,We, You, They | are | were | have | had |

## Irregular Verbs

**Irregular Verbs** have special forms to show the past.

**Irregular Verbs**

| Verb | Past tense | Past with helping verb |
|---|---|---|
| bring | brought | (has, have, had) brought |
| come | came | (has, have, had) come |
| go | went | (has, have, had) gone |
| make | made | (has, have, had) made |
| run | ran | (has, have, had) run |
| say | said | (has, have, had) said |
| take | took | (has, have, had) taken |
| think | thought | (has, have, had) thought |

- Some irregular verbs follow similar patterns.

| Verb | Past tense | Past with helping verb |
|---|---|---|
| ring | rang | (has, have, had) rung |
| sing | sang | (has, have, had) sung |
| swim | swam | (has, have, had) swum |
| begin | began | (has, have, had) begun |
| tear | tore | (has, have, had) torn |
| wear | wore | (has, have, had) worn |
| break | broke | (has, have, had) broken |
| speak | spoke | (has, have, had) spoken |
| steal | stole | (has, have, had) stolen |
| choose | chose | (has, have, had) chosen |
| blow | blew | (has, have, had) blown |
| grow | grew | (has, have, had) grown |
| know | knew | (has, have, had) known |
| fly | flew | (has, have, had) flown |

# ADJECTIVES

## Definition

An **adjective** is a word that describes a noun or a pronoun.

**Huge** lions stared at us. They seemed **angry**.

- An adjective tells what kind or how many. It can come before a noun or after a form of the verb *be*.

| | | |
|---|---|---|
| what kind | **Spotted** fawns were resting. | They looked **peaceful**. |
| how many | **Three** elephants were eating. | Monkeys did **several** tricks. |

- When two or more adjectives are listed together, use a comma to separate them, unless one of the adjectives tells how many.

**Large, colorful** parrots screeched. **Two white** geese honked loudly.

## Articles

*A, an,* and *the* are special adjectives called **articles**. *A* and *an* refer to any person, place, or thing. *The* refers to a particular person, place, or thing.

Let's take **a** trip. (any) It's time for **the** trip. (particular)

| Articles | |
|---|---|
| **a** | Use before singular words that begin with a consonant sound.<br>**a** jet **a** high step |
| **an** | Use before singular words that begin with a vowel sound.<br>**an** engineer **an** hour |
| **the** | Use before singular and plural words.<br>**the** answer **the** plans |

## Demonstrative Adjectives

*This, that, these,* and *those* are demonstrative adjectives. They tell which one.

- *This* and *these* refer to nouns close to the speaker or writer. *That* and *those* refer to nouns farther away.

**This** book is my favorite. **That** book is Ana's favorite.
**These** books belong in my room. **Those** books go back to the library.

| Demonstrative Adjectives | | |
|---|---|---|
| | **Singular** | **Plural** |
| Things that are close | this | these |
| Things that are farther away | that | those |

## Comparing with Adjectives

To compare two people, places, or things, add *-er* to most adjectives. To compare three or more, add *-est*. Use *more* and *most*, not *-er* and *-est*, with long adjectives.

ONE: Inky is a **cute** kitten. She is **playful**.
TWO: Inky is **cuter** than Toby. Toby is **more playful** than Inky.
THREE OR MORE: Grendel is the **cutest** kitten of all. Toby is the **most playful** of the three kittens.

- Change the spelling of some adjectives when adding *-er* and *est.*

| Rules for Comparing with Adjectives | |
|---|---|
| **1. Most adjectives:**<br>Add *-er* or *-est* to the adjective. | bright<br>bright**er**<br>bright**est** |
| **2. Adjectives ending with *e*:**<br>Drop the *e* and add *-er* or *-est.* | saf**e**<br>saf**er**<br>saf**est** |

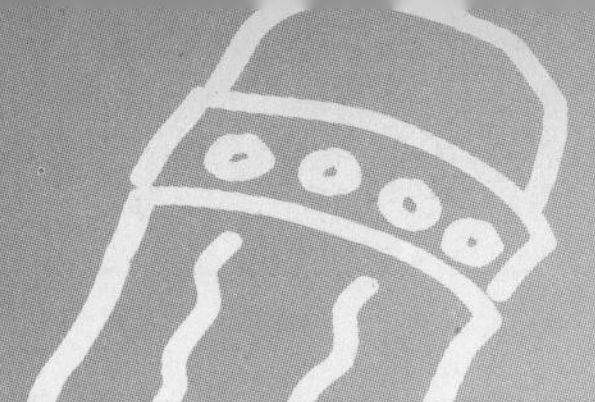



## Comparing with Adjectives (continued)

| Rules for Comparing with Adjectives (continued) | |
|---|---|
| **3. Adjectives ending with a consonant and *y*:** Change the *y* to *i* and add *-er* or *-est*. | busy<br>bus**ier**<br>bus**iest** |
| **4. One-syllable adjectives that end with a single vowel and a consonant:** Double the final consonant and add *-er* or *-est*. | fl**at**<br>fla**tter**<br>fla**ttest** |
| **5. Long adjectives:** Use *more* or *most* instead of *-er* or *-est*. | careful<br>**more** careful<br>**most** careful |

The adjectives *good* and *bad* have special forms for making comparisons.

- Use *better* and *worse* to compare two. Use *best* and *worst* to compare three or more.

ONE: The dress rehearsal of our play was **good**.
No one made a **bad** mistake.
TWO: Our first performance was **better**.
Our next performance was **worse**.
THREE OR MORE: Our third performance was **best**.
The second performance was **worst**.

| Comparing with *good* and *bad* | | |
|---|---|---|
| Describing one person, place, or thing | good | bad |
| Describing two persons, places, or things | better | worse |
| Describing three or more persons, places, or things | best | worst |

# ADVERBS

## Definition

An **adverb** is a word that describes a verb and tells *how*, *when*, or *where*.

HOW: The plane landed **smoothly** at the airport.

WHEN: **Soon** Jeff would see his grandparents at the gate.

WHERE: They were waiting for him **there**.

| How | When | Where |
|---|---|---|
| fast | tomorrow | here |
| hard | later | inside |
| together | again | far |
| happily | often | upstairs |
| quietly | first | downtown |
| secretly | next | somewhere |
| slowly | then | forward |

## Comparing with Adverbs

To compare two actions, add *-er* to short adverbs.

- Add *-est* to short adverbs to compare three or more.
- Use *more* or *most* with long adverbs or with most adverbs ending with *-ly*.

ONE ACTION: Janet will finish the book **soon**.
She will return the book **promptly**.

TWO ACTIONS: Janet will finish **sooner** than Jessie will.
She will return the book **more promptly** than Jessie will.

THREE OR MORE: Janet will finish **soonest** of all.
She will return the book **most promptly** of all.

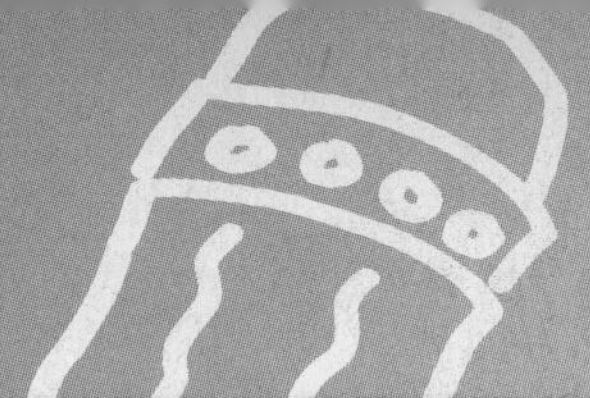

### Comparing with Adverbs (continued)

- Never use *-er* with *more*. Never use *-est* with *most*.

INCORRECT: Leslie skates **more smoother** than Roberto.
CORRECT: Leslie skates **more smoothly** than Roberto.

INCORRECT: Denzel works **most hardest** of all the students.
CORRECT: Denzel works **hardest** of all the students.

## PRONOUNS

### Definition

A **pronoun** is a word that takes the place of a noun.

Carl watches the swimmers.
**He** watches **them**.

Mary held Mary's blue ribbon.
**She** held **her** blue ribbon.

The swimmers listen for the whistle.
**They** listen for **it**.

Mr. Jones and I clapped loudly.
**We** clapped loudly.

### Subject Pronouns

There are seven **subject pronouns**. Some are singular, and some are plural.

| Subject Pronouns | |
|---|---|
| **Singular** | **Plural** |
| I<br>you<br>he, she, it | we<br>you<br>they |

Bill, will **you** hold the stopwatch?
Jamal and Andy, will **you** hand out towels?
Tania and I will record the times. **We** know what to do.
Carlton and Amy will cheer the team. **They** are very loud.

## Subject Pronouns (continued)

- Use **subject pronouns** as subjects of sentences.

  **I** would like to compete in a swimming race.

  **You** offered some tips.

  **They** have helped improve my speed.

- Use **subject pronouns** after forms of the verb *be*.

  The first swimmer into the water was **I**.

  Did Tina and Angelo win? Yes, the winners were **they**.

- When using *I* with another noun or subject pronoun, always name yourself last.

  **Mario and I** go to every swim meet.

  The ticket takers at the last meet were **Letty and I**.

## Object Pronouns

There are seven **object pronouns**. Some are singular, and some are plural. (Note that *it* and *you* may be subject or object pronouns.)

| Object Pronouns | |
|---|---|
| **Singular** | **Plural** |
| me | us |
| you | you |
| him, her, it | them |

Jeremy took Lupe and Carlos on a hike. He took **them** to Crystal Falls.

Dad gave the compass to Rebecca. Dad gave **it** to **her** last night.

Jeremy asked Leroy and me to carry the lunches. He gave **us** a pack.

- Use **object pronouns** after action verbs.

  Dad helped **her** build a campfire.

  They built **it** inside a circle of stones.

  Leroy showed **them** how to find dry sticks.

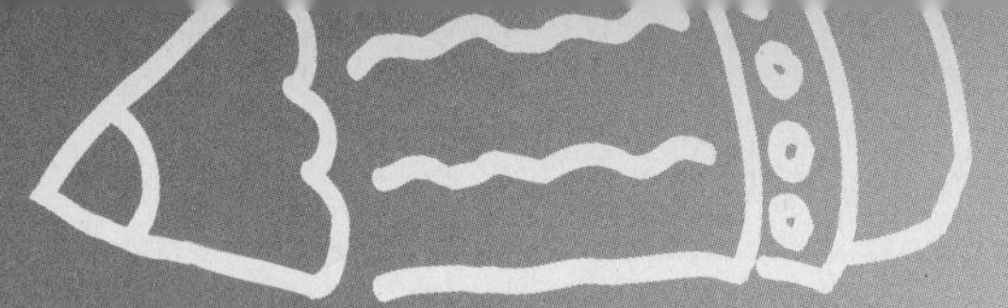

## GRAMMAR GUIDE

### Object Pronouns (continued)

- Use **object pronouns** after words such as *to*, *for*, *about*, *between*, and *after*.

  Will Jeremy cook dinner for **us**? I will eat after **you**.

  Arlyn will give the meat to **me**.

- When using *me* with another noun or object pronoun, always name yourself last.

  Dad showed **Jeremy and me** how to fish.

  The fish weren't biting for **him and me**.

### Possessive Pronouns

A **possessive pronoun** shows ownership.

Paul's pen is black. He keeps it in **his** pocket.

The blue notebook is Kate's. The pencil is also **hers**.

- There are two kinds of possessive pronouns. Some possessive pronouns appear before a noun. Other possessive pronouns replace possessive nouns.

**Two Kinds of Possessive Pronouns**

| Possessive pronouns used with nouns | | Possessive pronouns that stand alone | |
|---|---|---|---|
| my | **My** book is green. | mine | The green book is **mine**. |
| your | Clean **your** desk. | yours | **Yours** is messy. |
| his | **His** bike is blue. | his | The red bike is **his**. |
| her | This is **her** house. | hers | **Hers** is the gray house. |
| its | **Its** coat is shaggy. | its | The shaggy coat is **its**. |
| our | Those are **our** pens. | ours | Those pens are **ours**. |
| your | Take **your** sweaters. | yours | Leave **yours** here. |
| their | **Their** hats are red. | theirs | Thoses hats are **theirs**. |



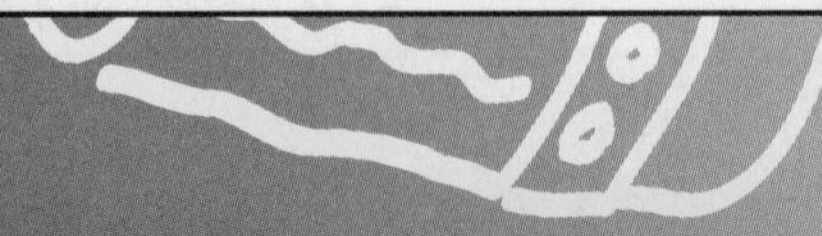

## Contractions with Pronouns

You can combine pronouns with the verbs *am*, *is*, *are*, *will*, *would*, *have*, *has*, and *had* to form contractions. A **contraction** is a shortened form of two words.

- Use an **apostrophe (')** to replace any letters dropped from the second word.

| Pronoun + Verb | Contraction | Pronoun + Verb | Contraction |
|---|---|---|---|
| I am | I'm | I have | I've |
| he is | he's | he has | he's |
| it is | it's | it has | it's |
| you are | you're | you have | you've |
| they are | they're | they have | they've |
| I will | I'll | I had | I'd |
| you will | you'll | you had | you'd |
| we would | we'd | we had | we'd |

- Do not confuse possessive pronouns with contractions that sound the same.

| Possessive pronouns | Contractions with pronouns |
|---|---|
| your = belonging to you | you're = you are |
| its = belonging to it | it's = it is |

**Your** new dog is really cute.
**It's** a dachshund.

**You're** very lucky.
**Its** body is long and low.

## Double Subjects

Do not use a noun and a pronoun to name the same person, place, or thing.

INCORRECT

Mary she is my sister

CORRECT

**Mary** is my sister.
**She** is my sister.

## ABBREVIATIONS

**Abbreviations** are shortened forms of words. Most abbreviations begin with a capital letter and end with a period. Use abbreviations only in special kinds of writing, such as addresses and lists.

### • Titles

Mr. *(Mister)* Mr. Pedro Arupe
Mrs. *(Mistress)* Mrs. Jane Chang
Ms. Carla Tower
Sr. *(Senior)* James Morton, Sr.
Jr. *(Junior)* James Morton, Jr.
Dr. *(Doctor)* Dr. Ellen Masters

**Note:** *Miss* is not an abbreviation and does not end with a period.

### • Words used in addresses

St. *(Street)*
Rd. *(Road)*
Ave. *(Avenue)*
Dr. *(Drive)*
Blvd. *(Boulevard)*
Rte. *(Route)*
Apt. *(Apartment)*
Pkwy. *(Parkway)*
Mt. *(Mount* or *Mountain)*
Expy. *(Expressway)*

### • Words used in business

Co. *(Company)*
Corp. *(Corporation)*
Inc. *(Incorporated)*
Ltd. *(Limited)*

### • Other Abbreviations

Some abbreviations are written in all capital letters, with a letter standing for each important word.

P.D. (Police Department)
P.O. (Post Office)
J.P. (Justice of the Peace)
R.N. (Registered Nurse)

## ABBREVIATIONS (continued)

- **States**

  The United States Postal Service uses two capital letters and no period in each of its state abbreviations.

AL *(Alabama)*
AK *(Alaska)*
AZ *(Arizona)*
AR *(Arkansas)*
CA *(California)*
CO *(Colorado)*
CT *(Connecticut)*
DE *(Delaware)*
FL *(Florida)*
GA *(Georgia)*
HI *(Hawaii)*
ID *(Idaho)*
IL *(Illinois)*
IN *(Indiana)*
IA *(Iowa)*
KS *(Kansas)*
KY *(Kentucky)*
LA *(Louisiana)*
ME *(Maine)*
MD *(Maryland)*
MA *(Massachusetts)*
MI *(Michigan)*
MN *(Minnesota)*
MS *(Mississippi)*
MO *(Missouri)*
MT *(Montana)*
NE *(Nebraska)*
NV *(Nevada)*
NH *(New Hampshire)*
NJ *(New Jersey)*
NM *(New Mexico)*
NY *(New York)*
NC *(North Carolina)*
ND *(North Dakota)*
OH *(Ohio)*
OK *(Oklahoma)*
OR *(Oregon)*
PA *(Pennsylvania)*
RI *(Rhode Island)*
SC *(South Carolina)*
SD *(South Dakota)*
TN *(Tennessee)*
TX *(Texas)*
UT *(Utah)*
VT *(Vermont)*
VA *(Virginia)*
WA *(Washington)*
WV *(West Virginia)*
WI *(Wisconsin)*
WY *(Wyoming)*

## TITLES

### Underlining

The important words and the first and last words in a title are capitalized. Titles of books, magazines, TV shows, movies, and newspapers are underlined.

The Call of the Wild (book) Cricket (magazine) Nova (TV show)
Treasure Island (movie) The Phoenix Express (newspaper)

Computer Tip: Use italic type for these kinds of titles instead of underlining.

## GRAMMAR GUIDE

### Quotation Marks

Titles of short stories, songs, articles, book chapters, and most poems are set off by **quotation marks (" ")**.

"The Necklace" (short story)
"Three Days in the Sahara" (article)
"Deer at Dusk" (poem)
"Home on the Range" (song)
"The Human Brain" (chapter)

## QUOTATIONS

### Quotation marks with commas and periods

**Quotation marks (" ")** set off a speaker's exact words. The first word of a quotation begins with a capital letter. Punctuation belongs *inside* the closing quotation marks.

- When a quotation comes last in the sentence, use a comma after the words that tell who is speaking.

  Linda whispered, "What time is it?"   Bill answered, "It's late. Let's go."

- When a quoted statement or command comes first in the sentence, put a comma inside the last quotation marks. Use question marks with questions and exclamation points with exclamations. Put a period after the words that tell who is speaking.

  STATEMENT: "It is almost lunchtime," said Angela.
  COMMAND: "Please put away your books now," said Mr. Emory.
  QUESTION: "When is our field trip?" asked Maria.
  EXCLAMATION: "I can't wait!" exclaimed Jeff.

### Writing a Conversation

Begin a new paragraph each time a new person begins speaking.

"Are you going to drive all the way to Columbus in one day?" asked Uncle Ben.

"I really haven't decided," said my father. "I was hoping that you would share the driving with me."

## CAPITALIZATION

1. Capitalize the first word of every sentence.

   What a wonderful day this is!

2. Capitalize the pronoun *I*.

   What can I do this afternoon?

3. Capitalize proper nouns. If a proper noun is made up of more than one word, capitalize each important word.

   Emily G. Messe　　District of Columbia　　Lincoln Memorial

4. Capitalize titles or their abbreviations when used with a person's name.

   Governor Bradford　　Senator Smith　　Dr. Ling

5. Capitalize family titles when they are used as names or as parts of names.

   We called Aunt Leslie.　　May we leave now, Mother?

6. Capitalize the names of days, months, and holidays.

   The meeting is on the first Tuesday in May.

   We watched the parade on the Fourth of July.

7. Capitalize the names of groups.

   Aspen Mountain Club　　International League

8. Capitalize the names of buildings and companies.

   Empire State Building　　Central School　　Able Supply Company

9. Capitalize the first, last, and all important words in a title. Do not capitalize words such as *a*, *in*, *and*, *of*, and *the* unless they begin or end a title.

   Secrets of a Wildlife Watcher　　"Growing Up"　　The Los Angeles Times

10. Capitalize the first word in the greeting and the closing of a letter.

    Dear Marcia,　　Sincerely yours,

11. Capitalize the first word of each main topic and subtopic in an outline.

    I. Types of fire departments
       A. Full-time departments
       B. Volunteer departments

GRAMMAR GUIDE

# PUNCTUATION

## End Marks

There are three end marks. A **period (.)** ends a statement or a command. A **question mark (?)** follows a question. An **exclamation point (!)** follows an exclamation.

The notebook is on the shelf. *(statement)*

Watch that program at eight tonight. *(command)*

Where does the trail end? *(question)*

This is your best poem so far! *(exclamation)*

## Apostrophe

Use an apostrophe (') to show ownership.

**1.** To form the possessive of a singular noun, add an apostrophe and *s*.

doctor's James's grandfather's community's

**2.** For a plural noun that ends with *s*, add only an apostrophe.

sisters' Boltons' families'

**3.** For a plural noun that does not end with *s*, add an apostrophe and *s* to form the plural possessive.

geese's men's children's mice's

Use an apostrophe in contractions in place of dropped letters. Do not use contractions in formal writing.

| | |
|---|---|
| isn't *(is not)* | I'm *(I am)* |
| can't *(cannot)* | they've *(they have)* |
| won't *(will not)* | they'll *(they will)* |
| wasn't *(was not)* | could've *(could have)* |
| we're *(we are)* | would've *(would have)* |
| it's *(it is)* | should've *(should have)* |

## Colon

Use a **colon (:)** after the greeting in a business letter.

Dear Mrs. Trimby: Dear Sir or Madam:

## Comma

A **comma (,)** tells your reader where to pause.

1. For words in a series, put a comma after each item except the last. Do not use a comma if only two items are listed.
   We made a salad of lettuce, peppers, and tomatoes.
   We made a salad of lettuce and tomatoes.
2. Use commas to separate two or more adjectives that are listed together unless one adjective tells how many.
   The fresh, ripe fruit was placed in a bowl. One red apple was especially shiny.
3. Use a comma before the conjunctions *and*, *but*, and *or* in a compound sentence.
   Some students were at lunch, but others were studying.
4. Use a comma after introductory words such as *yes*, *no*, *oh*, and *well*.
   Yes, it's a perfect day for a picnic. Well, I'll make dessert.
5. Use commas to separate a noun in direct address.
   Gloria, hold this light for me. Can you see, Joe, where I left my glasses?
   How was the movie, Grandma?
6. Use a comma to separate the month and the day from the year.
   I celebrated my tenth birthday on July 3, 1995.
7. Use a comma between the names of a city and a state.
   Denver, Colorado Miami, Florida
8. Use a comma after the greeting in a friendly letter.
   Dear Tayo, Dear Aunt Claudia,
9. Use a comma after the closing in a letter.
   Your friend, Yours truly,

**Quotation Marks** See Quotations, p. 310.

## PROBLEM WORDS

| Words | Rules | Examples |
|---|---|---|
| are<br>our | *Are* is a verb.<br>*Our* is a possessive pronoun. | Are these gloves yours?<br>This is our car. |
| doesn't<br>don't | Use *doesn't* with singular nouns, *he*, *she*, and *it*.<br>Use *don't* with plural nouns, *I*, *you*, *we*, and *they*. | Dad doesn't swim.<br>We don't swim. |
| good<br>well | Use the adjective *good* to describe nouns.<br>Use the adverb *well* to describe verbs. | The weather looks good.<br>She sings well. |
| its<br>it's | *Its* is a possessive pronoun.<br>*It's* is a contraction of *it is*. | The dog wagged its tail.<br>It's cold today. |
| set<br>sit | *Set* means "to put."<br>*Sit* means "to rest or stay in one place." | Set the vase on the table.<br>Please sit in this chair. |
| their<br>there<br>they're | *Their* means "belonging to them."<br>*There* means "at or in that place."<br>*They're* is a contraction of *they are*. | Their coats are on the bed.<br>Is Carlos there?<br>They're going to the store. |
| two<br>to<br>too | *Two* is a number.<br>*To* means "toward."<br>*Too* means "also" or "more than enough." | I bought two shirts.<br>A cat ran to the tree.<br>Can we go too?<br>I ate too many peas. |
| your<br>you're | *Your* is a possessive pronoun.<br>*You're* is a contraction of *you are*. | Are these your glasses?<br>You're late again! |

## ADVERB USAGE (See also Comparing with Adverbs, page 303.)

### Negatives

A **negative** is a word that means "no" or "not." Do not use two negatives to express one negative idea.

INCORRECT: We can't do nothing.
CORRECT: We can't do anything.
CORRECT: We can do nothing.

| Negative Words | | |
|---|---|---|
| no | no one | never |
| none | nothing | neither |
| nobody | nowhere | |

## PRONOUN USAGE (See also Pronouns, pages 304-307.)

### Double Subjects

Do not use a noun and a pronoun to name the same person, place, or thing.

INCORRECT: The food it was delicious.
CORRECT: The food was delicious.

### *I* and *Me*

When using *I* or *me* with nouns or other pronouns, always name yourself last.

Beth and I will leave. Give the papers to Ron and me.

### Compound Subjects and Compound Objects

To decide which pronoun to use in a compound subject or a compound object, say the sentence with the pronoun alone.

Lu and (*we*, *us*) ride the bus. (We ride the bus.)
Lu and we ride the bus.

I saw Dad and (*he*, *him*). (I saw him.)
I saw Dad and him.

# PROOFREADING CHECKLIST

Check your paper for mistakes. Use the questions below to help you. Correct any mistakes you find. After you have made the corrections, put a check mark in the box next to the question.

- ❑ **1.** Did I indent each paragraph?
- ❑ **2.** Does each sentence tell one complete thought?
- ❑ **3.** Do I have any run-on sentences?
- ❑ **4.** Did I spell all words correctly?
- ❑ **5.** Did I use capital letters correctly?
- ❑ **6.** Did I use punctuation marks correctly?
- ❑ **7.** Did I use commas and apostrophes correctly?
- ❑ **8.** Did I spell all the words the right way?

Is there anything else you should look for? Make your own proofreading list on a piece of paper.

## PROOFREADING MARKS

| Mark | Explanation | Example |
|---|---|---|
| ¶ | Begin a new paragraph. Indent the paragraph. | ¶ We went to an air show last Saturday. Eight jets flew across the sky in the shape of V's, X's, and diamonds. |
| ^ | Add letters, words, or sentences. | The leaves were red ^and orange. |
| ℓ | Take out words, sentences, and punctuation marks. Correct spelling. | The sky is bright ~~blew~~ blue. Huge clouds ℓ move quickly. |
| / | Change a capital letter to a small letter. | The Fireflies blinked in the dark. |
| ≡ | Change a small letter to a capital letter. | New York city is exciting. |